THE RICH DIE RICHER

AND YOU CAN TOO

The
RICH
DIE
RICHER

and You Can Too

WILLIAM D. ZABEL

WILLIAM MORROW AND COMPANY, INC.
New York

LIBRARY OF CONGRESS CATALOGING-IN-PUBLICATION DATA

Zabel, William D.
The rich die richer and you can too / William D. Zabel.
p.   cm.
Includes index.
ISBN 0-688-12350-3
1. Finance, Personal — United States.   2. Estate planning — United States.   3. Tax planning — United States.   I. Title.
HG179.Z33   1995
332.024 — dc20   94-34368
CIP

Printed in the United States of America

3   4   5   6   7   8   9   10

BOOK DESIGN BY PATRICE SHERIDAN

To my mother and father,
Anne and Louis Zabel,
who gave me love that
even the richest can't buy

Preface

Nearly every American wants to know how to accumulate and preserve wealth. This book focuses on how the rich get, live, and die richer, and how you can benefit from their wealth-creating, wealth-expanding, and wealth-preserving techniques.

And the rich have been getting richer. From $6 trillion to $10 trillion will be passed on over the next twenty years, with nearly $1 trillion to be transferred by the end of this decade. In effect, all the wealth that has been built up since World War II will pass in unprecedented amounts to the so-called baby boomers (age 34–48) and the generation before them, which has no special name (age 48–60).

During the 1980s the United States experienced a particularly massive growth and concentration of wealth. Between 1977 and 1989, the wealthiest 5% of U.S. families captured 74% of all after-tax income. By 1989 the wealthiest 1% owned more wealth than the bottom 90%. By the end of the decade, the term "decamillionaire" was coined to describe individuals with $10 million in assets, a group that quadrupled during the 1980s. From 1989 to 1992, the number of millionaire households, based on total net worth, rose by nearly a third from 2,818,000 to 3,683,000. *Forbes* has raised its minimum to $310 million to make its list of four hundred richest Americans, and regularly names quite a few billionaires. (One interesting study shows that the wealthy think it takes a median net worth of about $2 million to be "really wealthy" — almost four times the $565,000 cited by Americans as a whole.) How are so many Americans becoming richer?

Balzac's theory was that behind every great fortune there is a crime. Without arguing about exceptions to that provocative generalization, it certainly is hard to disagree with F. Scott Fitzgerald's observation that "the rich are different from you and me." Although I like Ernest Hemingway's simple rejoinder, "Yes. They have more money."

One might say: "Does it even matter? It's only money!" The eminent liberal Harvard economist John Kenneth Galbraith has said: "Money is a singular thing. It ranks with love as man's greatest source of joy. And with death as his greatest source of anxiety. Money differs from an automobile, a mistress, or cancer in being equally important to those who have it and those who do not." Certainly the power of money is seen everywhere and can affect everything — our lives, our loves, our family relationships. Shakespeare in *Timon of Athens* said gold can "make black white, foul fair, wrong right, base noble, old young." Much later, Marx pungently put it his way:

> The properties of money are my own (the possessor's) properties and faculties. What I *am* and *can do* is, therefore, not at all my individuality. I *am* ugly, but I can buy the most beautiful woman for myself. Consequently I am not *ugly*, for the effect of ugliness, its power to repel, is nullified by money. . . . I am a detestable, dishonorable, unscrupulous and stupid man, but money is honored, and so also is its possessor. Money is the highest good and so its possessor is good.

Perhaps that is why so many popular how-to books relate to creating money from real estate, from investing in the stock market, from starting your own business, etc., ad infinitum. There is little doubt that one should try to control money or it will, more often than not, control you and the lives of those who survive you.

Learning from the rich, who, by definition, can afford to master the opportunities to preserve, increase, and control wealth, can be helpful to most of us.

This does not mean, of course, that even the richest among us are always wise with their money. According to the *Forbes* 400, in October 1994, the second richest man in America was Warren Buffett, the folksy investor from Omaha, Nebraska, with an estimated net worth of over $9 billion. Yet his estate plan, as related in *Forbes*, reminds me of Samuel Goldwyn's alleged crack: "An oral contract isn't worth the paper it's written on." Buffett has left essentially his entire estate outright to his estranged wife, Susan, from whom he is separated but not divorced, on the oral understanding that she will at her death leave it all to a private foundation to carry out his charitable intentions. The fact that his wife could leave this inheritance to a future husband, lover, or friend or to a charity or charities not of Mr. Buffett's liking apparently does not worry him. Such trust is remarkable and probably to be commended, but it may be quixotic and, in any event, is certainly unnecessary. Why? Because, without changing the tax consequences, he could leave his estate in trust for his wife for her life, and require that at her death it go to his own charitable designee or designees. Nevertheless, in general, we can learn a lot from the ways the rich do deal wisely with their wealth.

This book is written from my perspective of having given legal advice for more than thirty years to the very rich, and its intention is to show how much can be learned from them. I think that both aspiring and existing capitalists can benefit from it. You will see that to a great extent most of us can, with some sophistication and planning, make estate and gift taxes essentially voluntary rather than mandatory. I can't, of course, reveal every technique, or clients might have no further need for my advice, and the Internal Revenue Service might focus unduly on matters it need not be troubled by. But most techniques can and will be openly discussed, and, in any event, new ones always need to be devised to adapt to changing tax laws and the shifting economic facts of life.

This book hopes to enlighten its readers by both real-life examples and detailed, clear explanations of specific money-saving techniques. The examples, the lessons they teach, and the questions they raise are many:

How did Abraham Lincoln, Pablo Picasso, James Dean, and Howard Hughes teach us the horribles of dying without a will?

What tax disasters did Howard Hughes and Campbell soup heir John Dorrance cause by dying without one established legal domicile?

How did Henry Ford II demonstrate in his estate plan the wrong approach to choosing and compensating trustees?

How did the matriarch of one of America's richest families, by her will, effectively rebuke those of her four sons who continued after her death to litigate against the others?

What can we learn from the lawsuit instituted on behalf of the two elderly daughters, six grandchildren, and eleven great-grandchildren of the late financier and diplomat, Averell Harriman, former Governor of New York, against his widow, Pamela Digby Churchill Harriman (now the U.S. ambassador to France), prominent Washington lawyers Clark M. Clifford and Paul C. Warnke, and trust adviser William Rich III for being "faithless fiduciaries who betrayed a trust and squandered a family's inheritance"?

Why did Bowie Kuhn, the former Commissioner of Baseball, buy an expensive Florida home on the eve of personal bankruptcy?

Why do George Soros and Walter Annenberg teach us how to give away money, while Doris Duke shows us how not to?

Why did Jacqueline Kennedy Onassis leave most of her estate to a CLAT (a charitable lead annuity) and not to her children?

Why would Groucho Marx have been well advised to have used a revocable or living trust?

Did the provision in the Donald and Ivana Trump premarital agreement prohibiting her from writing about him violate the First Amendment's free speech guarantee?

What did Steven Spielberg do wrong as sole director (and composer) of his prenuptial agreement with Amy Irving?

How did Aristotle Onassis use an ingenious trust device to give his then wife Jackie income without either of them being subject to U.S. income taxes?

Why did foam-cup tycoon Kenneth Dart give up his U.S. citizenship to become a citizen of Belize, a tiny Caribbean country known mostly for its scuba diving?

How did Andy Warhol's executor dramatically demonstrate the wrong way to compensate the estate's lawyer?

What kind of will did Sunny Von Bulow need to save her children ongoing anguish and great financial expense?

How does the decimation and rewriting of the will of Seward Johnson (of the Johnson & Johnson fortune) by all of his heirs warn us?

This book will answer many questions that you may or should have, including:

- How do the rich get rich and die richer? What specific techniques do they use that could be used by you—e.g., low-interest loans, personal residence trusts, and insurance?

- How do the rich give to charity, and what's the best way for them and you to do so? How can you take advantage of having your own charitable foundation?

- How much must you give, and how much should you give, to your spouse? How much of that can be given to a spouse free of estate and gift taxes? What legal form of gift should you use? In that regard, consider the marvelous QTIP Trust.

- How and when should a married couple lock in their respective $600,000 lifetime exemptions ($1.2 million in total) from federal estate and gift tax? Can they do it without giving up the income from the $1.2 million during their lifetimes?

- How much should you give your children?

- Can you pay, without gift tax, the educational and medical expenses of your children and grandchildren in addition to taking advantage of the annual gift tax exclusions for them (i.e., the $20,000 that a married couple can give each year to each of their children and grandchildren)?

- How can you make substantial gifts to your children and grandchildren *without paying any gift tax*?

- How can you restrict the use of money after the children get it?

- How can you use a "dynasty trust" for your descendants to take advantage of the exemption from the generation-skipping tax? Why is South Dakota the best state for a dynasty trust?

- What are the roles of trustee and executor, and how should you select them?

- Whom should you name as guardian for your children?

- Are revocable or living trusts an estate planning panacea? Why may they be advisable for the benefit of gay partners?

- When does one need a prenuptial or postnuptial or cohabitation agreement?

- What are the best estate and gift planning tax-saving techniques of the rich that can benefit you?

- Why are family "discount" partnerships currently the hottest technique with sophisticated estate planners?

- How do you provide for mistresses, paramours, or other secret beneficiaries?

- How can you protect the family business?

- How should you protect your assets from creditors? Why is Florida the favorite state of every potential bankrupt?

- What is an offshore APT (asset protection trust), and can you and should you use it?

- How much should fiduciary and legal services cost — i.e., what should you pay your executors, trustees, and lawyers?

- What is the last refuge of the rich to avoid all U.S. taxes?

- When does one need a living will and/or a health care proxy?

- How do you make the last words written about you both accurate and meaningful?

- What is an ethical will? Should you have one?

- Can you be sure your last wishes will be carried out?

In short, this book covers a very broad spectrum of matters relating to estate planning, including the selection of fiduciaries, practical and wise tax and other provisions for children's trusts, taxwise charitable giving devices, the advisability of pre- and postnuptial agreements, and methods of asset protection. Most chapters or sections are self-contained, and may be read in any order, so that the reader can easily pursue his or her particular interests. For example, one chapter uses three cases to explain the need for special legal precision in wills and trusts by showing the complicated and dire consequences that can arise from the misuse of one word: "issue." Since this book deals with a vast subject matter, there should be something of value in it for every reader, whether it is an analysis of the especially sophisticated and effective tax-saving devices (such as personal residence GRITs, GRATs, and family "discount" partnerships), or a discussion of the basic need for a health care proxy and living will, or advice on how much to pay fiduciaries and lawyers.

A major purpose of this book is to show that the money-saving techniques of the rich and powerful and many of the trust and estate problems and concerns they have are of practical interest to almost every middle-class American as well, in one way or another. Each of us can learn from the rich how to be richer — both materially and in other equally or more important ways — in the legacies we leave our children and all of our progeny.

Acknowledgments

This book would never have been written if my loving and intelligent wife, Deborah, had not decided a few years ago to go back to school. She, in fact, enrolled in and in due course achieved an MBA from the Wharton School, which required her to travel and attend classes in Philadelphia every other weekend for two years (not to mention all the necessary study time). Her admonition to me was "Why don't you write the book you've always wanted to write, and stay out of trouble." So I became determined to do the former, and try to avoid the latter.

Even with this apparent cornucopia of spare time, my legal practice, fortunately for me, remains so time-consuming and interesting that I still needed almost an extra year to finish this book. This additional time was especially necessary because I did it without the help of my able colleagues in our law firm, Schulte Roth & Zabel, who keep themselves busy enough practicing law. Nevertheless, the book is, in some ways, a product of all my years of legal practice and experience, and I do wish to thank some persons who have been very important to me along the way: my fellow remaining founding partners, Paul N. Roth, Daniel S. Shapiro, Stephen J. Schulte, John G. McGoldrick, and Burton Lehman; my primary mentor in the law, Leo Gottlieb; two great legal scholars and law professors, Austin Wakeman Scott and A. James Casner, who first taught me at Harvard Law School about the law of trusts and estates; many colleagues primarily in the trusts and estates department of our law firm, Kim E. Baptiste, Susan C. Frunzi, Ronald S. Kochman, Howard F. Sharfstein, Stephen C. Corriss, Susan S. Wallach, Debra R. Anisman, Susan Galligan, Jean A. Hegler, Sharon Soloff, Susan Blackman Tilson, Janie Farkas, William Zeena, Marnie Ginsberg, Maria L. Osmanski, Ewa Sabater, Amy Taub, Suzanne Kerner, Marty Spindel, Carol Sergis, and Laraine Ginsburg; and some important others for various reasons: my brother, Sheldon Zabel, Harris J. Amhowitz, Jon Golden, Jonathan M. L. Stone, Lynn Witkowski, Paul Rampell, Edgar A. Levenson, Raymond T. Heilpern, and H. H. Wilson.

My wife read many chapters and gave valuable advice about them. Our son, Gregory, was especially encouraging throughout, pushing me to keep at the book on many weekends when I felt like jettisoning the whole project. My sons, Richard and David, who have always been most loving and supportive, and both of whom are better writers than their father, made many helpful suggestions. They actually did some editing and research and deserve much credit for what may be the liveliest part of the book — Chapter VII. My irrepressible eighty-six-year-old mother read the entire manuscript, recommending infusions of humor as well as steering me to the data about the reign of my hometown, Sioux Falls, South Dakota, as the divorce capital of the United States, and about the remarkable life of Brigham Young's twenty-seventh wife.

Finally, my appreciation to those most helpful at William Morrow, especially Will Schwalbe, and also Gail Kinn, Jackie Deval, and Zach Schisgal.

One technical point that I should not need to mention but do so simply for the record. In the few instances where I refer to named persons whom I have represented in the past or now represent (such as Doris Duke and George Soros), everything related about them or their matters is from materials printed in the public press.

Perhaps my most difficult task in writing a book for laypersons was to explain complicated tax and other legal concepts in plain, comprehensible English. Having spent my entire career writing almost exclusively for lawyers, accountants, and financial planners in professional journals, this task was not easy. But I think that, for the most part, I have been able to make tax savings techniques intelligible to the nonlawyer. In trying to do that and all the rest entailed in writing this book, I have come to realize why my political hero, Winston Churchill, had this to say on the subject:

> Writing a book is an adventure. To begin with it is a toy and an amusement. Then it becomes a mistress, then it becomes a master, then it becomes a tyrant. The last phase is that just as you are about to be reconciled to your servitude, you kill the monster, and fling him about to the public.

So here it is. I fling it to you. I hope that you learn from it but also enjoy reading it.

—WILLIAM D. ZABEL

Contents

Section One

THY WILL
BE DONE

I

Wills

WHAT IS A WILL?

A will is a legal document containing your wishes as to the disposition of your assets after your death. Wills are ancient. Jacob, the father of Joseph, is thought by scholars to have made the first will (see Genesis 48, especially verse 22). Some say Noah had a will, but, as one wag asked, who were the disinterested witnesses? The oldest will of which there is a known copy is that of Uah, an Egyptian, made in 2548 B.C. Under the Code of Hammurabi in Babylonia, property, with only a few exceptions, had to pass to designated heirs on death. This was also generally true under the laws of Solon in Greece (Aristotle and Plato had wills) and under Roman law. Emperor Justin of the Byzantine Empire, one of history's greatest lawmakers, promulgated the Justinian Code, which prescribed the first formal requirements for wills.

A will is also, among other things, a symbolic emotional expression that can be a weapon, and occasionally it has been fired with venom.

Heinrich Heine, the German poet, left his entire estate to his wife on the condition that she remarry, because, Heine wrote, then there would be at least one man to regret his death. Similarly, a man named Septimus Daniel Gilbert in his will directed that he be buried in the same grave with his wife, and that his tombstone be inscribed "Daniel in the Lion's Den."

Some wills, in effect, wreak a kind of afterlife vengeance — sometimes in deed, sometimes in words, sometimes in both. Lord Redesale, an avid anti-Communist, left his estate to all but one of his daughters. He disinherited that daughter, Jessica, who had named her child Lenin. One American testator, Adolph J. Heimbeck, stated in his will: "I leave nothing to my two sisters Hazel and Katherine as they revere Franklin D. Roosevelt and the taxes caused by him more than equaled their share." Wealthy Kentucky horse breeder Leslie Combs bequeathed the bulk of his large estate to Lexington's Ephraim McDowell Cancer Research Foundation on the condition it remove its executive director, whom Combs detested. The foundation paid the director to leave and then got the legacy. Another man's will said: "To my son I leave the pleasure of earning a living. For twenty-eight years he thought the pleasure was mine, but he was mistaken."

Then there are whimsical wills. One wealthy American left all of his money to a chorus girl whom he had enjoyed watching in the theater. He never knew her, and the reason that this testator gave in his will for the bequest was that her turned-up nose amused him. He probably exited this world laughing.

Other wills are so malevolent that the deceased's estate is sued for "libel by will," or "testamentary libel" as the little-known tort is also called.

Perhaps the most vindictive will of all was written by a German who lived in Munich. It stipulated that a wake be held in an upper story of his residence. When his relatives gathered around the coffin, the floor collapsed, and most of the mourners were killed. It was later discovered that shortly before his death, the man had sawed through the supporting beams. Instead of taking his money with him, he took his heirs.

These are rather extreme examples, of course, and it is probably

" . . . and to my sister, Emma Bentley, who often said she would
bet a hundred dollars that a bunch of chorus girls would get
my money, I leave one hundred dollars."

safe to say that the average will is a conscientious attempt by the
deceased to benefit those persons or institutions he cherishes. On the
other hand, many persons die without wills.

DO NOT GO WILL-LESS:
PICASSO'S INTESTACY

Why do so many men and women refuse to make wills, or refuse to
sign them once they're written? Often intestacy (the state of dying
without a will) occurs because a person refuses to confront the fear of
dying. In many cases, it leads to a kind of intellectual paralysis, even
in normally efficient, rational adults. Will-making symbolizes to some
individuals a loss of power over their wealth and a lack of control over
their families. A will creates a relationship between the people you love

and the property you own, fixing the relationship immutably if the will is indeed your last. Many people, consciously or unconsciously, do not want to quantify their relationships. They would rather not decide whether to protect children with a trust or to give the property outright to them, how to divide the estate between the children or to make sure each grandchild gets an equal amount (providing for grandchildren per stirpes or per capita, in legal lingo), or how to apportion property among sets of children from different marriages or among such children and a second spouse.

I tell clients the obvious — that making a good will does not advance the date of death. But some seem to doubt it. One of Picasso's lawyers told me he urged the artist many times to make a will but that "he never did because of superstition. A way of avoiding death, one might say."

Many rationalize and say they do not have enough property to need a will. But the lack of one, even if the estate is modest, usually causes pain to the surviving members of the family and costs them money.

Intestacy means that state laws determine the estate's distribution, often with results contrary to what any thoughtful person would want. Children, for example, may inherit more than their mother. This was the case in Abraham Lincoln's intestacy. One-third of his limited estate went to his middle-aged widow, Mary Todd Lincoln, one-third to his elder son, Robert, who had just graduated from Harvard, and one-third to his younger son, 12-year-old Tad. Nor did the Lincoln family thereafter do well, so to speak, in estate and family law matters. The elder son, Robert Todd Lincoln, went on to amass a fortune as a lawyer, banker, and corporate official. In 1894, as president of the Pullman Palace Car Company, he defended the use of U.S. Army troops to put down striking workers. In 1875, in a highly publicized Chicago trial, Robert had his mother, Mary, committed against her will to a mental asylum. Robert and his wife, Mary Harlan Lincoln, had two daughters and one son, Abraham Lincoln II, who died at age 16 in 1890 of blood poisoning. Mary Harlan Lincoln left a large trust in her will for her descendants, which terminated in 1985 on the death of Robert Todd Lincoln Beckwith, a great-grandson of Abraham Lincoln and apparently his last living descendant. But Beckwith's young second wife, from whom he was divorced, contended that her 17-year-old son, Timothy Lincoln Beckwith, conceived two months after her marriage to Beckwith in 1967, was his son even though six years before the marriage he had had a vasectomy with a prostatectomy and was declared by doctors to be "completely sterile." The Mary Harlan Lincoln Testamentary Trust (then reputedly worth some eight figures) was to go to the American Red Cross, Iowa Wesleyan College, and the First Church of Christ, Scientist, but only if no Lincoln heir survived at her death. It has only recently been revealed that a considerable sum was settled on Timothy Beckwith (notwithstanding his very doubtful paternity), with regular payments and a lump sum payment at the end. Ironically, our perhaps greatest president's own parentage was questioned by William Herndon, his biographer and former law partner. Herndon determined that Thomas Lincoln was sterile and could not have fathered Abraham Lincoln. There has been speculation that Lincoln's true father was John C. Calhoun, a champion of states' rights, or even Samuel Davis, the father of Jefferson Davis, the President of the Confederacy.

The actor James Dean died in a car crash at age 29 without a will and before his reputation-making movie *Rebel Without a Cause* had been released. He had virtually no assets, but what he had (primarily a $100,000 insurance policy) and the legal right to licensing fees of his likeness went by intestate law to his father, Winston Dean, who had abandoned him early in his life after his mother died. These licensing fees reportedly generate $1 to $3 million per year for the undeserving father. Intestacy almost always causes heirs to incur needless legal expenses, extra death taxes, premiums for a fiduciary's bond, and the like. In our society, almost every person needs a will or an effective will substitute, such as a revocable trust, to protect his or her family and preserve property.

To this day, millions of persons have made wills, but sometimes it seems even more should have and did not. In addition to Lincoln, presidents Andrew Johnson, Ulysses Grant, and James Garfield died without wills. So did Chief Justice Frederick Vinson of the United States Supreme Court, who also did what some say is worse: he died broke. Thomas Jarman, considered by many to have been the world's greatest legal expert on wills, died without one. When Pablo Picasso died intestate at age 91 after a night of painting in his studio, he left approximately $300 million in assets.

Howard Hughes had even more wealth than Picasso, but he at least appears to have made a will, or wills, at one time or another. During the long and expensive litigation over the Hughes estate, fifty-two different documents were presented as wills, and four hundred prospective heirs surfaced to claim part of the estate. Leading the list of alleged wills was the infamous "Mormon will," a three-page handwritten document that turned up at Mormon headquarters in Salt Lake City. It was delivered there by Melvin Dummar, a substantial beneficiary under the purported will. He was a gas station operator, milkman, student, songwriter, and beer truck driver in the tiny communities of Gaffs, Nevada, and Willard, Utah. He claimed to have rescued Hughes in 1968 in a desolate spot near one of Nevada's most celebrated brothels, the Cottontail Ranch. Dummar became an instant celebrity—a movie and at least one book appeared on his unique role in the Hughes drama. The litigation was intense. A Nevada jury after seven months of testimony took only a few hours to brand the Mormon will a forgery. As a result, "laughing heirs" (indirect heirs who become totally unexpected beneficiaries), namely, twenty-one cousins, took Hughes's entire estate. These cousins avoided further litigation by a private settlement giving 71.5% to the maternal heirs and 28.5% to the paternal ones. When all was litigated and done, Hughes's not having a will (and also not having a clear legal domicile, as discussed later) generated almost fifteen years of litigation, approximately $30 million of legal fees nationwide, and millions in additional state death taxes (see discussion of Hughes's domicile problem in Chapter III, pp. 41–43). Quite an irony, particularly when many said the persons that Howard Hughes disliked most were lawyers and taxing authorities, and Hughes, by his own legal inactions, made both of them *de facto* substantial beneficiaries or additional laughing heirs of his estate.

But let us consider the Picasso intestacy. Roland Dumas, Picasso's personal lawyer for many years, asked Picasso several times to formulate a will, and Picasso refused. In addition to being superstitious, Picasso was amused at the thought that there might be extra complications after his death because he did not leave a will. Dumas told Picasso that if he did not sign a will, matters would indeed be very complicated after his death, Picasso's reply, with a twinkle in his eye, was: "Roland, it will be even more complicated than you think." Picasso's prediction came true.

While Picasso deliberately had no written will, he did leave a nuncupative or oral will, which can be valid under French law, donating his collection of paintings by other artists to the French government. Some of the heirs apparently had reservations about giving up this valuable collection, but there was sufficient evidence of Picasso's wishes that ultimately they were honored. Among the works were thirteen by Degas, one Renoir, two Cézannes, four Douanier Rousseaus, one Modigliani, two Braques, seven Matisses, one Miró, and others by Max Ernst, Marie Laurencin, and André Derain.

The most important matter to Picasso and the only item of property or art that he dealt with in a written instrument was his painting *Guernica*, called by John Canaday "the greatest social statement made in painting in this century." He directed that it be returned to Spain when its democracy was deemed reestablished.

Although Picasso's habit of retaining his art was known, no one quite expected the treasure trove that emerged from his closets after death. There were 1,885 paintings, 1,288 sculptures, 2,880 ceramics, 18,095 engravings, 6,112 lithographs, 3,181 linocuts, 7,089 drawings and an additional 4,659 drawings and sketches in 149 notebooks, 11 tapestries, and 8 rugs. These were Picasso's Picassos. In addition, he had residences, real estate, and cash.

No wonder that immediately upon Picasso's death, as he had foreseen, the complications began.

Picasso left as his heirs his widow, Jacqueline, and four children: Paulo, a legitimate child by his first wife, the Russian dancer Olga Koklova; Maya, the child of his mistress Marie-Therèse Walter; and Claude and Paloma, the children of another mistress, Françoise Gilot, now the wife of the biologist Dr. Jonas Salk. His unusual family tree helps us to understand the players in the estate imbroglio.

Jacqueline and the legitimate son, Paulo, quickly asserted their claims as sole beneficiaries of the estate, which was not surprising.

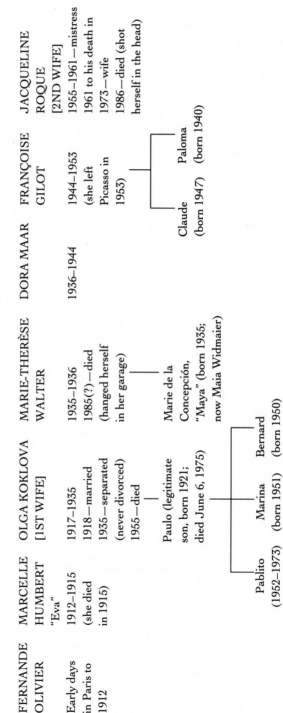

PABLO PICASSO FAMILY TREE

*(the seven most significant women
in his life and his children)*

PABLO PICASSO

*born October 25, 1881
died April 8, 1973 (at age 91)*

FERNANDE OLIVIER	MARCELLE HUMBERT "Eva"	OLGA KOKLOVA [1ST WIFE]	MARIE-THERÈSE WALTER	DORA MAAR	FRANÇOISE GILOT	JACQUELINE ROQUE [2ND WIFE]
Early days in Paris to 1912	1912–1915 (she died in 1915)	1917–1935 1918—married 1935—separated (never divorced) 1955—died	1935–1936 1985(?)—died (hanged herself in her garage)	1936–1944	1944–1953 (she left Picasso in 1953)	1955–1961—mistress 1961 to his death in 1973—wife 1986—died (shot herself in the head)

Paulo (legitimate son, born 1921; died June 6, 1975)

Marie de la Concepción, "Maya" (born 1935; now Maia Widmaier)

Claude (born 1947) Paloma (born 1940)

Pablito (1952–1973) Marina (born 1951) Bernard (born 1950)

Since 1964, each of the three children born out of wedlock had been effectively banned from Picasso's life, as were Paulo's children — Picasso's grandchildren. One tragic consequence of this was the death of Pablito, one of the rejected grandchildren, who swallowed what proved to be a lethal dose of a household cleanser after being denied access to Picasso's funeral.

And then the complications spread. Soon the three illegitimate children sued to establish their rights of inheritance. In 1971, Picasso had won a legal action in which he refused legally to acknowledge the paternity of his illegitimate children Claude and Paloma. The court based its finding on a then existing distinction in French law between children born out of wedlock and those born to couples of whom one member was still married to another spouse. When Claude and Paloma were born (as well as Maya before them), Picasso was separated from but still married to his first wife, Olga Koklova. It is thought that he never divorced her so as to preserve his right in her share of their jointly owned community property, which did, in effect, pass to Picasso at Olga's death in 1955.

A new French law was passed in 1972. Claude claims that "we had something to do with the passage of that law." This law in the case of an intestacy gave natural children the right to one-half of what a legitimate child would take if all of the surviving children had been legitimate, provided the deceased parent (Picasso) had been married at the time of their conception *and* had a legitimate child or children from such marriage. Picasso's sole legitimate son, Paulo, was the product of his marriage to Olga Koklova. Nevertheless, the question of whether the new law definitely applied to Picasso's natural children was not free from doubt. Litigation ensued in the court in Grasse.

French law added other complications. In intestacy, the surviving spouse, Jacqueline, had a right of usufruct (in our law an estate for life or a lifetime use of property) of one-fourth of Picasso's estate and also her community property rights to any assets acquired or created during the marriage, i.e., from 1961 through 1973. The surviving spouse's usufruct is calculated on a fictitious sum that includes all property that the decedent disposed of while alive as well as the property in the estate at death. The other heirs on posting bond can compel the surviving spouse to accept an annuity of equivalent value.

A further subtlety under French law with an artist's estate is that works created during the marriage but not put into commerce (probably meaning placed for sale) may not become community property to which the wife has rights. A French case involving the artist Picabia had supported the view that such works remain solely the property of the spouse who created them.

As one can see, there were many complex legal questions to be resolved. In addition, French law has several other rights not generally known or recognized in Anglo-American law, adding to the legal complexity of the Picasso estate. For example, the "Droit Moral" is a property right that passes to an artist's heirs to protect both the artist's reputation and the integrity of his or her work. In a complex, arcane way the heirs also obtain after death the Droit de Suite, which entitles them to a percentage of post-death sales in France of Picasso's works even though owned before Picasso's death by nonfamily persons, and Droits Patrimoniaux, which give the heirs substantial control over the post-death reproductions of Picasso's works.

Besides all these interlocking rights and issues, another factor well known to American heirs — the payment of death taxes — may have been the most persuasive motivation of the ultimate settlement.

France, like most countries, was entitled to a substantial portion of the estate as death duties (Droits de Succession), which range in France from 5% to a maximum of 60%. To sell art to pay the tax would have been nearly impossible and, of course, could have had a cataclysmic effect on the value of Picassos around the world. Fortunately, France had enacted a new law on December 31, 1968, allowing the government to accept works of art in lieu of death duties. The law was said to have been the ingenious idea of the late André Malraux. If so, there may be a great irony to it, since allegedly Picasso did not himself make a lifetime gift of a permanent collection of his works to France partially over personal pique at Malraux. When Picasso lost the Grands-Augustine studio in which he had previously lived for about fifteen years, Malraux had promised to intervene, but nothing was done. His pride wounded, Picasso forgot about the idea of a lifetime donation.

This tax law had already enabled French museums to obtain masterpieces by Rubens, Fragonard, and Cézanne. But nothing compared to the plethora of Picassos to be selected. (With such a law in our country, the burning of $1.5 million worth of paintings by Arizona artist Ted DeGrazia, allegedly because of potential estate tax problems, might have been avoided. There has been at least one unsuccessful attempt to pass a law to let U.S. artists pay their death taxes with their works of art. It would have applied to literary, musical, and other artistic works as well as paintings and sculpture. Mexico in addition to France utilizes this approach.)

The heirs in the overall settlement let the government select first its share of the master's art legacy (somewhat less than one-quarter of the total appraised worth). Chosen for what is now the largest and richest collection of Picasso's art in the world were 228 paintings, 149 sculptures, 85 ceramics, 1,495 drawings, 33 sketchbooks, 1,622 prints (including 111 monotypes), and 35 illustrated books, not to mention Picasso's gift of the works of other artists, which constitute a special display in the home of the Musée Picasso, the Hôtel Salé, a palatial seventeenth-century residence in the Marais district of Paris. The heirs also cooperated in the difficult selection process with Dominique Bozo, the first chief curator of the new Musée Picasso. Mme Bozo indicated that the "collection comprises a complete retrospective, without lacunae — dealing with Picasso's art in all of its movements and modes of expression. It embraces all media: painting, sculpture, drawing, notebooks, prints, and ceramics."

When the heirs were close to settlement, the legitimate son, Paulo, died in June 1975. There were then two new protagonists to reckon with — his surviving children, Marina and Bernard. After much wrangling involving many lawyers, a satisfactory formula was finally achieved, and the papers were signed on September 15, 1977, more than four years after Picasso's death. Of the huge balance of the estate and art after France's share (e.g., the government took 228 out of 1,885 of Picasso's paintings), the widow Jacqueline received about 30%; the two grandchildren, Marina and Bernard, each about 20%; and the three natural children, Maya, Claude, and Paloma, each about 10%. The estimated legal fees added up to over 10% of the estate.

The distribution of the remaining art was effected by another interesting nontestamentary device. There was a drawing of lots in which each beneficiary drew a lot and selected a painting, and ultimately, as the procedure continued, the values of the paintings were attributed to each beneficiary so that each got his or her appropriate share of the estate.

As with the case of Abraham Lincoln's estate, Picasso's heirs could have been saved enormous expense and difficulty with a properly executed and devised will and estate plan.

And if one is well advised, a will can be a kind of last hurrah. Thomas Jefferson used his will to expand his creation: the University of Virginia. George Washington freed his slaves. A transplanted Englishman, John Harvard, about three and a half centuries ago, in his will left his personal library and half of his estate to build a college on a one-acre cow yard in the then colony of Massachusetts Bay. Alfred Nobel, the inventor of dynamite and nitroglycerin, established by his will the most sought-after prizes in the world. Cecil Rhodes created the famous scholarships that bear his name.

Other wills have constructively perpetuated a family business or converted a private business empire into a dynamic charitable entity like the MacArthur Foundation. And a will, as explained in more detail later, can be used to regulate the personal conduct of relatives by the use of conditional bequests — bequests that result in disinheritance, say, for failing to complete an education, or for smoking, drinking, or even marrying certain prohibited persons.

To summarize, fear of death, inability to quantify loving relationships in terms of one's property, and repression of anger over loss of power and control are but a few of the many reasons why persons do not make wills. These reasons and most others are weak excuses for inaction.

The will-making experience can and should be a healthy and open confrontation with a person's true feelings about himself, his death, his property, and the persons and causes he loves. After all, the testator will be gone forever when his will takes effect; he will no longer be paying taxes or involved in family fights. Accordingly, one need not be a thanatologist to realize that he must get his psychological satisfaction from a life well lived and from an estate well planned to be a final, fitting expression of his philosophy of life.

In *Moby Dick*, Ishmael says after signing his will, "I felt all the easier; a stone was rolled away from my heart. Besides, all the days I should now live would be as good as the days that Lazarus lived. . . . I survived myself."

Without wills, gigantic estate battles at great cost can easily arise, as happened with the estates of Howard Hughes and Pablo Picasso.

Wills, then, are extremely important to any well-planned estate, and, in general, you should know what the will of your spouse or cohabitant provides so that you will not be surprised by its terms after he or she dies, or, even worse, find there is no will.

But even with a will there is no guarantee that a major family fight won't occur. As a lawyer who has specialized in trusts and estates law for more than a quarter of a century, I have seen much family madness over wills: a mother attacking her sons; a father clashing with his daughter; stepchildren assailing their stepparent; a family foundation turning against the spouse, children, and other family members of its own creator; brothers confronting sisters; uncles and aunts at war with nieces and nephews; and nearly every variation of the foregoing. A notorious case in point was the contest over Seward Johnson's will.

FAMILY FIGHTS OVER MONEY

The Johnson Will Contest

In real life there is no limit to what becomes contested when one dies. The Prophet's beard case decided in India in 1879 resolved a dispute among many claimants over a holy hair from the beard of Muhammad called the Aussaree Shareef. A sneezing bailiff might have made the decision moot. One man's will left his entire estate "all to mother." When he died, he left behind his real mother and a wife whom he had affectionately nicknamed "mother." Which mother wins?

To demonstrate the overall problem of effecting one's wishes by even a well-drawn will, I offer the notorious will contest involving the heirs to the Johnson & Johnson pharmaceutical fortune. J. Seward Johnson, Sr., died at age 87 in 1983. He was survived by his third wife, Barbara "Basia" Johnson (née Piasecka, 42 years his junior and a chambermaid in his home before marrying him in 1971), and his six children from two prior marriages.

His will was not particularly complicated: (i) most of his $500 million estate was left in trust for Basia for her lifetime; (ii) his six children were to receive no outright bequests (except for a small bequest of property to J. Seward Johnson, Jr.), as he had (he thought) amply provided for them many years before; and (iii) his private oceanographic research foundation, Harbor Branch, was also out in the cold at the discretion of Basia, as, again, he probably thought he had provided for it sufficiently during his lifetime.

A titanic litigation ensued, with the children (and, belatedly, the foundation) attacking the will, alleging the usual litany of grounds: testamentary incapacity, improper execution, undue influence, fraud, and duress.

For connoisseurs of will contests, if there are such, an interesting aspect of the Johnson case was the fact that Seward Johnson, in about thirty prior wills and codicils, had disinherited the attacking children. Generally, if a will is upset because of the decedent's incapacity, then his prior will is revived. His incapacity means that he could not legally revoke a prior will by means of his last will. (That is why, contrary to popular belief, you generally should not destroy your prior wills.)

One factor, among others, causing a settlement in the Johnson case was the possibility that the jury would find testamentary capacity on the part of Mr. Johnson (i.e., that he was competent at the time of its making), thus validating the will, but still invalidate the provisions for Basia Johnson on the grounds of her undue influence, fraud, or duress. If that happened, what would have gone to her instead would have passed to the children — as if there had been no will.

In any event, the parties decided to settle. The will was, to put it charitably, totally rewritten by the contestants. (It is surprising even to many lawyers that in a will contest the parties can completely rewrite the will by the terms of their settlement.) The result: any resemblance to Seward Johnson's actual last will seemed purely coincidental.

Mr. Johnson should be a veritable whirling dervish in his grave, because all of his expressed intentions were flouted. Basia received $300 million outright to do with as she wished and not in trust; five of the children received $5.9 million and J. Seward Johnson, Jr., received $12 million, causing death taxes substantially in excess of their legacies, since there is a tax on the taxes themselves (see pp. 209–210 for a discussion of tax on taxes); and the Harbor Branch Foundation received $20 million. Thus the U.S. government exacted, in total, additional death taxes of about $86 million that would not otherwise have had to be paid. Finally, the lawyers for the children insisted on payment of their fee of $10 million from the estate and received it as part of the settlement.

The Palm Springs Widow Case

After her remarriage, a rich Palm Springs matron, the widow of a member of an esteemed U.S. manufacturing family, in effect attacked her own two children and three stepchildren and their respective issue (her grandchildren) over the will of the deceased father-husband, who had died some ten years before. Technically the suit was against the two fiduciaries under the will: her stepson, a man of impeccable integrity and character; and a trusted, long-time family adviser of the same moral caliber.

Her major claim was that her marital trust under the will had been underfunded many years ago, and that she should now be paid a very substantial amount (about $25 million) from the children's and grandchildren's trusts because of the post-death appreciation of the Florida real estate held in those trusts. She made this claim even though she had been told at the time her trust was funded that she could receive a portion of that real estate; she refused it because it would not produce immediate income for her use. Any judgment for her would not only have taken property away from her own children, stepchildren, and grandchildren, but also have reduced their extremely valuable trusts, which because of the date of their creation were "grandfathered," i.e., exempted, from the new and heavy generation-skipping tax.

Her legal argument was that her marital trust was not supposed to

"*Now read me the part again where I disinherit everybody.*"

be a dollar amount based on the date-of-death values of the estate, but a fractional share of all assets of the estate, including their appreciation over the ten years since her husband died. Her lawyers threw up a potpourri of lesser claims and, to add fuel to the fire, made defamatory allegations against the stepson fiduciary, which were totally devoid of merit and, indeed, would have been libelous had they not been sheltered by the privilege of being stated in judicial pleadings. Her own two children, represented by eminent New York counsel, opposed her just as vigorously as did her stepchildren and their counsel.

After many months of skirmishing, one of the leading surrogates (judges of the probate courts where will contests are decided) of New York State wrote an opinion granting the fiduciaries summary judgment (judgment without a trial and based only on the papers submitted on the legal issue) against her, holding she was not entitled to a fractional-interest marital trust.

The mother-stepmother-plaintiff was ready to appeal and fight on — damn the expense and the law. Finally, the children, though victorious and confident about an appeal, in order to make peace and end the needless, expensive, and emotionally draining fight, agreed to a settlement.

What did she gain from it? Under the settlement she received not one dollar of principal outright. She will get income for life from a new trust that at her death goes back to all of the children, but she had to relinquish her previously held power to designate who would take at her death a substantial portion of the existing marital trust. Her total income from both her marital trust and the new trust will probably be less than it was before she started the acrimonious litigation, because now her marital trust must be invested differently and not, as before, when the whole family was friendly, solely to produce the most income for her. The family relationships will, of course, never be the same.

The decedent would, in my opinion, be appalled at what his widow has done. If she had discussed her "alleged" additional financial needs with the family rather than litigating, I believe, knowing the stepson-fiduciary as I do and the rest of the children, that she probably could have gotten a better deal than she ended up with without costing herself and her family several million dollars of legal fees that will never come back to any of them. In fact, even in the last settlement meeting, her new trust was reduced by an additional $250,000, which went to her lawyers on top of the $1 million they had already negotiated for their accomplishments.

Finally, how can one assess the cost of irreparable emotional damage? One must wonder if she has any real understanding of what she has done. I believe Winston Churchill once said that "it is better to jaw-jaw than to war-war"—which certainly is true with respect to most family differences over money.

This case and the Johnson case dramatically prove the point that will contests and other estate fights can result in different kinds of disasters for all concerned, with the most aggrieved party often being the decedent, who can no longer complain or explain.

Sometimes it is said pejoratively that only the lawyers benefit from these controversies. I am reminded of the British barrister who told his clients that he could win their will contest and in doing so would raise the law to the level of poetry. However, the family decided to settle early out of court, and the lawyer was heard to grumble that "the entire estate was frittered away on the beneficiaries."

The Terrifying Clause

Since even the best-conceived plan can still be contested by one's child, spouse, or other beneficiary, there is a somewhat neglected legal device for increasing the probability that your intent will be carried out. It is the so-called *in terrorem* or no-contest clause, which can be effective both legally and psychologically.

In terrorem—from the Latin—literally means "in fright, alarm, or terror." An *in terrorem* clause is intended to convince beneficiaries not to challenge a will (and in some jurisdictions a trust) for fear they will thereby forfeit all dispositions made for them, and perhaps also for their children and more remote descendants as well. Although a no-contest clause cannot automatically prohibit a will contest, it often discourages would-be challengers by significantly raising the stakes.

The general legal rule followed by a majority of the states is that *in terrorem* clauses are valid unless the challenger has probable cause for bringing the contest. Probable cause means "the existence, at the time of the initiation of the proceeding, of evidence which would lead a reasonable person, properly informed and advised, to conclude that there is a substantial likelihood that the contest or attack will be successful." Some states, like New York and California, enforce no-contest clauses even if there is a probable cause to attack the will, unless it is on the limited grounds of forgery or revocation by a subsequent will.

A number of jurisdictions go even further and hold no-contest clauses absolutely valid regardless of probable cause, namely, Alabama, Arkansas, Ohio, Massachusetts, Missouri, Rhode Island, and perhaps the District of Columbia (in dicta). Only Florida and Indiana prohibit *in terrorem* clauses in wills, and Florida recently expanded its prohibition to include such clauses in revocable or living trusts.

A no-contest clause should be considered whenever people who would have statutory rights of inheritance in the absence of a will are disinherited or receive less under a will than the law might otherwise give them. A no-contest clause should also be considered in situations in which significant bequests are made to nonfamilial beneficiaries. For example, if you leave the minimum share required by law to your spouse (albeit an estranged spouse) and the rest of your estate in a discretionary trust for your only daughter and also your two "companions," who are forty years your junior, your will, absent a no-contest clause, would be highly likely to generate an attack.

A no-contest clause will be more likely to discourage a will contest if the contestant is put at risk of losing something of real value. Thus, a parent may decide to leave a bequest to his disfavored child (even if it is less than what his favored children receive) so that the disfavored child would lose his bequest if he unsuccessfully contests the will. Of course, it may be difficult for the parent to determine how much is enough to prevent a contest but is not more than he can tolerate leaving the child. This parent could provide that if the disfavored child contests the will, then not only is such child to be disinherited but also that child's children (i.e., the parent's grandchildren) are to be disinherited. This form of the clause clearly raises the stakes, if it is effective under your state's law, and may well avoid a will contest, but each person must determine if and to what extent he or she really wants to punish the grandchildren for the actions of their parent.

As shown by the Johnson estate litigation, will contests are extremely costly, increase family tensions, make public otherwise private intrafamily squabbles, and may lead to a settlement vastly different from the decedent's wishes. Certainly, if there is any likelihood of a will contest, the *in terrorem* clause should be used.

An unanswered question about the use of these so-called no-contest clauses is their effectiveness to prevent attacks on agreements and property arrangements other than those set forth in the will that contains such a clause. In other words, to use the clause to stop legal actions other than a contest of the particular will containing the clause. For example, a will leaves a fixed sum to a surviving spouse but, if that surviving spouse attacks an earlier prenuptial agreement made with the decedent under which the surviving spouse had waived all or substantially all inheritance rights, then such surviving spouse forfeits the fixed sum provided in the will. Another unclear area is the extent to which these clauses can prevent claims against an estate such as for palimony, or stop an attack to set aside a gift or a contract entered into by the will-maker during his or her lifetime.

An interesting offshoot of these questions occurred quite recently involving the enormously rich Koch family of Kansas.

Fred C. Koch founded the business empire now known as Koch Industries — a diversified company with petroleum, hydrocarbon, chemical, chemical technology, agricultural, and mineral business groups. He died in 1967 survived by his wife Mary, and their four sons, Charles, Frederick, and twins, David and William. In the 1980s, full-fledged warfare broke out among the brothers. William made an unsuccessful takeover attempt in 1980, which his brother Frederick supported. William's twin, David, and his other brother, Charles, opposed them. Numerous other intrafamily lawsuits were filed in the 1980s. Eventually William and Frederick's stock interests in Koch Industries were bought out by the company in 1983 for a total sum of $770 million. Even after that apparent settlement, the litigation continued, including actions alleging that the $770 million was not fair value and that a family foundation was badly administered. Mary Koch was very distressed by all the litigation.

When she died in 1990, leaving the comparatively small estate of $10 million, her will gave almost all of her estate to her four sons in equal shares. But it also contained a special *in terrorem* clause — in this case, an antilitigation clause. It stated that if any of her sons involved in a litigation at the time of her death as a plaintiff against any of her other sons did not dismiss such litigation within six weeks of the date of her death, such plaintiff-son would forfeit his inheritance under her will. Frederick and William did not dismiss their major litigation against their brothers, Charles and David, but instead attacked the will of their mother, claiming, among other things, that the antilitigation clause causing them to forfeit their inheritance was against public policy in denying them access to the courts, was the result of undue influence by their brothers, and was unenforceable because of a conflict of interest by the lawyer-draftsman of Mary Koch's will. The Kansas Court of Appeals unanimously upheld the unusual clause.

Mary Koch in death not only expressed her great displeasure and pain over the family litigation but she also actually rebuked two of her sons — financially in a very small way, but psychologically and morally in quite another way. The *Koch* case is a legal precedent that all advisers to will-makers should know about and consider in litigious family situations.

While the *in terrorem* or no-contest clause is often effective to ward off will contests (and, perhaps in certain limited circumstances, other family litigation by the Koch forfeiture clause), there is a relatively new legal weapon for attacks on testamentary plans which should now be mentioned, and against which the *in terrorem* clause would not be effective.

Intentional Interference with an Inheritance

As previously mentioned, baby boomers (age 30–48) and the unnamed generation ahead of them (age 48–60) will be receiving trillions of dollars over the next several decades — $10.4 trillion, according to a recent Cornell University study. Annual bequests (gifts by will) are expected to increase from 1.5 million totaling $84.3 billion in 1995 to 3.4 million totaling $335.9 billion in 2015.

Some testators and testatrices may prefer to disinherit many of these boomers, and their older counterparts in favor of charities or others. The number of will contests or other attacks upon estate plans could explode exponentially, particularly because many persons harbor the false belief that they have a right to inherit. Quite the contrary, there is no constitutional or common law right of inheritance. In America children can be totally disinherited except in Louisiana, which has its inheritance laws derived from the Napoleonic Code (see p. 63). Nevertheless, many persons, both relatives and nonrelatives, believe that they have a vested right to inherit. This misconception, coupled with our litigious citizenry, will, I think, lead to a lot of business for lawyers and great costs to families who have to go through such legal battles.

For reasons ranging from the strict standards about who can contest a will to the previously explained no-contest or *in terrorem* clauses, a will contest may not be a practical option for many disinherited beneficiaries.

A previously little-used tort (a tort is a civil wrong, such as libel or negligence) known as intentional interference with the expectancy of inheritance may receive a lot more action in the next decade in the hands of talented trusts and estates litigators.

In plain English, this recognized tort holds that if one person can prove that the conduct of another has prevented him or her from receiving an inheritance, then the one who was denied the inheritance can sue the other. For example, I can foresee a child suing a charity because that charity has received most or all of his or her expected inheritance.

There are two major reasons why this kind of attack on an estate plan may proliferate. One, just alluded to, is that any person who can prove the elements of the tort can bring the action, while, for example in New York and many other states, only one who would inherit if the will were invalidated can sue to upset that will. Probably of greater importance is that the action may be brought before the will-maker has died. This is in sharp contrast to the law on will contests which, by definition, occur only after the death of the will-maker. I think that this tort of intentional interference with an inheritance might even provide a basis for a potential inheritor to stop a testator or testatrix from signing a new will or from making a gift which could effectively disinherit him or her. In any event, this relatively new tort may well lead to more and more litigation, before and after death, against the best-laid plans of numerous will-makers and estates lawyers.

II

Trusts and Fiduciaries

IN TRUSTS WE TRUST

Once there is a will, you may come into contact with the favorite legal device of estate planners, in or out of wills: the trust. Its provenance traces back to the Statute of Uses of 1536, in England, and many legal scholars deem it the greatest achievement of Anglo-Saxon jurisprudence. We do not boast about our concept of contract, because in most, if not all, systems of law there is such a concept, and in most civilized legal systems the concept seems to be as elastic and general as it is in ours. But no other system has as flexible a tool as our trust for making dispositions of property.

"Blind" trusts control the assets of leading public officials so their investments do not affect their governmental decisions.

A "rabbi trust" is a funding vehicle for nonqualified deferred compensation payments, whose name derives from the fact that the first trust for which the Internal Revenue Service issued a private letter ruling was one established by a synagogue to fund the pension benefits of its rabbi. An ever-growing portion of our nation's wealth is held in pension and profit-sharing trusts; billions more are held in charitable trusts. Special private trusts (a fair number of which I have created over the years) may be the only, or the most effective, way to provide for mistresses, illegitimate children, and other beneficiaries whose position is delicate. Later, you will learn of a little-known device used by the rich — the intentionally defective trust. In short, the purposes of a trust are as limitless as the imagination of lawyers and their clients. They can be created for any purpose that is not illegal, i.e., against public policy.

Trusts enable you to transfer to others (trustees) title to your property, either during your lifetime or at death, to be used for the benefit of third parties (beneficiaries). The two basic kinds of trusts are living (*inter vivos*) and testamentary, the latter being created at death by the terms of a person's will. The duties of the trustee are those the creator decides to impose, and the interests of the beneficiaries are what the creator chooses to give them.

In our country, trusts have a pejorative connotation to some, springing from the antitrust laws that were created to curtail and regulate monopolies, epitomized by John D. Rockefeller, Sr.'s famous Standard Oil Trust. Through the use of this Standard Oil Trust, Mr. Rockefeller crossed state lines with impunity and gained control of the entire U.S. petroleum market. These statutes really should have been called antimonopoly rather than antitrust laws. In my days at Harvard Law School, students dubbed the antitrust course "Antimonopoly Planning," ironically taking the more appropriate title from the "Estate Planning" course.

THE FIDUCIARIES: EXECUTORS, TRUSTEES, AND GUARDIANS

You should have a fundamental understanding of the functions of the three most important estate fiduciaries: executors, trustees, and guardians.

Executors and Trustees

An executor, as the word denotes, is the person (or institution) named in a will to execute or carry out the terms of that will. What this means is that the executor offers the will for probate in the relevant court. Probate is the legal process of proving before a competent judicial authority that a will of a decedent is genuine and valid. After the will is accepted in court, the executor collects and inventories the assets, has them appraised, pays the death taxes, if any, and distributes the assets in accordance with the will's directions. During the administration of the estate, the executor must also invest the assets, including determining whether to retain or sell existing investments. Depending on the size and complexity of the estate, its administration will vary from two years to as much as ten years or more.

Family members, professional fiduciaries (banks and trust companies), trusted friends, lawyers, and accountants are usually named as executors. While lawyers and accountants perform much of the actual work in any event, they need not necessarily be named executors.

A trustee is the fiduciary who holds trust property and administers it for the benefit of the trust's beneficiaries. Usually, the term of a trustee is much longer than the term of an executor, since trusts often last for the lifetime of a person, or until a child reaches a designated age. As with executors, one rounds up the same suspects for trusteeship — family members, banks, trust companies, friends, lawyers, and accountants.

There seems to be a commonly held view that an executor or trustee must be an expert investor of money. That ability is a plus but not a necessity. An ordinarily intelligent person is not prohibited from serving as an executor or trustee merely because of a lack of expertise in investment matters. Your fiduciary can hire a money manager, just as you can, or can be directed to consult a designated expert or experts. Such a person, as executor or trustee, must take reasonable steps to obtain competent advice and formulate a prudent investment strategy for the trust.

The most important qualities of an executor or trustee are integrity and judgment. He, she, or it should command the respect and confidence not only of the testator but of the beneficiaries.

The duties of executors and trustees are not only business and financial but also human and personal. The fiduciary should be one who will take a personal interest in the welfare of the beneficiary; one who will conscientiously, with gentleness, firmness, and wisdom as circumstances require, carry out the wishes of the decedent and protect the assets of the estate or trust.

There is a popular canard articulated by many lawyers, accountants, and financial planners that you should not use a bank or trust company as your executor or trustee. The basic argument goes that these corporate fiduciaries cost too much, are too impersonal, and are not good at investing the estate's assets.

My experience has taught me that established banks and trust companies can make the very best fiduciaries. As institutions, they are not subject to many of the frailties of the individual as executor or trustee — aging, ill health, death, and conflict of interest (intrafamily, economic or otherwise). To the extent a corporate fiduciary were to do something out of order, then it, unlike many individual executors and trustees, should have substantial assets to compensate for any wrongdoing or negligence. Many do have good investment capabilities, or, if not, they can also be directed to hire particular money managers. Over the years, I have worked with most of the top New York banks, and also with some of the leading Swiss and other foreign-owned banks with U.S. subsidiaries or offices which handle trusts and estate matters. I think that in any substantial or complicated estate their services can be invaluable and well worth their customary charges. A very intelligent compromise position, often used by the sophisticated client, is to have co-fiduciaries — an individual family member or members or other trusted individuals together with a bank or trust company.

In the Averell Harriman case, the trustees of the nine Harriman family trusts were three individuals — Clark Clifford, Paul Warnke, and William Rich III — who apparently had agreed to serve without being paid commissions. The gravamen of their alleged breach of trust was a bad investment in a rural New Jersey resort hotel, The Seasons Resort and Conference Center (née the Playboy Hotel), leading to losses of over $20 million. These trustees were also charged, among other things, with fraud in concealing the losses, and conflicts of interest (especially with First American Bank of which Clifford was chairman and Rich a director), alleged to be "the only lender to recoup its entire investment [of $18 million]"). The litigation could go on for years. Several points can already be made:

1. If an independent bank or trust company had been a co-fiduciary, would this mess have occurred? I doubt it.

2. Trustees who do not get paid for their services may give you only what you have paid for.

3. Why did the three named trustees resign without first obtaining a release from liability, either informally or through a court accounting? I can't understand it. Without the protection of a release the new trustees have now been able to sue them. I would never have allowed a trustee in the Harriman situation to resign without first obtaining some legal protection from liability. Even if a release could not be obtained, either in or out of court, the trustees (by not resigning and seeking an accounting) would have had the use of the trust funds to defend themselves in the court fight rather than being forced to use their own assets to pay lawyers to defend their actions as trustees.

4. Finally, Pamela Digby Churchill Harriman, the widow of Averell Harriman, was sued although she was not a trustee of the trusts. The theory for suing her is that she became a de facto trustee by being a general partner of the investment partnerships that invested the assets of the nine Harriman family trusts involved in the litigation. Beware of your actions in investing trust funds that may make you liable as if you were a trustee. Pamela Harriman apparently personally lost $3 million on the same disastrous hotel investment. On the facts available as of November 1994, it will be very difficult to find Pamela Harriman personally liable for the acts of the actual trustees.

Guardians

A final category that is dramatically important when death comes unexpectedly, as it often does, is a guardian for minors. When death comes to a parent who leaves behind minor children, the role of the guardian becomes essential. Technically, there can be one guardian for the person and one for the property of your children. The latter provision is not often used, because any substantial property for a minor is better held in trust than by a guardian, who, depending on local law, must give the minor all such property outright at 18 or 21. The guardian of the person is the surrogate parent with whom the child will live. There could hardly be a more important parental decision, even though the universal hope, of course, is that the guardian will never serve.

Everyone should realize that parents who do not name guardians are leaving the choice to the local court having jurisdiction over such cases. One wealthy Connecticut couple perished during a storm while sailing. They left a will but had named no guardian for their two children. The 3- and 5-year-old youngsters immediately became the objects of a family squabble. Within days of the deaths, a grandmother, two aunts, and an uncle had petitioned the probate judge for custody of the children. The judge appointed as guardian the maternal aunt who had taken the children into her own home after the accident, and who had children of her own near the ages of her sister's children.

In one of my cases, a rich woman designated her equally rich brother to be guardian of a young Vietnamese girl whom she had adopted. When the woman died a few years later, the brother refused to take the child. The decedent had always said that her brother had agreed to be the guardian, but one could not be sure. It is, of course, the height of irresponsibility to name guardians (or executors or trustees) without obtaining their prior consent to act. Because of the money involved in this case, a real donnybrook ensued, including an attempt to gain custody by the decedent's estranged husband, whom she was trying to divorce at the time of her death. Ultimately, with the help of a compassionate judge, the child was placed in the home of an American professor, his Asian wife, and their two children. She has since become a strong, productive, happy person and recently finished her college education.

Customarily, a blood relative is chosen as guardian, but that is not always the wisest choice. One should look for someone who shares the same traditions and values. For example, if a child is accustomed to certain religious training and an emphasis on the value of education and his guardians disregard this prior upbringing, the harm to the child is obvious.

Should the trustee and guardian be the same? It can be helpful, but it is not necessary. Often the best guardians may have limited financial acumen or experience. Because trustees and guardians may disagree, it is advisable to try to leave directions, even if only by prec-atory memoranda (memoranda expressing one's wishes), to tell the trustee what to do — for example, about advancing money when the trustee's and the guardian's judgments differ. Whose judgment should control, and under what circumstances?

In which home should the guardian raise the children — yours or the guardian's? Should there be an outright cash legacy to the guardian or guardians as a token of appreciation and to create goodwill? Have you chosen a couple, or really only one of the couple? And if you wanted both of the couple, should they later be replaced by your sec-ond-choice guardian if divorce or death separates them? Should money be made available to increase the size of the guardian's home? To help educate the guardian's children so they will not be second-class citizens to your children? To hire extra household help? (In one case, new guardians who lived far away from the children's home brought along the children's housekeeper to help provide continuity.) To raise the children with certain basic religious training?

In the last analysis, choosing a guardian is much more a question of common sense than of law, but doing it wisely can be a precious gift to your children.

THE WRONG TRUSTEE?
THE HENRY FORD II CASE

The importance of the selection of a fiduciary was vividly demonstrated
in the imbroglio over the estate of Henry Ford II, who died at age 70
in September 1987, a resident of Palm Beach, Florida. Most of his
estate, estimated to be about $350 million, was disposed of by means
of a revocable trust rather than a will, a commonly used device by
many testators for, among other reasons, privacy—the trust, unlike a
will, is not filed in the probate court and need not be made subject to
public scrutiny. (See Chapter VI on the overall efficacy of using a
revocable trust in estate planning.) His will was a relatively simple
eight-page document primarily "pouring over" all and any assets to his
revocable trust that he had not already put in it during his lifetime.

Essentially all of this trust was to be used for his widow's lifetime
benefit, with a guaranteed minimum yearly after-tax income of $1.5
million, to be adjusted for inflation. She is the only person entitled to
income from the trust, which controlled 8% of the voting stock in the
Ford Motor Company. In addition, the trustees could, in their discretion, give her principal to maintain her standard of living. At her death,
the trust principal is to be distributed equally among the Ford grandchildren, who now number six, skipping his three surviving children,
Edsel Ford II, Charlotte Ford, and Anne Ford Scarborough. Ford
explained in the trust that the children had already been amply provided for.

The automobile magnate named three trustees: his widow (and last
of his three wives), Kathleen Duross Ford, a 48-year-old former model;
his son, Edsel; and a Detroit businessman, Martin Citrin, whose wife
was a close friend of Kathleen's. Not long after Ford's death, Mr.
Citrin shot himself in the head—fatally. The only named successor
trustee was William H. Donaldson, an eminent New York businessman
of previously unquestioned integrity, who was a founder of the Wall
Street investment banking firm Donaldson, Lufkin & Jenrette, chairman of the Ford Foundation's finance committee, an undersecretary of
state under presidents Gerald Ford and Richard Nixon, and a trusted
friend of Henry Ford II.

The successor trustee appointment of Donaldson set off a gigantic brawl when Kathleen Ford attacked him, claiming that he should not be allowed to serve because he allegedly refused to accept his appointment without a $1 million annual trusteeship fee. She wanted another trustee named in his place. Mr. Ford had named no successor to Mr. Donaldson. Edsel and the rest of Henry Ford's family all supported Mr. Donaldson. They claimed that the $1 million was only an estimate of the maximum his fee would be in his first year and that it "would be substantially reduced in subsequent years" and even in the first year "if circumstances warranted."

While Mrs. Ford's lawyer said that the fight was "pure and simple" over Mr. Donaldson's fees, Donaldson's lawyers and the family contended that Mrs. Ford feared Donaldson's independence as a cotrustee. Court papers allege that Mrs. Ford told Donaldson that she did not want him to act unless he "would agree to act in her personal interest and not evenhandedly." Mr. Donaldson had also told Mrs. Ford's personal attorney that he should resign as lawyer for the trust because his personal representation of her created "conflicts of interest." Shortly thereafter, Mrs. Ford instituted her lawsuit.

The litigation was eventually settled, with Mr. Donaldson staying on as trustee, as one is sure Mr. Ford wanted. However, he was to serve only for a limited period of approximately three years from the time of settlement.

If you accept at face value Mrs. Ford's lawyer's statement that the fight was only over trustee's fees, the whole thing could have been avoided if Mr. Ford had stated the compensation that he wanted the independent trustee to receive either in all events or if the other trustees could not unanimously agree about it. Such an arrangement would not be at all unusual. Quite the contrary, with a trust this size it is advisable not to leave fiduciary fee questions unsettled. And with hindsight a specific fee provision in the Ford trust could have eliminated the only asserted grounds for what seemed, in any event, a legally impoverished attack on the designated trustee. The Ford case seems to prove the importance of being clear about fiduciary fees, particularly in family situations in which the other trustees or the main beneficiaries are known not to be friendly with each other. (None of Mr. Ford's children attended his 1980 wedding to Kathleen.) The Ford case also supports the proposition that when and if it is possible and practical, the testator should name fiduciaries who he knows are personally respected by his beneficiaries as well as by himself. But then no one knows with certainty how his beneficiaries will behave when he is gone and his money is left behind.

Henry Ford had said that "the most unattractive thing he found in life was families airing their dirty laundry in the press." The press in general, and the Detroit newspapers in particular, but also the *Wall Street Journal* and the *New York Times*, had a field day with the spectacle of a Ford family fight over money and power.

Besides all the laundry airing, such as the much-publicized dispute over whether terry-cloth furniture covers should be paid for from Mrs. Ford's own income or from the trust, Mr. Ford's privacy was invaded by various other disclosures. In a 1986 amendment to the trust, Ford mandated that if he was ever kidnapped, total control over all efforts to free him was to vest in Arjay Miller, who had been president of Ford but whom Mr. Ford had apparently kicked upstairs in 1968. Mr. Miller left the company in 1969 to become head of Stanford's graduate business school.

For his funeral, Henry Ford II instructed: "There should be music — and, in this connection, a black jazz band playing 'When the Saints Go Marching In' for a recessional, for I do not wish to be remembered only in a solemn fashion." He also wished to be cremated "and the ashes scattered from a helicopter on the waters of the Detroit River, opposite Detroit Renaissance Center." Apparently this was done, but the privacy that everyone agrees Mr. Ford had zealously sought by the use of his private trust was destroyed as soon as the trust was filed as an exhibit to his wife's court petition against Mr. Donaldson.

So, once again, as with the case of J. Seward Johnson, Henry Ford II would, one might think, be aghast at the remaking of his estate plan because of the litigation among his heirs and fiduciaries with these results: his designated trustee, William Donaldson, to serve for only a relatively short term; Donaldson's successor to be anyone's guess, but certainly not Henry Ford's own selection; his widow to receive not the

$1.5 million yearly minimum income as adjusted (plus discretionary principal payments) but instead the minimum provided by Florida law (estimated to be $10.5 million per year); his most private wishes and property dispositions to be known to every newspaper reader in America; and the ongoing administration of his estate to be enveloped by the miasma that is the usual remnant of such acrimonious family litigation.

The Henry Ford case teaches us that the best estate plan will not work if the main beneficiary cannot get along with the designated fiduciary (here, a trustee) and also that the compensation of the fiduciaries of your estate should be discussed and agreed upon *before* death, not after.

III

Estate and Gift Taxes

THE PRESENT FEDERAL TRANSFER TAXES

Surprisingly, most wealthy persons badly underestimate how heavily their estates will be taxed. A recent survey by U.S. Trust Company of New York shows the average estimate was only 24%. In fact, the range for federal death taxes is more likely 37% to 55%. In order to appreciate the relevance of and the need to avoid estate and gift taxes, consider for a moment the current federal gift and estate tax (transfer tax) rates:

$0 to $600,000	- no tax
$600,001 to $750,000	- 37%
$750,001 to $1,000,000	- 39
$1,000,000 to $1,250,000	- 41
$1,250,001 to $2,000,000	- 45
$2,000,001 to $2,500,000	- 49
$2,500,001 to $3,000,000	- 53
$3,000,000+	- 55

There is an added 5% estate tax surcharge on $10 million to $21.04 million in an estate that, in effect, wipes out the benefit of the usual $600,000 exemption.

Each citizen has a one-time exemption of $600,000 from either federal estate or gift tax and, in addition, can give $10,000 each year free of gift tax to anyone in the world. (A married couple can give anyone $20,000 per year regardless of which spouse actually furnishes the money or property.)

It often, but not always, makes sense because of the tax bracket swing to make certain (assuming you have enough money) that each spouse has assets of at least $3 million in order to lock in the lower estate tax brackets (37% to 55%) in the estates of both spouses. Furthermore, in 1992, for example, 56% of estate tax returns of gross estates of over $5 million were audited, perhaps another reason to try to keep the estates of both spouses below that figure, if practicable.

But federal transfer taxes are not the only concern.

STATE TRANSFER TAXES

State death and gift taxes must also be taken into consideration. Depending on the size of your estate, the federal government grants you a credit, up to a certain maximum, for the payment of state death taxes. The states then charge you at least this credit amount — usually called a "soakup" tax because that's what the states do. In Florida, Nevada, and Arizona, the most popular retirement states, this state death tax credit is the only other death tax one pays. On an estate of $1 million with all of it going to a child of the decedent, this state death tax credit is $33,200.

But in about twenty-two states, the taxing authorities want more. Five of them — including New York and Massachusetts — impose separate, often substantial estate taxes. Seventeen others, such as Kentucky and Connecticut, levy inheritance taxes that can be even more sizable. Many of these states tax you even if your estate is under $600,000. Inheritance tax rates vary widely depending on the recipient of the inheritance, e.g., whether the recipient is a family member or unrelated. One Pennsylvania resident adopted his own brother to save inheritance tax because of the lower rates on inheritance by a child. Most states exempt everything left to a surviving spouse, though Delaware, Michigan, Pennsylvania, and Tennessee do not. New Hampshire offers an exemption to spouses, parents, children, and grandchildren and their spouses but taxes all outsiders at a high 18% flat rate.

Consider the following state death taxes on a $1 million estate left entirely to your child:

Most states (imposing only the state death tax credit)	$ 33,200
North Carolina	35,000
Kansas	41,750
Indiana	51,900
New York	53,500
Delaware	55,250
Ohio	58,100
Pennsylvania	59,880
South Dakota	71,250
Iowa	71,825
Connecticut	77,935
Kentucky	84,550
Massachusetts	107,000

So, not only do federal estate taxes hit you hard, but these state death taxes can too.

Interestingly enough, only six states (and the Commonwealth of Puerto Rico) have gift taxes. These states are Connecticut, Delaware, Louisiana, New York, North Carolina, Oregon, and Tennessee. These state gift taxes are quite important to take into account for persons living in these states, because giving money is cheaper taxwise than leaving it to your heirs by will. For example, if you are subject to tax at a 50% estate and gift tax bracket, and you give $500,000 to your children, the gift tax would be $250,000. To leave the same $500,000 to your children by your will would take $1 million, since the 50%

estate tax is on the entire $1 million while the gift tax is only on the gifted amount of $500,000. For older persons, the best estate planning is often to make substantial gifts, especially in those states with no separate gift taxes — bearing in mind, however, the cost of the loss of the use of the money that paid the gift taxes for the rest of the giver's lifetime.

THE ISSUE OF DOMICILE

Today more and more Americans have residences in two or more states. Often one state is the place of original domicile, such as New York or New Jersey for many, and the second residence is often in a so-called retirement state such as Florida, Arizona, or California.

What many persons do not seem to realize is that it is legally permissible for both states (and even more than two) to tax your worldwide assets at death if your legal domicile is not clear. In fact, such states in a brutal combination blow could technically — and legally — wipe out your estate with their taxes.

Take the well-known case of the Campbell soup heir who got himself into thick trouble with the tax collectors over the issue of his domicile. In that celebrated case, New Jersey and Pennsylvania both claimed John T. Dorrance, an heir to the Campbell soup fortune, as their domiciliary, and each state collected approximately $17 million in inheritance taxes in the 1930s. Fortunately for his descendants, the family soup product was so popular that the Dorrance family fortunes were later resuscitated. His grandson, John T. "Ippy" Dorrance III, is determined to avoid the tax sins of his ancestor by means of expatriation (see Chapter XIII); he has become a citizen of Ireland, also residing in the Bahamas and Devil's Tower, Wyoming. If his plan works, at his death the bulk of his $1.2 billion fortune will be subject only to 2% Irish death taxes instead of the 55% U.S. estate tax.

Probably the most famous case of this kind is the Green Domicile Case. Four states — Texas, Massachusetts, New York, and Florida — claimed Colonel (by the grace of a Southern governor) Edward H. R. Green, the only son of the notorious millionairess Hetty Green, as a domiciliary, with the cumulative federal and state death tax bills exceeding $37 million ($1 million more than Mr. Green's estate). Fortunately for the beneficiaries, the Supreme Court of the United States in 1936 accepted, at the petition of Texas, original jurisdiction over the case, because the total state tax claims exceeded the gross estate and because the dispute was between two (or more) states.

Hetty Green had died in 1916, the richest and most detested woman in the United States, with a fortune estimated at between $100 and $200 million. She had left her entire estate to her children, whose lives she had essentially ruined — her daughter, Sylvia, and her son, Edward. They were aptly described in a delightful book about Hetty and her family by Arthur H. Lewis, *The Day They Shook the Plum Tree* (Harcourt Brace, 1963):

> Colonel Ned, a six-foot-four-inch, three-hundred-pound, wildly eccentric, one-legged son who blithely tossed away $3,000,000 a year on yachts, coins, stamps, diamond-studded chastity belts, female teenage wards, pornography, orchid culture, and Texas politics, and a frightened, eremitic daughter, Sylvia Wilks, who kept a $31,000,000 cash bank balance that earned no interest.

A special master, John S. Flannery of the Washington, D.C., bar, appointed by the U.S. Supreme Court, held hearings for nearly two years with 385 witnesses in behalf of the four competing states, four million words of testimony, and 2,855 exhibits. The special master ruled in favor of Massachusetts, and his opinion was upheld by the U.S. Supreme Court, avoiding the total eradication of Colonel Green's estate. Given the notoriety of the case, the final decision cost one state attorney general the highest office in his state (Texas) and helped lift another into a governor's mansion (Massachusetts). In its opinion the Supreme Court specifically noted that it was long established that such situations of double taxation of estates were part of the federal system and were constitutional.

Let us consider a person with homes in Texas and California. (If we used Texas and Maine we could discuss former President Bush's domiciliary status.) Where is this person domiciled for tax purposes? How is domicile defined?

The federal definition of "domicile" reflects the meaning of the term as it generally applies for state tax purposes as well:

> A person acquires a domicile in a place by living there, for even a brief period of time, with no definite present intention of later removing therefrom. Residence without the requisite intention to remain indefinitely will not suffice to constitute domicile, nor will intention to change domicile effect such a change unless accompanied by actual removal.

Both Texas and California have their own estate taxes. In the case of a domiciliary of either state, all assets (excluding real estate and tangible personal property, i.e., physical objects such as art and furniture, actually located outside of the state) owned by the decedent, wherever situated, are subject to the state estate tax. This definition means that stocks, bonds, partnership and other business interests, and other intangible assets are subject to the estate tax of the state of domicile.

If a state claims that the decedent was domiciled in it and assesses a full state estate tax, the executor of the estate may challenge that assessment in the state's courts. If the executor loses, however, and the courts of Texas (in our example) determine that the decedent was a Texas domiciliary, California will not be bound by that decision. Instead, it is legally permissible for the California courts to determine that the same individual was actually a domiciliary of California. If this were to happen, both states would assert the right to tax virtually the entire estate, and they can still succeed under present laws.

That is exactly what happened to the Howard Hughes estate.

Howard Hughes died in 1976. The State of Texas claimed him as a resident even though Texas officials admitted that Hughes had spent no more than forty-eight hours in the state after 1926. Disputing the claim was the State of California, where Hughes lived between 1925 and 1966, and where the death tax rate was 24%, compared to 16%

in Texas. Hughes's heirs contended that he was domiciled in Nevada, which has no estate or inheritance tax. The combined death taxes would not have wiped out the estate (as they would have in the Green case), and so the U.S. Supreme Court refused to decide which state (probably Nevada) was Hughes's tax domicile. After millions in legal fees and three trips to the U.S. Supreme Court, eventually a compromise was reached by the states whereby Texas received $50 million in cash and California received $44 million in cash plus a $75 million parcel of land near the Los Angeles Airport.

Texas Attorney General Jim Mattox boasted that the settlement would finance the annual cost of operating the state's agriculture department, public utilities commission, and attorney general's office. Less ecstatic was Hughes's first cousin William Lummis, who has ably administered the estate on behalf of the heirs. Said Lummis: "I think they nicked us pretty good."

There are state statutes allowing taxing authorities to compromise death taxes with the taxing agencies of the other state or states. But these statutes are not mandatory. And such a compromise might likely result in a higher total tax than would have been imposed if the decedent had had only one domicile. That is what eventually happened in the case of the Howard Hughes estate.

So, at best, the risk of inconsistent determinations of domicile might be ameliorated by negotiations after the client's death that may result in combined state death taxes that are somewhat less than full taxes owed to both states based on domicile in each but are likely to be larger than a single domiciliary tax would be. At worst, attempts to compromise may be unsuccessful, and there appears to be no remedy for the client's estate to the specter of double state taxation unless the combined rates of federal, California, and Texas estate taxes, including interest, exceed the sum of the net assets available for the payment of the taxes. Even then, the estate itself has no remedy, but must, as in the famous Colonel Green case, instead rely on one of the two states to commence legal proceedings invoking the original jurisdiction of the U.S. Supreme Court.

In short, even the best-case scenario involves lengthy and costly post-death proceedings and the serious possibility of double taxation.

It is thus advisable for every person with assets to determine which state is more likely to be successful in asserting domicile after his or her death and to sever as many ties as possible to the other state or states so as to minimize the risk that another state will successfully assert that he or she was a domiciliary there. Bear in mind that the fact that a person during lifetime has had no problems with more than one state over income taxes does not mean a conflict about domicile will not arise over death taxes when, after death, assets need to be legally transferred to the person's heirs in more than one state.

UTILIZING YOUR $600,000 ONETIME EXEMPTION

At the time of this book's publication, but perhaps for not much longer, each person has a onetime $600,000 exemption from federal gift or estate tax (technically known as the "unified credit"), which can be used to benefit one's children (or any other person). The exemption is not $600,000 per child but a total of $600,000. So, if you have three children, you could now give each of them $200,000 (not $600,000) free of gift tax. Your spouse can do the same, even if he or she uses your money. However, if your estate is more than $10 million, this exemption is phased out at death, so one should use it now, because although in such cases the $600,000 can be added back at death, the future appreciation on the $600,000 will not be. Furthermore, everyone who can afford to should consider using the exemption now, since it may well be eliminated in the next tax legislation. There is no lobby fighting for it.

Many middle-class or even so-called upper-middle-class persons are loath to remove irrevocably $1,200,000 or even $600,000 from the assets available for their economic support. But these valuable exemptions, which will in time no doubt disappear, can be utilized now, with the taxpayer couple keeping most of the economic benefits, if they simply know what they are doing.

Thus, one spouse creates a trust of $600,000 for the other, with income payable to the beneficiary-spouse, and principal also if the trustee so determines (or the beneficiary-spouse takes it pursuant to an acceptable standard for principal withdrawals for tax purposes). The beneficiary-spouse can be a cotrustee of such trust. Meanwhile, the other spouse creates another $600,000 trust, with some technical differences required for tax purposes to avoid the so-called reciprocal trust doctrine, but with equal economic benefits available for the other beneficiary spouse. Accordingly, during the joint lives of the two spouses there need be no loss of income or even of principal if necessary. Nevertheless, if the trust is properly drawn, all of the trust income and all of the principal *and its appreciation* can remain out of the taxable estates of the spouses and go to the benefit of the children and other family members.

This technique of reciprocal spousal trusts is probably the most conservative use of the two $600,000 exemptions, but it will appeal to many who are always uncertain, psychologically or in reality, about the economic future.

If, in addition, you wish to keep a string that can bring back the money to you if you need it — and I mean all of the money, both $600,000 trusts — you need to use certain foreign trusts also known as asset protection trusts or APTs. (See Chapter XI, p. 189, for a discussion of these trusts.)

THE GENERATION-SKIPPING TAX: DYNASTY TRUSTS

Historically, in America, families of great wealth, like the Rockefellers, the Du Ponts, the Fords, and the Kennedys, passed wealth down for generations without death taxes by the simple expedient of the use of family trusts. These trusts, in most states, could last for the maximum period of time allowed by the so-called Rule Against Perpetuities, a rule of law arising out of an English statute going back to 1536. In effect, this rule prohibits trusts from continuing beyond a period defined with reference to an ascertainable class of persons living at the time the trust was created, e.g., all of the then living descendants of Joseph Kennedy. In that example, such a trust could last no longer than twenty-one years after the death of the last survivor of such designated Kennedy descendants. This allowed trusts to last for eighty to one hundred years and, more important for death tax purposes, for three or even more generations of one's family.

And the trust, being the uniquely creative legal instrument that it is, could by its terms practically give each descendant the equivalent of outright ownership without the death tax effects of such ownership. Thus, such a generation-skipping trust, say one of the many for the late President Kennedy, could provide as follows: all income would be paid to him; any or all of the principal could be paid to him or used for his benefit in the discretion of a friendly trustee; the president could also take down principal equal to 5% of the trust in each and every year he chose to without the trustee's consent; and he could direct, with unimportant limitations, how the trust property passed at his death among his spouse and descendants. Then, at his death, there would be no death taxes on his trust, and there would be ongoing trusts of similar terms for his children, John and Caroline, which would mean no death taxes at their subsequent deaths. And on and on, only subject to the time-period limitation of the Rule Against Perpetuities. The use of these trusts is what essentially all the wealthy American families did to avoid death taxes for many generations.

To eliminate the generation-skipping trust, the greatest estate planning technique since the inception of the federal estate tax in 1916, Congress in 1986 invented the federal generation-skipping tax ("GST tax"), which is a new tax at a flat rate of 55%. The GST tax is to make sure that no property skips a generation without being taxed. For example, say you had a large estate, with children who were already provided for, and you wanted to leave it directly to your grandchildren. Under the new law, this estate would essentially be taxed twice. There would be a GST tax on what went directly to the grandchildren at your death (as if it had first passed to your children, was taxed, and then went to grandchildren, and was taxed again), *plus* the applicable estate tax on your estate. (See later discussion at pp. 160–162 explaining how Jackie Kennedy Onassis avoided this double tax by the creative use of a charitable lead trust in her will.)

However, there is a very important exemption from the GST tax of $1 million per taxpayer-donor (not per grandchild-recipient). Thus, a married couple together have a total exemption of $2 million. If they use it all at once, e.g., by direct gifts to adult grandchildren, there will be gift taxes (not a GST tax) on $800,000, because the couple together have only $1.2 million of exemptions ($600,000 each) from gift tax.

How does one best take advantage of the GST exemption?

One method of growing popularity is to use a so-called dynasty trust (sometimes called a perpetuities trust) for this purpose. It is an irrevocable trust created for the benefit of the creator's ("grantor's") descendants, and funded with property to which the grantor allocates all or a portion of his GST exemption. If the grantor is married and his or her spouse participates in making transfers to the trust, as previously indicated a total GST exemption of $2 million is available. (To avoid any current gift taxes, a couple might wish to use only their maximum current exemption of $1.2 million for such a trust.)

Once exempted, property transferred to the trust, including all appreciation in value and all accumulated income, remains free from further federal transfer taxation for as long as it remains in trust, which can be for many generations. Given the effects of compounding, a successfully invested trust can accumulate to a value of hundreds of millions of dollars, which can be made available to future-generation beneficiaries undiminished by estate or generation-skipping taxes. For example, assuming growth at an annual after-tax rate of 7%, a dynasty trust of $2 million would double every ten years as follows:

10 years	$ 4 million
20 years	8 million
30 years	16 million
40 years	32 million
50 years	64 million

Like old generation-skipping trusts, a dynasty trust is typically structured to continue in existence for the maximum period of time permitted under applicable state law. Under the laws of most states, this legal maximum is limited by the Rule Against Perpetuities. But South Dakota, Wisconsin, and Idaho have eliminated this rule, and so in those three jurisdictions these dynasty trusts can last in perpetuity, or forever.

South Dakota (my state of origin) is the most advantageous, because it has no state income taxes, unlike Wisconsin and Idaho, where rates go as high as 7% to 8%. In due course, perhaps South Dakota will become a home to dynasty trusts like Delaware now is to corporations. After all, South Dakota was once (long before Nevada) the divorce capital of the United States, particularly from about 1880 to 1893. In fact, my hometown, Sioux Falls (the Queen City of the upper-north Middle West), was the place that the then rich and famous came to get divorced since the South Dakota divorce law required only ninety days of residence and a claim of incompatibility.

A dynasty trust may be created during the grantor's lifetime or at death. The advantage of using the GST exemption is magnified if it is used during the grantor's life, because once property is transferred to a dynasty trust and exempted, all appreciation and accumulated income generated by the property until the grantor's death will be exempt as well. This additional accumulation should normally result in more property being held in the trust by the time the grantor dies than could be placed there initially at the grantor's death. However, creating the dynasty trust during life will result in a taxable gift by the grantor and may require the payment of a gift tax. In order to avoid gift taxes, many individuals prefer to fund a dynasty trust during life only to the extent of the available unified credit (maximum of $600,000 for an individual, or $1.2 million for a married couple), with the balance of the available GST exemption amount ($400,000 for the individual grantor or $800,000 for the married couple) funded at death.

Lifetime funding of a dynasty trust may have additional benefits as well. Because the trust is irrevocable, future changes in the transfer tax laws should not affect it. Thus, the grantor is assured of receiving the benefit of the GST exemption and any unified credit used in funding the trust, and those benefits cannot be eliminated if such exemption or credit is reduced in the future. If the GST exemption is increased at some future time, it should always be possible to add to the trust.

A dynasty trust may take any one of an indefinite number of forms, depending on the desires of the creator. For example, all of the property can be held as a single fund for all descendants, or it can be split into separate trusts, such as one trust for each child of the grantor and his or her family line. It is not necessary at all that the trust property be "locked up" with no benefits available during the trust term. Indeed, in a typical trust, the income and principal are made available at the discretion of the trustee to one or more beneficiaries during the period of the trust's existence, according to whatever standards of distribution the grantor prefers, so the trust assets should be viewed as readily available to the family.

The most common way to use the GST exemption in wills is for each spouse to create a separate $1 million trust from which the surviving spouse will receive all income for life. Upon the death of the surviving spouse, the trust principal will pass to separate lifetime trusts for the grantor's children. Although the trust will be subject to estate tax on the surviving spouse's death (which would be paid from such spouse's other assets), as with the dynasty trust, it will never be taxed again. The key therefore is to allow the trust to grow to the greatest possible extent for future generations. Thus, if the children have adequate income and other financial resources, the income in the GST trust can be accumulated and the trust will grow accordingly. Then, on the children's death, it will benefit the grantor's grandchildren tax-free, regardless of its value at that time. And on and on for as long as the trust can last.

A very effective way of taking advantage of the GST exemption is to fund a dynasty trust with life insurance. Thus, assume a 45-year-old donor creates a dynasty trust and has it purchase a $20 million life insurance policy on the donor's life. The total premiums on this policy will be $1 million payable over ten years. Each time there is a premium payment, the donor allocates $100,000 of the GST exemption to it, so that the entire trust is fully exempt from the GST tax once the premiums have been paid in full (but the donor will have to pay a total of $153,000 in gift tax on the last four premium payments, which are not covered by the $600,000 lifetime exemption).

When the donor dies, $20 million in insurance proceeds flows into the trust. The trust principal is then invested for growth, and all income is accumulated during the lifetime of the grantor's children. Thirty years later, on the death of the last surviving child of the donor, the trust is worth $70–$80 million, all of which will pass transfer tax-free to the donor's grandchildren and more remote issue (such as great-grandchildren). The result is a transfer of tens of millions of dollars for a total transfer tax cost of $153,000. And, of course, all of these numbers could be doubled if the donor's spouse originally joined in the gift.

One highly effective means of taking advantage of the $1 million GST exemption is to create a charitable lead unitrust (CLUT). A CLUT is a trust that pays an annual amount to charity for a period of years, with the trust principal then passing to the donor's family or other designated beneficiaries. The amount charity receives each year is equal to a fixed percentage of the trust principal as revalued each year. Thus, as the trust grows, so does the amount charity receives.

With a CLUT, it is possible to leverage the GST exemption and thus leave more than $1 million to grandchildren and more remote descendants without a generation-skipping tax being imposed. This leveraging arises because the charitable deduction deriving from a CLUT is equally applicable for both gift tax and generation-skipping tax purposes. For example, assume a doting grandmother has already provided amply for her children and now wants to put aside $3 million for the eventual use of her grandchildren. She also has a private family foundation that she would like her descendants to have the benefit of using for their philanthropic causes.

She could take the $3 million and put it in a CLUT that pays a 5% unitrust amount (i.e., 5% of the value of the trust as determined each year) annually to the family foundation for a twenty-year period. Assuming that the applicable IRS interest rate is 7.6% at the time the CLUT is created, the grandmother would receive a gift tax charitable deduction of approximately $2 million with respect to the CLUT, leaving a taxable gift of $1 million. (The gift tax charitable deduction is equal to the present value of all the payments charity will receive, assuming a 7.6% interest rate.) If she has never used any portion of her $600,000 exemption, a federal gift tax of $150,000 would be due. However, because the gift is only $1 million, she could allocate her $1 million GST exemption to it and thereby avoid a generation-skipping tax from ever being imposed on the trust.

Now let us assume the trust principal grows at an after-tax rate of

7% per year. At the end of the twenty-year term, the grandchildren will receive approximately $4 million tax-free. In addition, the grandmother's family foundation will receive approximately $3,750,000 over the twenty-year charitable term. Thus, for a gift tax cost of only $150,000, the grandmother has transferred $4 million to her grandchildren as well as built up a sizable foundation.

I should note that this device is really only for those who are charitably inclined. Had the grandmother simply given the grandchildren $1 million and let it grow at the same 7% after-tax rate for twenty years, the grandchildren would end up with only $200,000 less than they do with the CLUT. However, when you consider that the foundation also receives $3,750,000, the particular benefit of a CLUT can be seen.

For all who can afford it, as with utilizing the current $600,000 exemption from federal gift and estate tax, the $1 million GST tax exemption per grandparent should be locked in now by one or another technique discussed herein or others beyond the scope of this section.

Section Two

HOW TO
GIVE IT
AWAY

IV

Dispositions to Spouses

When Brigham Young died in 1877 with an estate estimated at $2.5 million (a huge amount in those days, when $1 million was really worth something), he had a different problem from most of us. He was survived by seventeen wives and forty-four children. To attain fairness, he divided his estate into equitable shares among sixteen of the surviving wives, and the children of deceased wives. Brigham Young disinherited the remaining surviving wife, Ann Eliza Webb Young, who was the only wife who had sought to divorce him (actually she eventually was granted an annulment after an intense four-year litigation). Ann Eliza, his twenty-seventh and last wife, became an avid antipolygamist, lecturing on the subject throughout the country. While Ann Eliza raised no objections to her exclusion from Brigham Young's estate plan, seven of his surviving wives and daughters objected to a payment by the executors of $1 million to the Mormon Church, which he had allegedly borrowed during his lifetime. The contestants eventually reached an out-of-court settlement, proving again that no one on this earth, regardless of his or her spiritual powers, can rest assured that their estate plan will not be attacked after their demise.

Even among our multimarried populace in which divorce seems to end every other marriage, the usual question — very unlike that faced by Brigham Young — is how to provide for the one surviving spouse, assuming any prior divorce settlements, including their requirements for post-death payments, have been honored.

TRANSFER TAXES

Before 1982, when a new unlimited marital deduction was introduced into federal estate tax law, most persons left their spouses at least one-half of their estate — the old maximum allowable estate tax marital deduction — and left the rest to their children or perhaps to charity, or both. For example, when John D. Rockefeller III died in 1978 in an automobile accident, he left half of his estate to his wife and half to charity, thus avoiding all federal death taxes. Others put the second half of their estate in trust for both their spouse and children.

Today, there is no limit to the quantity of property that can be transferred from one spouse to another without federal gift or estate tax, either during life or at death, provided that the surviving spouse is a citizen. (In November 1988, new federal gift and estate tax restrictions were enacted on transfers to a noncitizen spouse.) However, you must stay apprised of your state's death and gift tax laws, because they may not conform to the federal law.

YOUR LEGAL OBLIGATIONS TO YOUR SPOUSE

So, for tax purposes, you can leave as much as you want to your spouse free from federal death taxes. But what is your legal obligation? In the absence of a binding prenuptial or postnuptial agreement, each state's law must be consulted to determine the so-called statutory, or forced share rights, of a surviving spouse. In every common-law state except Georgia, you must leave a certain amount to your surviving spouse. For example, in Florida the surviving spouse is entitled to 30% outright of all assets passing under the decedent's will, while in New York the statutory share is one-third of a defined net estate that includes various assets passing outside the will such as jointly owned property.

(In New York until September of 1994 this one-third could be put in trust for the surviving spouse with income only to be paid to such spouse for life, and with the trust principal then passing to whomever the testator has named.)

In many states, a surviving spouse's rights at death to a statutory share of the deceased spouse's estate can be avoided or substantially reduced by sophisticated evasive techniques including the use of a revocable trust as a will substitute. See Chapter VI, pp. 77–84.

There is also a strange irony in the laws of many states, namely, that a spouse's rights on divorce can be substantially superior to his or her rights of inheritance at death. Under the equitable distribution statutes of both New York and Florida, a spouse in a divorce can get outright (and not in trust) up to one-half of the property accumulated during the marriage. Under special circumstances I have actually had to advise clients to consider divorcing their spouses in New York and Florida in order to be able to obtain much fairer shares of their spouses' estates that they could not (and were told by their spouses they would not) get if they stayed married until death did them part.

Eventually, the forced share rights of a spouse on death and divorce will probably be brought into harmony, as they more or less already are in community property states like California and Arizona.

This difference between spousal rights on divorce and on death is the key to understanding the intensely bitter but quite interesting litigation between Lillian Goldman, the widow of New York City real estate tycoon Sol Goldman, and her own four children, particularly her daughter Jane and her son Allan, who are executors of the estate.

THE SOL GOLDMAN ESTATE BATTLE

Sol Goldman's estate has been estimated to be worth $1 billion, double the size of the J. Seward Johnson pharmaceutical fortune. It was the largest estate ever fought over in the New York County Surrogate's Court, at least before the current dispute over the Doris Duke estate.

Properties owned by the estate include the Stanhope Hotel on Fifth Avenue, the Hyde Park Hotel on East 77th Street at Madison Avenue, the Hotel Gramercy Park, and numerous parcels that are valuable in themselves but apparently could be developed into even more valuable assets. At the heart of the controversy was whether the real estate empire would stay one vast income-producing trust, as Mr. Goldman directed, or will be divided, not quite like Gaul, but with Mrs. Goldman taking one-third of the estate outright and free of trust instead of the then statutory minimum one-third share in trust for her lifetime as provided for in Mr. Goldman's will. In fact, the children argued that their mother may be entitled to nothing. Lillian Goldman's lawyer, in the hyperbole that typifies these fights, said the case is "the most revolting show of filial greed I have ever seen."

To appreciate the case and the truly remarkable legal volte-face that occurred, some background is needed. Mrs. Goldman moved out of their Waldorf-Astoria Towers suite in 1983, and sued Sol Goldman for divorce. But thereafter, in 1984, she signed a reconciliation agreement with him. The agreement, among other things, was to give her $1 million in cash within a week, an additional $5 million by April 1989, ownership of a New York City apartment of her selection, and one-third of his estate outright when he died. Within about one week, Mrs. Goldman refused a $1 million check and disavowed the agreement, saying it was procured by fraud between her own divorce lawyer, the late Roy Cohn, and her husband's divorce lawyer, Raoul Lionel Felder. She based this attack on a letter that she found in her husband's jacket from Cohn to Felder stating: "After the job we did for the Goldmans — including saving Sol's exposure of 3 or 4 hundred million dollars equitable distribution, I was shocked and deeply hurt that he would offer me $100,000 for all these months of work." Cohn demanded $300,000, saying such a figure would be "the best bargain" Mr. Goldman had ever struck.

The ensuing trial lasted nearly three years. (I was an expert witness at the trial on New York inheritance rights and on the methods that Mr. Goldman might be able to use to avoid satisfying the agreement's provision leaving an outright one-third of his estate to Mrs. Goldman.) It seemed clear that the real issue at stake was Mrs. Goldman's desire to take, under the New York equitable distribution law, up to one-half of Mr. Goldman's property outright (estimated to be about $500 million) in the divorce action rather than the one-third outright in the agreement.

Mr. Goldman achieved a complete victory in September 1987. The court held that the agreement was both valid and enforceable, also finding that the Cohn letter did not prove fraud but merely the twin peccadilloes of greed and braggadocio. Sol Goldman died on October 18, 1987, twenty-six days after the judgment was entered, leaving a will giving Lillian the then minimum New York spousal share, one-third in trust for her lifetime.

What happened next is that the sides flipped their positions. Mrs. Goldman moved in court to enforce the agreement that she had attacked so vehemently, obviously preferring the one-third outright under the agreement to the lifetime trust of one-third under the will. The children asserted two main arguments: (i) their mother had breached the agreement, and even though the agreement was upheld as valid, she could not enforce it against the estate; and (ii) since she had legally "abandoned" their father, she was not even entitled to the third in trust under the will.

The children's lawyer, with diplomatic understatement, said that while the children were taking "hard positions," they would never put their mother "in the poorhouse."

As usual in these cases, much of the battle seemed psychological. Some say, for example, that Mrs. Goldman felt her husband dominated her for forty years, and she was not about to be dominated by her children as executors. One might think that with the death of Mr. Goldman, the family would have put aside the rancor of the divorce litigation and settled the estate matter. But, as is often the case, the bitterness from these family disputes can, like a congenital disease, pass from one generation to the next. Eventually, in July 1994, the case was settled, and the family agreed on a division of the real estate properties. Interestingly, if Mrs. Goldman's property rights on divorce and on death had been legally the same under New York law, none of this might have happened, and a reconciliation agreement in 1984 could have worked.

TECHNIQUES TO PROVIDE FOR YOUR SPOUSE

Regardless of your situation or how you view your legal obligation to your spouse, there are several ways to give whatever amount of your estate you determine. The simplest way is to give it outright with no strings attached. Another way is the old form of marital trust, the so-called general power of appointment trust, whereby the surviving spouse receives income for life and can direct, either by will or by a lifetime transfer instrument, the distribution of the marital trust property to anyone in the world.

A major problem with the old marital deduction forms was that the tax law required the surviving spouse to have the power of ultimate disposition. This meant that the surviving spouse could give the property to his or her new marital mate, rapacious relatives, or any others who, from the first spouse's point of view, would be undesirable. It also meant that the surviving spouse might be unduly pressured by a future spouse or children or others to leave them the marital deduction property.

A very popular method to avoid these problems came in with the unlimited marital deduction in 1982 — the so-called QTIP trust. In simple terms, a life income interest for the surviving spouse can qualify for the marital deduction even though the deceased spouse can determine in his or her will what happens to the property at the death of the surviving spouse.

Now, in general, if a testator puts "qualified terminable interest property" in a trust for his or her spouse, an executor can elect to have such property qualify for the marital deduction if certain conditions are met:

1. The surviving spouse must be entitled to all the income from the entire interest (or from a specific portion thereof), payable annually or more frequently, for a period measured solely by the spouse's life. For example, income interests for a term of years — or terminating on the surviving spouse's remarriage — will not qualify.

2. There must be no power in any person (including the spouse) to appoint any of the property to anyone other than the spouse during the spouse's lifetime. The surviving spouse, or a third party, may direct distribution of the property if the distribution takes effect only after the death of such spouse. (It is quite common to give the surviving spouse some power to dispose of the property, but usually only to the issue — children, grandchildren, etc. — of the marriage or to such issue and to charity. Sometimes the surviving spouse may be allowed to appoint to each child — but only equally, or with no more than a certain percentage difference, say 15%, between each child's share, and only a percentage of the total to charity.)

3. A trustee can be given the power to invade principal, but only for the benefit of the surviving spouse. Also, such spouse can have a lifetime power of withdrawal to himself or herself. Of course, thereafter such spouse can give the property to anyone — subject to possible gift tax depending on the size of the gifts.

In addition, there are numerous combinations of the foregoing — for example, one-half outright to the spouse and one-half in a QTIP trust, or one-half in a QTIP trust that passes automatically to the children at the death of the surviving spouse and the other one-half in another QTIP trust which the surviving spouse can appoint to the children only, or to the children and to charity.

"A rose by any other name would smell as sweet,"* said "lawyer"

---

* See Robert Frost (with the marital deduction no doubt in mind):

> The rose is a rose,
> And was always a rose,
> But the theory now goes
> That the apple's a rose,
> And the pear is, and so's
> The plum, I suppose.
> The dear only knows
> What will next prove a rose
> You, of course, are a rose —
> But were always a rose.

Shakespeare, but the marital deduction in its QTIP form is not simply a rose by another name. It has become a far, far sweeter and yet, at the same time, thornier estate and gift tax planning device, best availed of by the thoughtful and the well-advised.

Having decided how much to give one's surviving spouse does not always determine how much one tells the spouse. In most marriages, the more disclosure and discussion the better, but I have seen enough not to be dogmatic with that generalization or any other in the field of estate planning.

V

Dispositions to Children

GIVING TO CHILDREN GIFT-TAX-FREE

As previously mentioned, you may give $10,000 per year to any number of children or other persons free of gift tax; with the consent of your spouse, $20,000 per year to any person, even if all the funds come only from the assets of the donor spouse.

This tax rule was relatively easy to understand, I thought, until I gave a lecture to a group in Palm Beach. I explained the universality of the $10,000 annual gift tax exclusion by saying that one could, for example, give that amount to everyone in the telephone book. At the end of the lecture, in the question-and-answer period, a little old lady in the back of the room raised her hand and asked me somewhat hesitantly if she could give $10,000 per year to her daughter. I answered that I thought I had explained that she could even give $10,000 to everyone in the telephone book. "Yes," she said, "but my daughter has an unlisted number!"

*"We're all wondering, Gramps, when your race is run
and your day is done, who gets the glue?"*

These annual exclusion gifts should obviously be given as early as possible in January of each year so death during that year will not preclude the gifts. Many persons seem to make these gifts at the end of the year during the holiday season, which may make sense sentimentally, but certainly not in terms of good tax planning. There is a current fear that the annual exclusion may soon be limited to a total of $30,000 per couple.

In addition to this annual exclusion, you may pay—free of gift tax—an unlimited amount for tuition expenses (not room, board, etc.) at an educational institution and for the medical care of a child or any other person. However, the payments must be to the educational institution and to the provider of medical services, not to the child or other beneficiary. Also, you may not create a trust to pay for such future expenses in order to try to get a gift tax exclusion now. However, you may be able to prepay, on a discounted basis, four years' tuition or a whole series of needed medical treatments.

One can also give one's lifetime exempt amount ($600,000) to one's children, either outright or in trust. However, as indicated later, there are various tax-saving ways to leverage — i.e., enlarge — the value of these exemptions by the use of trusts such as GRITs (personal residence trusts) or GRATs.

YOUR LEGAL OBLIGATION TO YOUR CHILDREN

In the United States, you can totally disinherit your adult children in every state except Louisiana. The Bayou State in its constitution provides forced heirship rights, rights that are derived from the Napoleonic Code from the time when Louisiana was a French colony. A sole surviving child with forced heirship rights is entitled to one-fourth of the estate; two or more such children split half. This forced portion is called *legitime*. Legislation to limit forced heirship rights only to children under 23 and those of any age who are incapacitated because of mental or physical infirmity was declared unconstitutional in 1993 by the Louisiana Supreme Court. If you want to disinherit a child in Louisiana, among the accepted legal reasons are attempted assault against the parent, conviction for certain felonies, refusal to ransom a parent detained in captivity, and — best of all for parents who complain about never hearing from their children — failure to communicate with a parent without just cause for more than two years after adulthood.

ATTACHING STRINGS

As more and more Americans accumulate vast wealth, they worry about leaving inheritances that will stifle their children's initiative, depriving them of the pleasure and satisfaction of self-achievement — particularly of earning a living. They do not want their issue to become financial parasites sitting around waiting for their trust monies. Commodore Vanderbilt's grandson William, heir to some $60 million in

1885, said that "inherited wealth . . . is as certain death to ambition as cocaine is to morality." William was a living illustration of the truth of his own observation: an indifferent businessman and dedicated *bon vivant*, he died of a heart attack at a fashionable French racetrack in 1920.

Warren Buffett, the Nebraska billionaire investor, believes that setting up heirs with a "lifetime supply of food stamps just because they came out of the right womb" is harmful to them. It has been said that he thinks the right amount to leave children is "enough money so that they would feel they could do anything but not so much they could do nothing." This balance is a difficult golden mean to achieve. Buffett reasons that for a college graduate "a few hundred thousand dollars" should be enough. Many, and not just his daughter Susan (quoted as saying, "Well, I feel I've learned the lesson"), will disagree with him. Certainly no one can be dogmatic about how much is enough. In a March 1994 survey of affluent Americans by U.S. Trust Company of New York, respondents said that $5.5 million was the most money that an individual could inherit without the inheritance having "a detrimental effect on the values of that person." (How many children and adults would be overjoyed with only $5 million?)

However you formulate the problem of how and how much to give to children, generalizations are difficult, and your solutions depend partly on how Draconian a view you take of the fact that your heirs are members of the so-called Lucky Sperm Club. Thus, the strictest approach is to allow no money, either income or principal, to go to a child until age 30 or so, which approach presumably forces the child to work at least for a time. One mollification of this approach is to allow principal to be invaded to meet the child's important needs, such as health and education costs. Some grandparents condition gifts to grandchildren upon graduation from college.

Another alternative is to give one portion of principal upon graduation from college or at a certain age (often 25) with nothing more until after age 30. This delayed or stepped distribution forces the child's attention on the best use of the first principal distribution and presumably will allow him or her to learn about handling money without risking the entire trust.

*"Luckily for you, your grandfather's remarkable vision
of the future was limited to the oil business."*

But beware of the borrowing heir, because some states do not recognize spendthrift provisions restricting assignment of principal by trust beneficiaries. Even if such restriction is allowed, creditors can still get the principal when it is actually paid over to the beneficiary. Consider using a clause that allows the trustee to defer distributions of principal if the child-beneficiary has previously assigned rights to principal to creditors. (See the discussion of the "crisis clause," p. 75.)

Generally, I think it is advisable to give your trustees broad discretion to use income and principal for a child without restricting distributions to emergencies. In this way, trustees can deal with situations unforeseen when the will or trust was drafted.

An approach that several of my more thoughtful wealthy clients have recently adopted incorporates the following elements in their children's trusts:

1. The annual earned income (as defined) of the child is matched (or even doubled or tripled) by payments from the trust. In some cases, the matching of earned income is capped at a certain amount per year, e.g., $100,000.

2. A basic standard of living is guaranteed by a minimum, mandatory monthly income payout. This payout can be pegged to a cost-of-living index in order to take inflation into account. (Such a provision can be controversial as to both its efficacy and its amount. One Maryland semibillionaire guaranteed his children a yearly income no greater than the salary of the President of the United States — presently $250,000.)

3. In addition, the trustees have broad discretion to pay or apply both income and principal to, or for the benefit of, the child. The use of this clause could make unnecessary the minimum monthly payment to guarantee a certain standard of living. Nevertheless, most clients seem to prefer the use of the minimum standard of living clause rather than only allowing the trustees to do what they believe the parents would have done.

4. Such trusts usually terminate when a child attains a certain age.

There are, of course, many problems with all of this. The issues are both philosophical and subjective. Take the definition of "earned income," which is to be matched to create incentive for the great desideratum — a child who earns his or her own income. (As writer Dorothy Parker noted, "The two most beautiful words in the English language are 'check enclosed'!")

Should windfall income from one "lucky" investment be excluded? What about one large real estate commission or finder's fee? One very smart real estate magnate specifically wanted real estate commissions excluded and income limited to salary and other such compensation for personal services actually rendered.

What of the child who successfully pursues a teaching career or becomes a great research scientist, both careers with relatively low income by our society's standards? One parent solved this problem by making distributions totally discretionary under his will and by leaving an explanatory memorandum that provided, in part, as follows:

> With respect to distributions of trust income, it is my wish that you use such distributions to provide an incentive to my children to be economically productive. To the extent practicable, you should match their own earnings with income from the trust. I realize, however, that there may be circumstances where this policy will not be desirable. If, for example, a child of mine should choose to become a college professor or enter government service, he or she should not be penalized for choosing a worthwhile and productive career in a field where the monetary rewards are not great. My primary concern is that the children's inheritance from me not be used to undermine their ambition and initiative. If a child is failing to live up to his or her capacity to lead a productive life, then I want you to make or withhold distributions of income in a way that will encourage a change in attitude.

HOW TO RESTRICT MONEY AFTER THE CHILDREN GET IT

Many parents, even if they feel their children are responsible — essentially defined as gainfully (if not fully) employed — want to make sure that after substantial assets are distributed to them these assets do not end up with their children's spouses in the event of divorce or their child's death.

Premarital Contracts

One way to try to keep property in the immediate family is by means of premarital contracts. A related question is whether parents should impose premarital agreements on their children. My personal view is that in most cases, such psychological pressure is not justifiable.

A willful child may well say no, and marry without a premarital agreement primarily to spite the parents.

Such a use of the so-called golden umbilical cord may be disastrous, choking the relationships between the parents and the child and the prospective spouse. Particularly with first marriages, it is dangerous to force these contracts, although, in my experience, such force often seems to work, especially if the contracts are limited to cover only specific family business assets or trusts.

If a child refuses to execute a prenuptial agreement, the parents might consider creating incentives for the child to enter into the agreement. One way is for them to threaten to discontinue making transfers, both during their lifetimes and upon their deaths, to the child unless the desired agreement is signed. If the parents prefer to use a carrot rather than a stick, they can offer to provide specified financial benefits to the child or the spouse if they sign the agreement.

Alternatively, the parents can utilize trusts for this purpose. Either the provisions of the trust or perhaps a separate letter to the trustees of the trust would prohibit distributions of trust income and principal unless the child has in force and abides by the provisions of a valid prenuptial agreement. In this way, any revocation or amendment of the prenuptial agreement or failure by the child to honor it would cause the trustees to discontinue making distributions.

Even if a child executes a prenuptial agreement, there is the question of how to ensure that the agreement is not secretly revoked or amended. One relatively little known way to avoid this possibility that I have often recommended is for the parents or family trustees to be signatories to the prenuptial agreement. The agreement would state that they have an interest in its enforcement, e.g., in order to continue the harmonious operation of the family business or to preserve the family trust's assets. The prenuptial agreement should provide that as a result of such interest, the agreement cannot be amended or revoked without the written consent of the child, his or her spouse, and the interested parents (or the legal representatives of their estates).

As an alternative to including such provisions, the parents may prefer to have the child execute a prenuptial agreement and then enter into a side letter agreement. The letter would provide that the parents have an interest in the existence and enforceability of the prenuptial agreement and that, accordingly, the child agrees not to amend or revoke it, or to give more to his or her spouse than the agreement requires, without the written consent of the parents or the legal representatives of their estates.

A side letter might be less desirable than a provision in the agreement itself. The parents can more easily enforce the provisions if their interest and the rationale for such interest are clearly stated and acknowledged by both the child and a prospective spouse prior to their signing it. On the other hand, such a provision might also be more susceptible to a determination by a court that undue influence was exerted by the parents on the prospective son- or daughter-in-law, making the agreement void and unenforceable.

In either case, parents in such circumstances should be aware of the possible public policy issues that arise in this context. As a general matter, the law provides that you are forbidden from using your property as a means to coerce an estrangement between family members. (For example, if X, by an otherwise effective will, bequeaths $1 million "to my brother B on the condition that he never communicate or associate with our sister S," the condition would be invalid and the gift to B would be unrestricted.)

A family relationship does, of course, include a relationship by marriage. You cannot validly make a bequest to your son or daughter on the condition he or she divorce your son-in-law or daughter-in-law. Such a condition is against public policy, and your child would take his or her inheritance free of the condition.

Special Conditions on Bequests

In general there are practically no limits on the kinds of conditions you may impose on gifts and bequests to your children. The law prohibits only those that are contrary to public policy or otherwise forbidden by law.

The recent will of a somewhat eccentric Floridian conditioned his only child's trust inheritance on the following: that his son be a registered Republican and a member in good standing of the Loyal Order of the Moose, never change his surname, be employed in one of his family's corporations or in the "legal or financial profession," have his wife sign a postnuptial agreement waiving all interests in the son's assets, and attend a Christian church with his family not less than twice monthly. Without getting into the wisdom of each of these conditions, none of them seems to be illegal.

In one extraordinary case a woman was left a substantial bequest of the income from a trust "as long as she is above ground." After her death, her loving and thoughtful husband, not wanting her below ground (it seems for more thoughtful than loving reasons), kept her in a glass case inside the house, thereby managing to continue the annuity for an additional thirty years.

Twenty-nine-year-old German automobile heir Otto Flick inherited 40% of the Mercedes-Benz fortune on the condition that he never be seen driving any car other than a Mercedes. That condition seems reasonable.

Charles Millar was a prim and proper Canadian bachelor lawyer with a devilish sense of humor. After a series of prankish bequests, including leaving each Protestant minister in Toronto a share of stock in a local brewery, he left the bulk of his substantial estate "to the Mother who has . . . given birth in Toronto to the greatest number of children" within ten years after his death. Thus began the so-called Stork or Baby Derby. As a group of mothers wearily approached the finish line procreating incessantly, Millar's second cousins and even more distant relatives contested the will as against public policy. The Canadian Supreme Court upheld the will, proclaiming that promoting procreation, even in this unusual way, was a legally valid purpose. No wonder one sage observer of humankind called a will "wealth's last caprice." Four prolific Toronto mothers, each with nine children born during the ten-year period, shared the estate. Each of them probably deserved the whole thing. Another woman claimed ten births, but her record was somewhat blemished in that only five of the children were also her husband's. She and another woman, who had ten children in the period but four of them were stillborn, were given consolation awards. They deserved more!

A sophisticated, highly educated New Yorker was denied membership in an exclusive men's club. His will disinherits his only daughter if she ever marries a member of that club or anyone who had an ancestor or close relative, as carefully delineated in the will, who was a member. This, too, is a legally valid restriction. (Ironically, Groucho Marx, who once said he would not want to join any club that would accept him, considered his membership in the Hillcrest Country Club in Beverly Hills valuable enough to pass on to his son.)

Religious and Racial Restraints on Marriage

A relatively common reason for disqualifying a child from inheritance is that the child has married outside of a designated religious group. As a general rule, such a condition is enforceable if it does not unreasonably restrict the choice of persons one can marry or, in effect, operate as a total restraint on marriage. If a condition is found to be invalid, the beneficiary takes the gift or bequest as if he or she had complied with the condition.

Fairly often over the years I have had clients who wanted to restrict bequests based on their children marrying within a particular religious group. The parent may also condition the bequest on the requirement that a beneficiary neither embrace a particular faith nor marry a person of that faith. Again, these restraints have been upheld. In a relatively recent case in Oregon, a prohibition on either becoming a Catholic or marrying a Catholic was upheld. There seems to be no constitutional law prohibition on such restraints.

Sometimes these religious conditions have a quixotic quality. Hariette Stormes left $350,000 for a scholarship at the University of California at Berkeley limited to Jewish orphans majoring in the aeronautical sciences. Not surprisingly, the scholarship went unused for some years, and recently the terms of the bequest were broadened.

There are usually deep emotional and psychological forces at work in cases of religious intermarriage. These restrictions are not generally a matter for rational debate; nor are most other religious issues. For example, try to talk a person who has lost most of his family in the Holocaust out of prohibiting his heirs from marrying non-Jews. The question does arise — it has recently been an issue of intense debate in

Israel—of who is a Jew. Sometimes the complexity of defining the permissible religious marriage makes people rethink the wisdom of such restrictions. In my experience, few who feel deeply about the subject will be deterred.

Assuming the prohibition of marriage on religious grounds would be upheld, the legatee might try to cohabit—without marriage—as a means to avoid the restraint. A restraint against cohabitation is not automatically implied, since the courts read these restrictions as narrowly as possible. To avoid the evasion of such restrictions, the testator must include a restraint on cohabitation without marriage with a prohibited person and define in the will or trust what constitutes cohabitation.

A more controversial condition is a prohibition on marrying someone of another race—in our society, usually a black or an Asian.

Amazingly enough, black-white marriages (miscegenation) were prohibited by statute until 1967. In that year, the U.S. Supreme Court, in *Loving* v. *Virginia*, a case in which I participated, unanimously struck down the antimiscegenation statutes then still in effect in nineteen states—mostly Southern and "border" states, but also including Indiana and Wyoming. At that time, no other civilized country had such laws except the Union of South Africa.

All of the states with miscegenation laws prohibited black-white marriages. Other "races" that have been included in the various laws are Mongolians, Chinese, Japanese, Africans, Malayans, Native Americans, Asiatic Indians, West Indians, mulattoes, Ethiopians, Hindus, Koreans, mestizos, and half-breeds. The laws bordered on burlesque. The Arizona law, repealed in 1962, at one time so restricted a mulatto that he could not marry anyone, even another mulatto; then it was changed so that a mulatto could marry an Indian but could not marry a black, a Caucasian, or another mulatto.

Who was a black under such laws? A man could be black in Georgia because he had a one-half black great-grandmother, and by crossing the border into Florida, become a white because Florida made him a black only if he had a full black great-grandmother. The most common definition used an unscientific percentage-of-blood test that usually classified a black as "any person of one-eighth or more Negro blood." If a blood test is to be used and one-eighth Negro blood — whatever that means — makes you black, why does not one-eighth white blood make you white?

In short, the statutory definitions of blacks were sometimes contradictory, often nonexistent, and usually a combination of legal fiction and genetic nonsense nearly impossible to apply as a practical matter. None of the statutory definitions was sufficiently precise to meet the constitutional requirement of due process — which nullifies a criminal statute that is so vague that men of common intelligence must guess at its meaning and differ about its application. It is of little surprise then that in the *Loving* case, the U.S. Supreme Court consigned these anachronistic antimiscegenation laws to legal oblivion.

In 1984, in the case of *Palmore* v. *Sidoti*, in which I also participated, a divorced white father sought to remove his 3-year-old daughter from the custody of his white ex-wife when she married a black man. The state court counselor recommended a change in custody because this lifestyle was "unacceptable to the father *and to society*" (emphasis in original).

Agreeing that the main concern was the best interests of the child, the Supreme Court unanimously ruled that racial considerations could not constitute grounds for a custody decision. Thus, in this case, the Court stated, "The Constitution cannot control such prejudices but neither can it tolerate them. Private biases may be outside the reach of the law, but the law cannot, directly or indirectly, give them effect."

With this constitutional law background, it would seem that private racial discrimination in wills and trusts would not be tolerated by our courts. But, to the surprise of many, the cases are not so clear on how far our courts will go to invalidate or refuse to enforce private racial discriminatory clauses in wills and trusts.

Most of the cases have arisen relating to charitable trusts rather than to racial restrictions on inheritances of private persons.

Stephen Girard, a wealthy Philadelphia merchant who died in 1831, created in his will a charitable trust to establish a school for "poor male white orphan children." The City of Philadelphia administered the trust through one of its agencies. When two black boys sued over being denied admission because of their race, the U.S. Supreme Court said that a public agency could not, consonant with the equal protection clause of the Fourteenth Amendment, administer a racially discriminatory admissions policy. Private trustees were then appointed by the aptly named Orphans Court of Philadelphia County, and Girard College was allowed to continue its segregated operation — with the U.S. Supreme Court, in effect, acquiescing by refusing to hear an appeal.

Finally, however, a decade later the school's discriminatory policy was again challenged and the U.S. Court of Appeals for the Third Circuit said the policy was unconstitutional. Even though the trust was no longer administered by state or city officials, past governmental involvement over 126 years (1831 to 1957) had affixed an irrevocable public identity to the trust. But again, the U.S. Supreme Court denied the application for an appeal.

In another leading case, U.S. Senator Augustus O. Bacon had devised land to the city of Macon, Georgia, to be used as a park for white persons only. When a constitutional attack was launched by black citizens, private trustees — as in the Girard precedent — were appointed to run the park. The U.S. Supreme Court reversed, however, holding that certain matters were municipal in nature — too public for private management, at least if they have acquired a public character.

The land subsequently was returned to the private heirs of Senator Bacon because the Georgia Supreme Court ruled that his specific charitable intent — a park for whites only — could not be carried out. The doctrines that allow a court to alter a trust that has become illegal, impossible, or impracticable of fulfillment were held to be inapplicable because Senator Bacon had made his specific intent so clear. The U.S. Supreme Court affirmed the determination of Georgia's highest court.

So where are we? It still may be constitutionally possible to establish a valid, purely private trust for the benefit of one race only — if a private trustee is designated from the beginning. The trend in American law, however, is so strong against racial discrimination, buttressed by the various civil rights statutes of Congress, that today, in my opinion, a court would not — and should not — enforce a racial restriction on marriage in a will or trust, as a matter of public policy. The court could do so without resolving, or even reaching, the constitutional law issues.

The "Crisis" Clause

Even though you have determined to let a child have all of his or her inheritance outright at a certain age or on meeting a certain condition, serious consideration should be given to using an escape clause or what I call a crisis clause. For example, assume that at age 35, when the trust is to terminate, a child is in the midst of a drug or alcohol crisis or even in an angry and costly divorce litigation. The following kind of clause may be appropriate and wise:

> . . . if my Trustees determine that it would not be in such child's best interests to distribute to such child any part of the principal at the time specified, my Trustees are authorized to retain such principal and to continue to hold it in trust as long as they shall deem advisable, including the lifetime of such child. During such continuing period of trust, my Trustees will have the same powers over income and principal as set forth in this Subdivision.

Without this clause, a court battle can ensue over withholding principal, and customary boilerplate provisions will not justify a long withholding, even though it would be in the best interests of the child.

PRESERVING CONTROL OF FAMILY BUSINESSES

In times of hostile takeovers, a major concern of families of great wealth has been to protect their self-created, closely held financial empires from "business predators." One child's desiring immediate monetary gratification or acting out other psychological needs can cause the breakup of the family holdings.

Over the years, Lester Crown, head of the very rich Chicago family that owns real estate, hotels, and 23% of General Dynamics, and his late father treated their assets as a common pot for their extended family. They distributed shares and limited partnership interests to Lester's seven children and his uncles, cousins, brothers, nieces, and nephews. He fears that "one of these days we're going to get hit in the back of the head because we did this." If he were to start over, he might set up a single trust to give everyone a life income but to preserve control over his empire.

In addition to the single-trust concept, other techniques are used to try to preserve family control and keep a business private. One example is the plan of Minnesota billionaire Curtis Leroy Carlson. His companies, which include the Radisson hotels and TGI Friday's restaurants, had 1988 sales of $5.3 billion, and he is the sole shareholder. He has created a holding company whose shares at his death will be divided equally among his two daughters and seven grandchildren.

The holding company board has Mr. Carlson as chairman and seats filled by both daughters, their husbands, and a grandchild from each family. It will also include outsiders. Mr. Carlson wants to prevent a takeover and is well aware of what has happened in other families as ownership has been spread among heirs. He says: "Someone's going to want to take their cash and go."

Heirs will have that choice, but they must sell their shares only to the holding company pursuant to a stipulated formula. A more immediate threat could be an intrafamily fight over policy, in which case they must submit to binding arbitration.

VI

The Revocable or Living Trust: An Estate Planning Panacea?

From time to time, articles appear lauding the benefits of revocable (or living) trusts and urging all people of sound mind to create them. Many persons, for example in Florida, a haven for persons with substantial estates (and, as later explained, for those with creditor's rights problems), feel they are unsophisticated and not well advised if they do not have one. When one of these articles is printed, I often receive a barrage of calls from clients asking why their estate plan does not include one of these miraculous devices.

A revocable trust is created by an individual (grantor) during his or her lifetime containing instructions about the management and disposition of assets (and the income from such assets) during life and at death. The grantor can act as his own trustee, with a successor to serve in the event of death or incapacity. A revocable trust, as its name denotes, can be revoked or amended, in whole or in part, by the grantor at any time.

Although the revocable trust is a useful estate planning device for some individuals, the benefits of using a revocable trust instead of a will as your primary dispositive instrument should be analyzed carefully on a case-by-case basis. Some of the advantages of these trusts, like Mark Twain said about the rumors of his death, are highly exaggerated or even nonexistent. For example, one mythical advantage is that a revocable trust is a tax-savings device. All property in a trust over which the grantor retains control is subject to claims of the grantor's creditors and is taxable, as though the assets were owned outright. The living trust saves neither income nor estate taxes. In fact, in certain complex situations involving substantial assets, there are special tax aspects that favor a will over a revocable trust: (i) to avoid the application of the "throwback rules" on the income of an estate earned during its period of administration; and (ii) to get better tax treatment on capital gains, where the residuary beneficiaries of an estate are charitable entities.

A revocable trust can contain provisions taking effect at death that do save taxes — for example, dispositions that take advantage of the marital deduction, the charitable deduction, and the federal unified credit. But the identical tax-savings provisions can instead be contained in a will.

Furthermore, a revocable trust funded during the grantor's lifetime involves administrative and legal expense, although there is no gift tax on transfers of property to it.

When the revocable trust is created, title to the grantor's homes, bank accounts, securities, businesses, and other investments usually are transferred to it. There are no significant benefits, as a general rule, of nominally funded revocable trusts. The transfers of title may cause problems in certain situations, for example if the grantor wants to refinance his home and a lending institution or an insurer insists that title be in the name of an individual, or in a case when the title to a jointly owned home is changed in order to put it in trust. When the trustee is someone other than the grantor, separate income tax returns must be prepared and filed for the trust, which entails additional expense. Also, unless the grantor or someone willing to forgo a commission is the trustee, there will be current trustee's fees.

Although a revocable trust is more costly during the grantor's life, the argument perhaps most frequently made for it is that enormous savings are achieved at death, primarily because the assets in the trust are not part of the grantor's probate estate.

In the 1970s, Norman Dacey, a nonlawyer, wrote a best-selling book, *How to Avoid Probate*, that had as its main thesis the advisability of using a revocable trust, primarily to avoid lawyers' and court fees. This result may or may not be true, depending on the facts of the situation and the state in which the grantor resides.

While the term "probate estate" refers only to that portion of a decedent's assets that pass under a will and are administered by a court, it should be kept in mind that the nonprobate assets in a revocable trust are part of the decedent's taxable estate and must still be taxed, managed, and distributed to beneficiaries—albeit under the terms of the revocable trust rather than under the terms of the will. These trust assets also remain subject to any claims by the grantor's creditors. If the grantor's probate estate is insufficient to pay creditors and estate taxes, the trust or even the trustee, personally, may be legally responsible for the payment of such taxes and debts. Furthermore, many individuals create revocable trusts and never transfer their assets to the trust. As a result, all of their assets will still pass through probate as if no revocable trust were in existence.

Let's say a New York State grantor has $3 million in assets. In the first place, the grantor would need a will even if most of his assets were already in a revocable trust. The function of the will would be to specify the disposition of all property not in the trust (jewelry, automobiles, furniture, insurance and pension benefits payable to the estate, etc.) and to name executors or personal representatives (and guardians, if minor children are involved).

In a state where attorneys' fees are not statutorily set, the legal fees for representing the estate would be fairly constant whether or not a revocable trust were used. A savings in legal time charges might arise, however, because title to the decedent's trust assets would not have to be transferred to the estate, but this time was already charged by the attorney during the grantor's lifetime.

All other lawyers' functions—tax planning, tax audits or litigation, valuations, etc.—would remain the same. Similarly, court costs and filing fees would involve some savings, but only an insubstantial amount. Filing fees to probate a will disposing of a $3 million estate are $1,000 in New York. If only $50,000 of the $3 million passed under the will and the rest was in a revocable trust, the filing fees would be $225.

It should be pointed out, however, that in states like California, where the statutory legal fee to settle an estate in court is $110,000 on a $10 million probate estate, or in Florida, where the statutory legal fee is less for nonprobate assets (1%) than for probate assets (2%), it seems that money might be saved by diminishing the size of the probate estate. But, despite indications in popular literature to the contrary, even in California and Florida the savings on probate legal fees are not great except in the context of large estates. Furthermore, even though the statutory legal fees are deemed reasonable by the courts in California and Florida, that does not necessarily mean that attorneys are able to charge those amounts for administering an estate. In many cases, attorneys will agree to administer an estate on an hourly time charge basis rather than for a statutory legal fee.

Although statutory fees for executors (or personal representatives) and trustees appear to be quite different, these differences may be illusory. For example, in New York, if an individual dies with a probate estate of $3 million, his executor would be entitled to a statutory commission of $84,000. If the same individual had a probate estate of only $50,000 and a revocable trust worth $2,950,000, his executor would only receive a commission of $2,500, but his trustees would receive $12,750 for each year the trust continues, plus up to $30,000 (1% fee) for paying out the principal.

It is difficult to say which is the better deal. Obviously, if the trust continues for some time, the annual commissions received by the trustee when added to the payout commission could easily exceed an executor's commission. Further, the executor or the trustee of the revocable trust, particularly if a bank is acting, may require extra compensation of as much as one full executor's commission on the death of the grantor because of the extra work involved in connection with administering the estate. There also may be, in some situations, an accounting for the revocable trust on the grantor's death, causing additional legal fees and other expenses.

In certain situations and jurisdictions, however, a revocable trust is the preferred primary method of estate planning — for example, if privacy is a paramount consideration. In most jurisdictions, the content of a will is public information but the dispositions contained in a trust remain private, unless the trust is contested and becomes the subject of litigation, as in the Henry Ford II case. In at least several states, however, a copy of the trust may have to be filed with the local probate court as an exhibit to the estate tax return filed for the deceased grantor's estate. Also, if the trust holds title to real property that is subject to a mortgage loan, the lending institution or the title company, or both, may require that a copy of the trust be recorded in the local county clerk's office. The trust also may be subject to public disclosure in the event creditors seek payment of the grantor's debts from the trust, or if the grantor files for protection under the bankruptcy laws.

Furthermore, if an executor or personal representative whom an individual wishes to name in his or her will is ineligible to qualify in that jurisdiction, or if an executor or personal representative who qualifies but who lives in another jurisdiction is required by the courts to post a bond in order to act, a revocable trust may be a solution.

There are also, from time to time, special uses for a revocable trust that solve a particular estate planning need. One rich investor used certain money managers who traded daily and with great success, making very small percentage points or often even less than one percentage point a day, but using vast sums often highly leveraged. Even a quick probate — in some states they can be accomplished in a few days — could be highly costly in lost trading profits, so this titan of Wall Street put those investment accounts into a revocable trust so that his death would not cost (his heirs) even one day's profits (or, I suppose, losses).

Another lifetime advantage of a living trust in complex estates is that if the trustee is a bank or a person other than the client, the trust may be used to familiarize the trustee with the assets and peculiarities of the estate prior to the client's death. Similarly, the client and, perhaps, other trust beneficiaries can evaluate the management and investment abilities of the particular trustee.

Some advocates of the revocable trust say it is particularly well suited for gay partners, because their relationship is generally not recognized by the civil law, which may result in more frequent challenges to their property arrangements if they are set forth only in a last will and testament. A living trust, being a legal entity established during the life of its creator, may prove harder to attack than a will, especially if the trust has existed and been operative for some years before its creator's death. The gay partner can be the cotrustee or only trustee of the trust and thus be in control of the assets at the time of death of the creator or his or her complete incapacity prior to death. This control could be vitally important if family members attack the partner's inheritance for homophobic or for simply venal reasons. At least in such cases the partner will be in control of the funds to try to ward off an unwarranted attack. (In smaller financial situations, a durable power of attorney could be just as effective without the lifetime costs of creating a revocable trust. A power of attorney, however, unlike a revocable trust, does not survive the death of its creator and, in practice, may not be accepted by certain financial institutions.)

There is debate in legal circles if, in fact, a revocable trust is more difficult to upset than a will. The grounds for attack are essentially the same — undue influence, duress, fraud, or incapacity. There is some authority that the burden of proof may be more difficult to sustain by the attacker of the living trust. Each case is primarily its own special situation and will, in general, depend on its peculiar set of facts. But it may be said that if it is done correctly, the revocable trust can in many cases be made more difficult to upset than a will. Also, unlike a will, it can more readily provide the primary beneficiary — for example, the gay partner — with the funds to fight the fight while it is occurring.

Probably the most compelling general reason for recommending the use of a revocable trust is the orderly and expeditious management of an elderly person's affairs or the affairs of someone otherwise unable or unwilling to manage his or her property. The grantor can manage his or her assets, perhaps with the help of a bank or trust company as cotrustee, and then, in the event of the grantor's mental or physical incapacity, the cotrustee, without the need for any further legal proceeding, simply continues to manage the assets and pay the income therefrom for the grantor's benefit. In many cases, if the elderly grantor does not want the burden of investment management the cotrustee can do all the work.

A revocable trust can eliminate the need for a court-appointed conservator or guardian, avoiding the so-called Groucho Marx problem. In his 80s, in spite of his legal opposition, Mr. Marx was declared incompetent by a Los Angeles court. At the time, he was living with a woman named Erin Fleming, who asserted that Groucho wanted her as his guardian. After an unpleasant court battle, a relative was appointed as his guardian. With a living trust, he could have specified whom he wanted to manage his affairs if he ever became incapacitated. A revocable trust is far less expensive and less embarrassing than a guardianship or a conservatorship proceeding.

Of course, during the lifetime of the grantor, the same purpose can be achieved by the use of a durable power of attorney — a short document appointing another individual as an "attorney-in-fact" to manage your affairs. New York and some other states now permit a "springing" power of attorney, which would not take effect until the incapacity arises. Nevertheless, depending on the composition of an individual's assets and his or her relationship with other family members, the creation of a revocable trust generally would be better and more efficient for this purpose than such a power of attorney. A power of attorney, whether durable or not, generally terminates immediately at the death of the individual who created it, and the assets that were "managed" by the attorney-in-fact will have to pass through probate. In addition, a trustee may be held legally to a much higher standard of responsibility in the administration and management of the grantor's assets than an attorney-in-fact. In many instances, according to the terms of the trust, the trustee may have greater flexibility and discretion in managing the grantor's assets. In addition, a durable power of attorney may not suffice and may be impractical if the individual has numerous bank accounts and securities accounts and each institution wants to use its own power of attorney form.

In Massachusetts, the creation of a revocable trust is standard practice and is done primarily to avoid the court appointment of a guardian, who can cause unnecessary expense, delay, and problems by second-guessing every decision. In addition, the creation of a revocable trust in Massachusetts sidesteps the requirement of a yearly formal accounting that is imposed with respect to trusts created under wills.

In the District of Columbia, revocable trusts are also commonly used, apparently to avoid certain inefficiencies of the local probate courts.

For what might be called Machiavellian estate planning, there are some states, such as Illinois, Connecticut, Michigan, Ohio, and Florida, where the revocable trust — unlike a will — may still be used to bar the grantor's surviving spouse from obtaining a statutory share of such trust property at the grantor's death.

In certain other circumstances, a revocable trust can be used to choose a jurisdiction with favorable laws to govern the disposition of assets, particularly if the law of the state where probate is required is less favorable — say, to the operation of a grantor's business or with respect to his creditors' rights. The advantage of this technique is that complications, delay, and expense may be avoided in the probate proceedings, depending on the states involved.

Despite the recurring appearance of articles touting the revocable trust as an estate planning panacea, it is by no means advisable for everyone, may well be inadvisable for many, and should always be evaluated on a case-by-case basis.

VII

The Need for Legal Precision
in Estate Planning

There is no more important legal document than a will. And in the preparation of no other legal document is the inaccurate or misleading use, or even *location*, of a word or phrase more serious or potentially damaging. This danger is particularly great because a will, unlike most contracts, cannot be changed after it becomes effective — on its maker's death. Few people spend enough time with their lawyers going over the language of a will and its relationship to their specific family situations. To demonstrate what care should go into even the definitional, or "boilerplate," provisions of a will or a trust, consider the three hypothetical trust and estate cases below, where ambiguity about one word, "issue," led to arcane and Byzantine legal problems. They are based on real situations, but all names and facts have been completely altered.

*"What sort of will would you like to have, Mr. Fignewton? . . .
Short and simple? . . . Or one that will go clear to the
Supreme Court?"*

THE ADOPTED ISSUE

Samuel Kradel III was a success by most standards. He was rich, lived
in an elegant New York City townhouse, and was a partner in a pres-
tigious investment banking firm. At 56, he had never married but had
never lacked female companionship.

When I saw him about his legal problem, he had been living for
some time with the "love of his life"—the latest and longest-lasting in
a series of affairs. She was a beautiful 29-year-old French girl named
Nicole, and she wanted financial security. Nicole had given Sam an
ultimatum: provide it or terminate the relationship. She said, "Your
money is more important to you than I am"; he said, "My money is
more important to you than I am." The importance of money seemed
to be primarily in the eyes of the holder (or would-be holder).

Nicole gave Sam two choices: (to him a Hobson's choice): marriage or a substantial, immediate, and irrevocable money settlement. Sam liked neither but not for the reasons you might expect. He was certain marriage would destroy the beautiful relationship. And although he was well off, he did not want to part with substantial assets. I advised him such a gift to Nicole without marriage would cost him large gift taxes (federal and New York) as well as the loss of the assets and their income if the relationship were to go sour. Furthermore, he was a devoted alumnus of Yale (no virtue to me as a loyal Princetonian) and had, a few years before, committed to leave nearly all of his estate to Yale.

We reviewed his financial situation in great detail to see if there were some way to give Nicole economic security while preserving both Sam's bachelorhood and his personal estate for his own benefit and the future benefit of that school in New Haven.

Sam was the beneficiary of a substantial trust created under the will of his late grandfather. Sam was to receive the income of this trust for his lifetime. At his death, the property in the trust was to pass to Sam's "issue." The grandfather had been from Ohio, and — here's the catch — his will did not define the word "issue." If Sam died without issue, the trust property was to pass to some second cousins who lived in Ohio and about whom Sam cared not a whit.

I advised Sam to adopt Nicole.

In many states, the word "issue" includes adopted persons as well as the natural offspring — assuming the relevant will or trust neither prohibits adopted persons as "issue" nor defines them as persons adopted under a specific age, bearing in mind the "Lolita adoption" (older man adopting a younger woman) problem. In forty-nine states and the District of Columbia (and various foreign countries), you can now adopt an adult. (South Dakota has no procedure for adult adoptions.) Of course, the circumstances under which adults may be adopted vary greatly from state to state.

American law even has reported cases (in Kentucky) of a husband legally adopting his wife and vice versa. In each instance, the adopted spouse was able to take the remainder of a trust, having become the "issue" of his or her own spouse.

It is mind-boggling what enterprising Americans have done to avoid what Justice Oliver Wendell Holmes called "the price of civilization" — taxes. For example, a younger brother in Pennsylvania adopted his older brother in order to affect inheritance rights and realize death tax savings. Colorado and Georgia authorize adopting to make the adoptee an heir.

Various famous persons have also adopted adults. As he neared death, W. Somerset Maugham adopted his male secretary, Alan Searle, in an attempt, albeit unsuccessful, to limit his natural daughter's inheritance rights under French law. In November 1988, the late billionairess Doris Duke, then 75, adopted 35-year-old Chandi Heffner, with whom she had been living since 1985. The adoption seemed to presage Ms. Heffner's becoming a major heir of the daughter of James Duke, tobacco tycoon and the benefactor of Duke University. Miss Duke, as she preferred to be called, had been married twice, but she had no surviving children, her only child having died at birth. Later the adoption of Ms. Heffner turned sour. Yet, as most persons know, you cannot divorce a child, even an adopted one. So, instead, Miss Duke disinherited Chandi, saying in her will (she died in October 1993):

> I am convinced that I should not have adopted Chandi Heffner. I have come to the realization that her primary motive was financial gain. I believe that, like me, my father would not have wanted her to have benefited under the trusts which he created, and similarly, I do not wish her to benefit from my estate.

Chandi Heffner is contesting the will as I write this book.

Not long ago, a battle was waged over the $180 million fortune of the late Lydia Mendelsohn Buhl Morrison, heiress of the Fisher Body automobile fortune and the only child of its former head, Louis Mendelsohn. At question was the validity of her adoption of adult twin Spanish boys, Carlos and Pedro.

At a bullfight in Madrid in 1967, Lydia and her second husband, the late Thomas J. Morrison, became enamored of a 12-year-old boy. They had no children, although Lydia had two children of her first marriage, Lydia Buhl Mann and C. Henry Buhl III. The Morrisons tracked down the parents of the boy and asked to adopt him. The parents agreed, if the Morrisons would also take the boy's twin brother.

The Morrisons brought the boys to the United States, where they were raised primarily in Detroit and Palm Beach. But they were not formally adopted until 1973 in New York. The boys were 18 by that time, and Michigan law then prohibited adult adoptions, while New York allowed them.

Lydia Morrison left her personal estate of $60 million, including her dog, Rocky Sylvester Stallone, Jr., to Carlos and Pedro. At stake was the $120 million Mendelsohn trust that, at Mrs. Morrison's death, was to be divided among her "issue."

Her natural children claimed all of the trust on the ground that Carlos and Pedro should not be deemed to be "issue" because their adoptions were illegal. The natural children said their mother misrepresented to the New York adoption court that she was a resident of New York when she was a legal resident of Michigan. After the New York Family Court denied the natural children right of access to the adoption files, the case was finally settled out of court.

In another notable case, Robert David Lion Gardiner, part owner of the 3,300-acre Gardiners Island off eastern Long Island, announced that he intended to adopt a wealthy young cousin, so that the descendants of his niece, Alexandra Gardiner Creel Goelet, will not be the sole heirs of the island. The niece's attempt to enjoin such an adoption in advance of its happening was denied by the New York County Surrogate's Court. (Rumor had it that, to be safe, Mr. Gardiner had an alternative prospective adoptee referred to as a "spare heir.")

Adoptions of adults become more complicated where sexual relations are — or seem to be — involved. Statutes in Florida and New Hampshire prohibit a homosexual from adopting an adult or a child. (The constitutionality of these statutes has not been tested in the courts.)

A Rhode Island court denied a petition of a married man to adopt a married woman because "to implement an adoption between persons whose relationship is essentially that of paramours . . . is to concede that the legislature of Rhode Island intended a sardonically ludicrous result." Lower court cases in New York had gone both ways on the permissibility of adult homosexual adoptions. But in 1984, the state's highest court, the New York Court of Appeals, denied the petition of a 57-year-old male who sought to adopt a 50-year-old male with whom he had a twenty-five-year relationship. So today it seems that in New York, a homosexual cannot adopt his or her partner.

To get back to Sam Kradel, Sam and I decided he should adopt Nicole to make her his "issue," thereby elevating his own status from sugar daddy to adoptive father. This stratagem, if it worked, would assure her economic security at Sam's death, as she would then inherit Grandpa Kradel's $2.5 million trust fund.

While Sam lived, he would continue to support her in the affluent style to which she had become accustomed. Even if they broke up during Sam's lifetime, this would not undo the adoption. Sam relaxed, thinking he had the best of all possible worlds — Nicole now, Yale later, and both without marriage.

But it was not that simple. Sam told Nicole of this plan, and she told her lawyer. Her lawyer called me. He had only one question: could we assure Nicole that the Ohio relatives would not contest her rights to the trust fund on Sam's death? If they did, would we give a legal opinion that she would be considered "issue" for purposes of Sam's grandfather's will? In other words, was she economically protected? (Fortunately, he did not ask other legal questions, such as whether the adoption could convert a merely illicit relationship into an incestuous one.)

The legal question here would be: what did Sam's grandfather intend when he used the word "issue"? Only blood offspring? If Sam had married and adopted a young child, would not the child inherit on Sam's death? What of a lovely mistress who made the testator's favorite grandchild very happy? As between Nicole and the relatives in Ohio, some of whom were not even born when the grandfather died, who should take the trust property?

A major difficulty is that no one can ask Sam's grandfather — or prove what he intended. He probably had no specific intent about this question because he never thought his grandson would adopt an adult

American mistress, let alone a French one. But if he had thought of it, what would old Sam Kradel have wanted? Should we go back and study his sex life for our answer? Did he have a mistress, or at least a few flings? Would he have thought his grandson was, in effect, robbing the Kradel fortune?

One could argue this case either way. I know which side I'd prefer to argue, but Nicole and her lawyer did not care which side I'd prefer. She wanted financial protection without having to win a favorable legal decision after Sam's death to get it.

Nicole was upset; Sam was distraught. I was in the middle, neither upset nor distraught but not happy. Lawyers very much want to solve their clients' problems, not exacerbate them.

So, another approach was decided on. I would go to Ohio and negotiate with the presumptive heirs to give them — or anyone claiming through them — a portion of the trust on Sam's death if they would not contest Nicole's status as "issue." These Ohio relatives were not well off, so perhaps for a promise to pay, say, $250,000 we could assure Nicole, if she survived Sam, the remainder of the trust.

The Ohio relatives did the same thing Nicole had done. They consulted a lawyer. He wanted them to get at least 50% of the trust. Too much, said Nicole's lawyer. Sam naturally agreed. Intensive negotiations began. Before a settlement could be agreed upon, it appeared that Nicole had lost much of her enthusiasm for her lover.

As a final agreement was about to be reached by the lawyers, Nicole reached out to a new provider, who promised her both marriage and economic security, and she moved out on Sam. He has never quite recovered, although it is an exaggeration in human terms to say he is suffering.

I suppose the moral of this, if any, is that it is better to marry the woman you love than to adopt her so you can leave all your money to Yale. (Now, if it were to Princeton, my alma mater, that would be a different story.)

In any event, if Sam's grandfather had carefully defined the word "issue" in his will, Sam's only alternative, for better or for worse, might have been marriage.

*"Believe me, Sam, it is better to marry the woman you love than
to adopt her so you can leave all your money to Yale."*

THE ARTIFICIAL ISSUE

As a man approaches his death, he often becomes obsessed with
leaving behind one particular legacy — a son of his blood to bear
his name. This particular obsession seems to cross religious and
ethnic lines. The male heir has been a great desideratum in many cul-
tures and seems to continue to be even in this modern age, when to
most sensitive, educated people a person's worth is not related to
gender.

So, I was not unduly surprised when Benjamin Internestein proclaimed to me his need for a male heir. But I was somewhat surprised
by his proposed method.

A fairly often used method is adoption of a blood relative. A Japanese billionaire, Shoji Uehara, head of Taisho Pharmaceutical, was adopted by his uncle, who had started and built his great enterprise with the motto "Business Is War." Sonless Shoji adopted his son-in-law Akira to have his own direct male heir to the business empire. The adoption cycle will stop at Akira, as he and Shoji's daughter have three sons.

Seiji Tsutsumi, the extraordinary Japanese billionaire poet-entrepreneur, used adoption in a time-honored way in his country. He wanted to marry a former geisha (now Asako Tsutsumi), but knew the union would be socially unacceptable. He arranged for a prominent friend to adopt her, which gave legitimacy to their subsequent marriage.

Adoption is not what Ben had determined to do. He was a very successful man. His corporations had made him a centimillionaire. At age 69, he had been happily married to his charming wife for more than forty years and had two loving daughters and three grandchildren. When this obsession began to haunt him, he offered his daughter and son-in-law a great deal of money if they would change the grandson's name to Internestein. The son-in-law refused: even though he was not a man of principal, he was a man of principle.

Ben had thought of another way. Working for one of his corporations was a young single woman about 30. She had told Ben she wanted to adopt a child but was having great difficulty because she was single. She was also concerned about making enough money to support the child comfortably.

Ben asked her if she would have a child with him if he made certain that the child would always be well provided for (and, as a consequence, her standard of living would also be elevated). He hastened to explain that he wanted only a son, but that his doctor believed this result could be relatively certain if artificial insemination were used. Ben's male sperm would be separated by a centrifugal process so that the insemination should create a son. The prospective mother agreed on the condition that a trust of $2 million be created to support Ben's "artificial" issue for his life.

Ben was very happy, believing that he could fulfill his need to have a son. He wanted to know if I thought there were any legal problems with his proposal. Before answering, I asked what his wife thought of all this. He said that he had persuaded her to go along with his wishes. The daughters, who knew he had provided well for them, were, however, incensed and had tried without success to dissuade him. But he was obsessively determined to procreate a son.

Ben had already thought out some of the problems. If it were determined by amniocentesis that a girl was to be born, the mother could, if she wished, bear it, accept $250,000 instead of the $2 million trust, and agree that she would never seek more support for the child. There were serious legal problems with this approach.

An alternative proposal was that she could have an abortion if the sex of the unborn child were determined to be female. However, Ben was quite certain that the artificial insemination technique would result in a male birth. If it were a son and if he ever changed the Internestein surname, the trust, of course, would end and revert to Ben's family.

I told Ben that I did have a serious problem with this plan. As Ben conceived it (so to speak), the trust was to be created now and to become irrevocable on the birth of a son; or, if no son were born, the trust property would revert to Ben. In purpose and effect, the trust was to promote the birth of a child born out of wedlock, now often referred to as a nonmarital child.

There is a doctrine in the Anglo-American law of trusts that a trust cannot be created for an illegal purpose. For example, you cannot create a trust to run a gambling establishment or establish a house of ill repute where such enterprises are illegal. Would Ben's trust be legally enforceable and effective?

"Don't tell me what it's *not*," retorted Ben. "With what you charge, you ought to be able to find a legal way to do this, or I'll find a lawyer who can!"

Since Ben was willing to acknowledge his paternity and support the child, was the trust really illegal or against public policy? Even if it were, who could attack it? His wife would not. His daughters would, but on what ground? He was free to disinherit them totally under New York law and the law of every state except Louisiana, so on what basis would they have standing (after Ben's death) to attack or set aside the trust?

If the trust were to be created by contract on the condition that a son be born, the son might have third-party rights (so-called donee-beneficiary rights) to enforce the creation of the trust. Again, the law of contracts has doctrines on the unenforceability of illegal contracts or contracts that are against public policy. Would the doctrines apply to this unique case?

Eventually, even though we determined the trust should be enforceable under U.S. laws, we recommended what seemed to be a more legally effective way to carry out Ben's plan. He would establish an offshore trust in a jurisdiction whose law would not recognize an attack on the trust based on the concept that it was against public policy.

A son was born, and some years later Ben died happy, knowing that there was a young boy growing up with his name and of his blood. And, of course, Ben had been careful how he defined "issue" in his will and other legal instruments, because of the existence of his special "artificial issue." Ben's son is, so far, a happy, economically secure boy. There are worse things than being a rich little bastard.

And one of the worst may be having one parent too many. Take the next case, a most unusual one.

THE UNEXPECTED ISSUE

A distinguished older gentleman—let us call him Patrick Natterson— came to see me at my office. He was in his 70s, tall and elegant, and he told me a story that was extraordinary even after all the stories that I have heard over my many years in the field of trusts and estates. Mr. Natterson came from a different city, and the problems that he wanted to tell me about arose out of the marriage of his niece to a young man approximately a year before our meeting. The niece was from his wealthy established family, and her new husband was a scion from an equally well off clan. Accordingly, the two of them had the wedding of the year in their city, attended by all of its social elite. Both families were delighted that these two beautiful young people were forming a union. After the wedding, they went off on a honeymoon, and when they returned, the bride was pregnant. Again, everyone was very pleased, because she had not intended to pursue a career, and there would now soon be a new young heir to the two great family fortunes.

About nine months thereafter, the baby was born. It was a boy, and, quite unexpectedly, he was black. Mr. Natterson then told me what had happened. The night before the wedding there had been two parties — a bachelor party and a bachelorette party. At the bachelorette party, a male black dancer had been a participant and had done a striptease for the ladies in attendance (analogous perhaps to what was going on at the bachelor party). Apparently, at some time during that evening, the bride, in a moment of indiscretion, had sexual relations with the black dancer. It was not clear to me, and I did not press the question, whether she had gone off on the honeymoon forgetting the incident because of being very inebriated, or simply thought there was no risk of pregnancy. In any event, the dancer was the probable father of the child, although legally, as every law student knows, the husband of the mother was, by law, strongly presumed to be the father.

The human tragedy that followed was devastating. The mother of the bride had a nervous breakdown and required institutional care. The mother of the groom also went into a psychological state of shock. The groom asked the bride for a divorce. The question of what would happen to the innocent infant boy had not been resolved at the time of my meeting. Nearly everyone wanted the boy put up for adoption. In the world that we live in, it is hard to believe that the reactions would have been the same to a child born out of wedlock to the groom as a result of his bachelor party, but, again, I did not pursue this because it was not relevant to our discussion.

In fact, I next asked Mr. Natterson why he had come to see me. His answer was precise and to the point. He said that he was consulting me as an independent lawyer in another city to assure great confidentiality. He wanted legal advice, and was also seeking such advice on behalf of an older member of the groom's family, because various trusts in his family and trusts in the groom's family would be affected by the legal status of this unexpected issue. The reason was that under the terms of the trusts of both families, upon the death of the bride or the groom or others, property would pass to "issue," not specifically defined, and in some of the older trusts to "lawful issue," also not specifically defined.

What was the legal status of the quite unexpected issue—the baby boy?

Historically, the presumption was that illegitimates were not included in a class gift to "issue" in a will or trust unless there was some specific intent in the instrument to include them. Connecticut was the first state to reject this general rule excluding illegitimates from a class gift to children or issue, and was alone until New York followed suit in 1976. Now, the trend, but still not the majority view, is to construe wills and trusts to include illegitimates in such class gifts absent a contrary intent expressed in the document. In fact, in light of certain U.S. Supreme Court cases in the '70s and '80s, a rule or statute that presumes legitimate and not illegitimate persons are included in a class gift to issue may well be an unconstitutional denial of equal protection of the law.

Many states have adopted a statutory rule of construction including illegitimates in accordance with such states' statutory rules on intestate inheritance, i.e., rules on the persons who take the estate of a person dying without a will. For example, in Florida, a person born out of wedlock is deemed a lineal descendant of his natural mother and also of his father if (i) the natural parents marry each other; or (ii) paternity is determined by adjudication, before or after the death of the father; or (iii) the father acknowledges paternity in writing. Thus, Natterson family trusts passing to the "issue" of the mother of the boy would probably be read to include the boy.

However, the trusts that pass to "lawful issue" would seem to pass only to children not born out of wedlock. There are two New York cases to that effect but few, if any, cases in other jurisdictions. There seem to be no cases in Pennsylvania or Florida, for example. An interpretation that reads "lawful issue" to cover all descendants would seem to make the word "lawful" meaningless.

Of course, this case is more complicated than it may seem. The unexpected issue was technically born in wedlock, and such a child is presumed to be legitimate and presumed to be the child of his natural mother (Mr. Natterson's niece) and her husband. This presumption exists regardless of whether conception occurred before or after marriage, and it is one of the strongest known to the law. It was a conclusive presumption at early common law: "If a husband, not physically incapable, was within the four seas of England during the period of gestation, the court would not listen to evidence casting doubt on his paternity." Today, the presumption can be overcome by blood group and other scientific tests — so-called HLA (human leucocyte antigen) and DNA tests. Human cells have twenty-three pairs of chromosomes, which carry genetic markers known as human leukocyte antigens. Since a child's antigens must come from either the mother or the father, the occurrence of an antigen in the child and the alleged father indicates a high probability that the alleged father is, in fact, the biological father. While standard blood tests have an exclusion rate of 50% to 60%, the use of both the blood test and the HLA test can indicate exclusion with a rate of accuracy above 90%.

Newer tests, known as DNA typing, have been developed. In the DNA tests, known now to all as a result of the O. J. Simpson trial, a blood sample is analyzed, and since the chances of two people having the same "DNA fingerprint" can be 1 in 15 billion, it seems that one could determine conclusively whether a particular man is or is not a child's father.

Then there is the issue of standing — who can challenge the presumption of legitimacy. Obviously, many of these issues are beyond the scope of this book.

As our research continued, the mother reluctantly opted to place her baby boy for adoption. In New York, but only since 1986, an adoption would make the child a stranger to any natural relatives for purposes of inheriting a disposition in a will or trust, whether executed before or after the order of adoption. That is not the case in several states. In any event, this unexpected issue case demonstrates, once again, the need for great care in the use of the English language in defining even the most basic terms of a will or trust.

THE WILLS OF LITERARY TITANS

Can one find such precision in the wills of great literary figures? Unfortunately, such wills generally lack a prose style or even poetic phrasing. It becomes obvious upon reading their wills that the titans of literature were severely inhibited by their lawyers. Nearly all are as commonplace as the will of, for example, a businessman who cannot compose a clear sentence, writing as if he thinks that syntax is the name of a corporation involved in the manufacture of oral contraceptives (Syntex).

Many distinguished writers of literature were trained as and some practiced as lawyers, including Aristotle, Donne, Flaubert, Kafka, Wallace Stevens, and possibly Chaucer. And one would think that the real prose writers and poets would have imposed on their legal advisers some of their own literary style and love of the language. But it is the other way around. Lawyers down through the centuries have by means of their legerdemain convinced literati to put their wills in the stilted and often arcane legal language of the times.

William Shakespeare's will in its primary disposition for his eldest and most favored daughter reads in part:

I give, will, bequeath, and devise unto my daughter Susanna Hall [various specific properties are listed] and after her decease to the first son of her body lawfully issuing and for default of such issue to the second sons of her body lawfully issuing and to the heirs males of the body of said second son lawfully issuing, and for default of such issue the same so to be and remain to the fourth, fifth, sixth, and seventh sons of her body lawfully issuing, one after another, and to the heirs males of the bodies of said fourth, fifth, sixth, and seventh sons lawfully issuing in such manner as it is before limited, to be and remain to the first, second, and third sons of her body and to their heirs males [etc., etc., *ad nauseam*].

The rest of Will's will is equally dull, and written in the same style. Its only interesting aspect is an interlineated clause apparently added at the time of signing by which Shakespeare made his only bequest to his wife, Anne Hathaway, leaving her his "second best bed, with the furniture." Some thought this humorous; others scandalous. Was this because their union was a so-called "shotgun marriage," their eldest

child's baptismal date being only six months from the date of the marriage license bond? Anne Hathaway was 7 years older than the 18-
year-old Shakespeare whom she allegedly seduced. Were there other
reasons that explain this unusual and small testamentary disposition?

Scholars have differed for centuries about it. Probably the correct
view is that the "second best bed" was the more comfortable marital
bed while the "best bed" was in the guest room for visitors. Also, Anne
may have had under local law substantial dower rights in the property
outside of any bequests in the will. But evidence for several theories
exists, and we cannot be dogmatic about what the will reveals of the
true nature of Shakespeare's marital relationship. We can conclude that
Shakespeare's lawyer could have used more precise or informative language to describe the marital bequest. Or perhaps it was Shakespeare
himself who should have been more precise. For evidence that he spent
his "lost years" pursuing the law, see *Shakespeare's Hidden Life: Shakespeare at the Law (1585–1595)*, by W. Nicholas Knight (Mason &
Lipscomb, 1973).

Virgil's will was uninspiring and commonplace, but it contained
what could have been a disastrous direction to his executors to burn
the text of the *Aeneid* because he had not finished it, having said "poetry
is nothing if not perfect." Fortunately, Virgil's executors, Varius and
Tucca, were wiser than he; being apparently nonperfectionists, they
did not heed the direction, for the *Aeneid* was unfinished only as was
Schubert's famous symphony or Turner's *Canal at Chichester*.

The will of the French satirist Rabelais, who died in 1553, contains
the ambivalent clause "I have no available property, I owe a great deal;
the rest I give to the poor." It is more difficult to confirm this para-
doxical provision than Rabelais's alleged reply to a messenger from
Cardinal Jean du Belay, sent to see how Rabelais fared in his last
illness: "*Je vais chercher un grand peut-être; tirez le rideau, la farce est jouée*"
("I'm going in search of a great perhaps; lower the curtain, the comedy
is over").

One wishes those one admires to die with the same style and wit
that graced their lives. Oscar Wilde may have done so even if without
a recorded will. This story is told in differing versions but with the
same punch line. When Wilde was without money and dying, syphilitic

and in pain, staying in a mean little room in the Hôtel d'Alsace in Paris, a friend came to visit him. Wilde was lying in bed and, though suffering, he was sipping champagne from a fine long-stemmed glass. "My word, Oscar, what are you doing?" Without hesitation came the reply: "I am dying beyond my means."

Not so cool was the poet John Donne, who died in 1631. His will was made "in the fear of God, whose mercy I humbly beg and constantly rely upon in Jesus Christ, and perfect love and charity with all the world, whose pardon I ask from the lowest of my servants to the highest of my superiors. . . ." He left £500, whose interest was to be applied "for the maintenance of my dearly beloved mother, whom it hath pleased God after a plentiful fortune in her former times to bring in decay to her very old age." He also wrote a separate, bittersweet poem entitled "The Will," perhaps because none of his poetry was in his own will:

Before I sigh my last gasp, let me breathe
Great Love, some legacies; I here bequeath
  Mine eyes to Argus, if mine eyes can see;
If they be blind, then Love, I give them thee,
My tongue to Fame; to ambassadors mine ears;
To women or the sea my tears;
Thou, Love, has taught me heretofore
  By making me serve her who had twenty more,
  That I should give to none, but such as had too much before.

My constancy I to the planets give;
  My truth to them who at the court do live;
Mine ingenuity and openness
  To Jesuits; to buffoons my pensiveness;
My silence to any who aboard have been;
My money to a Capuchin:
Thou, Love, taught'st me, by appointing me
To love thee, where no love received can be,
Only to give to such as have an incapacity.

Montaigne, the great essayist who died in 1592, was said to have done what many testators would do if they could. Realizing he was dying, he called all his valets and servants and other beneficiaries-to-be to his bedside. There he paid to each of them the bequests he had given to them in his will, thus avoiding any obstacles his executors or others might have raised against satisfying them after his death.

The danger in this approach to testamentary giving is the unpredictability of death. If death does not occur, anticipatory benevolence can lead the donor to financial disaster. A farmer in Suffolk, England, being very ill, followed the advice of his affectionate relatives to give them his money (and also avoid legacy duties). He did so, and later regained his health but not his wealth. The farmer had to seek relief from his local parish.

Most famous United States authors, including Mark Twain, Whittier, Longfellow, Emerson, Emily Dickinson, Melville, and Faulkner, left conventional wills written in standard legalese. Harriet Beecher Stowe's will also was unremarkable both in its style and provisions, leaving everything to her children with one puzzling exception: "I make no provision out of my estate for my daughter Georgiana at her special request." (Shades of Cordelia!)

Although Walt Whitman revised his will a number of times before his death in 1892, starting in 1873, the will was unnoteworthy except for leaving his much-admired silver watch to Peter Doyle, a young and intimate friend, "with much love." Yet after a period of distance and incommunication, Peter was supplanted as Walt's boy protégé by Harry Stafford, who is reported to have reinvigorated the aging poet with "wrestling matches" and other youthful entertainments, which Whitman was only somewhat discreet in writing of. In the last will, Harry ultimately got Walt's watch as well as having won his affection.

F. Scott Fitzgerald, a loyal Tiger to the end, died while reading the *Princeton Alumni Weekly* (scribbling notes about the football team) and eating a chocolate bar. The first line of his handwritten will, apparently written without the assistance of a lawyer, read: "Part of my estate is first to provide for a funeral and burial in keeping with my station in life." Later, he crossed out the word "funeral" and inserted "cheapest funeral" followed by "without undue ostentation or unnecessary expense." In fact, he died with few assets and a reputation that was on the decline. He asked to be buried with his family in a Catholic cemetery in Rockville, Maryland, but his lifestyle and status as a "nonbeliever" caused the bishop to raise objections, and he was buried instead in nearby Union Cemetery. He had $700 in cash at the time of his death, $613 of which went to the undertaker. After paying off a number of large debts, his remaining assets of under $35,000 were left to provide for his 19-year-old daughter, Scottie (Frances Scott Fitzgerald), and wife, Zelda, lasting them seven years. Zelda also received $50 per month pension as the widow of a veteran. Various provisions relating to her benefit are conditional upon whether "she shall regain her sanity."

There is little to note about the other provisions of the will, although his executor, John Biggs, in seeming reference to Fitzgerald's change of fortunes between the time his will was written and his death, said: "He left the estate of a pauper and the will of a millionaire."

Samuel Johnson's will, as copied by Boswell, was an interesting testament, but as usual in these cases not up to the testator's lifetime literary standards. No wonder, coming from a man who said, among other things, "It is better to live rich, than to die rich," and "Life is very short, and very uncertain; let us spend it as well as we can." As you might guess, he put off doing his will almost to the very end. While it exhibits his generosity, both the will and codicil were written in an ordinary legalistic way.

Dr. Johnson, as he became known even though he was no doctor (his M.A. from Oxford, which he left early because of poverty, was only a belated honorific), left a will written on December 8, 1784, and a lengthier codicil written the next day. The codicil contained one striking provision: "I bequeath to God a soul polluted by many sins, but I hope purified by Jesus Christ." Johnson left the bulk of his estate "in trust" for the benefit of "Francis Barber my man servant, a negro." Barber was from Jamaica and had been brought to England in 1750 by Colonel Bathurst, the father of a good friend of Johnson. The colonel in his will gave Barber his freedom, and he entered Johnson's service in March 1752. They were great friends, and Barber served Johnson with two relatively brief interruptions until Johnson's death in 1784.

Samuel Johnson influenced the will of George Bernard Shaw, who died in 1950 at the age of 94. His detailed will, which did at least have some literary flair in spots, begins with rather precise burial instructions:

> I desire that my dead body should be cremated and its ashes insepa-
> rately mixed with those of my late wife now in the custody of the
> Golders Green Crematorium and in this condition inturned or scat-
> tered in the garden of the house of Ayot Saint Lawrence where we
> lived together for thirty five years, unless some other disposal of them
> should be in the opinion of the Trustee more eligible. *Personally I prefer
> the garden to the cloister.*

His will stated he desired that no method of commemorating him should suggest that he "accepted the tenets peculiar to any established church or denomination." He also requested that no memorial should "take the form of a cross or any other instrument of torture or symbol of blood sacrifice."

Of greatest importance to Shaw was to replace what he called Dr. Johnson's alphabet with the "Proposed British Alphabet" of forty letters. Shaw's primary bequest of the residue of his estate was to create a trust for the scientific investigation of his new phonetic alphabet, including preparing the text of his play *Androcles and the Lion* in it, to determine how much time and effort would be saved by using this alphabet. (Mrs. George Bernard Shaw, perhaps not to be outdone in providing eccentric bequests, left $263,200 "to polish the manners of the Irish.")

There was a contest of the will on the grounds the alphabet trust was too vague, a nice irony given the decedent's reputation as a great craftsman of the written word. Eventually a compromise was reached by which only a limited portion of the estate would be used for the alphabet reform plan. A competition was held and a phonetic alphabet selected. The play *Androcles and the Lion* was published and distributed as requested. Of course, the possibility of acceptance of the new phonetic alphabet seems as remote now as in 1957 when the competition was held.

Shaw concluded his will:

. . . I also record my regret that my means are not sufficient to provide for material pledges of my regard for the many friends, who as colleagues in the Socialist movement or as artists cooperating with me in the performance of my plays or otherwise have not only made my career possible but hallowed it with kindly human relations.

In fact, the noted Socialist was quite a capitalist. His estate was £367,233 (or $1,028,252 in 1950). After his death, it is estimated that the Shaw estate earned in excess of $2 million from the Broadway production of *My Fair Lady*, which was the musical version of his play *Pygmalion*, and more millions from the sale of the movie rights. Thus he could have made many Socialist colleagues so-called laughing heirs or drinking heirs. That, after all, would have pleased the irreverent Shaw, who was, as he himself said, "only a beer teetotaller, not a champagne teetotaller." Not that Shaw always had the last word. He once sent Winston Churchill two tickets to the opening night of one of his plays, inviting him to "bring a friend if you have one!" Churchill replied: "Thanks for the tickets. I can't attend the opening night but shall go to the second performance, if there is one."

Lillian Hellman, a careful wordsmith, named certain persons in her will to be "literary property fiduciaries," but no literary property was set aside for them to administer, leading the New York surrogate in a proceeding to interpret the will to say that "while [Lillian Hellman's] literary works can be characterized as creative genius, her will cannot." And that has been true of the wills of most literary geniuses.

AVOIDING
TAXES —
EVERY CITIZEN'S
RIGHT

VIII

How the Rich Do It —
i.e., Get Richer

There is a plethora of intricate devices that can create substantial savings in income, gift, and estate taxes, and most of them have been designated by acronyms. Here is how some of the most effective ones work.

LOW-INTEREST LOANS

One of the best devices is one of the oldest and simplest: low-interest loans to children. This long-favored estate planning technique depends on the government's required interest rates which can vary greatly. This simple, risk-free device is ideal for investors who are capable of generating returns in excess of the relatively low interest rates the government requires on short-term (three years or under), mid-term (over three to nine years), and long-term (over nine years) loans.

The concept could not be more straightforward. An individual (the "lender") makes a loan to his children (or a trust for their benefit) and the children then pay him the lowest permissible interest that will not result in an imputed income or gift tax under the Internal Revenue Code. The lender, who presumably is a sophisticated investor, then invests the borrowed funds for the children with a view toward out-performing the stated interest rate on the loan. To the extent that he is successful, he will have succeeded in making a tax-free transfer of the surplus to the children.

For example, assume the required interest rate on a mid-term loan is 5.34%. Next, assume a lender makes a $1 million, nine-year loan to his child, with interest payable annually at 5.34% and principal payable in one lump sum at the end of the loan term. The funds are then invested for the child and earn an average after-tax return of 15% annually. At the end of the loan term, the child will be left with ap-proximately $1.6 million, after the loan has been repaid in full. And since no gift was involved, no tax will be due on that amount.

An even better result can be achieved if the lender forgives the payment of a portion of the interest and shelters the resulting gift from gift tax by using his $10,000 annual gift tax exclusion ($20,000 if the lender is married). Thus, in the above example, if the lender is married, he or she can have the child pay only $33,400 in annual interest instead of the $53,400 he or she is obligated to pay, with the remaining $20,000 being a tax-free gift. If the child's interest obligation is decreased in this way, the amount that will be left at the end of the loan term will increase to approximately $1.9 million.

The required interest rate on the loan will fluctuate monthly and will depend on the term of the loan. In February 1994,* the required rates for annual interest payments were as follows:

Short-term loans (less than or equal to three years)	3.96%
Mid-term loans (over three years but not more than nine years)	5.34%
Long-term loans (over nine years)	6.33%

---

* These rates change monthly and can vary greatly over time. Thus, the rates for November 1994 are 6.34% for short-term loans, 7.45% for mid-term loans, and 8.01% for long-term loans.

The tax consequences of this transaction are also very simple. Since no gift is involved, there is no gift tax. If the lender dies during the loan term, the principal balance of the loan will be includable in his or her gross estate, just as if the lender had not made the loan.

The lender will have to pay income tax on the full amount of the interest payable on the loan, even if the lender uses the annual gift tax exclusion to forgive a part of such interest. The children may or may not receive a corresponding deduction, depending on, among other things, whether the interest is investment or mortgage interest.

A deduction for mortgage interest on up to $1 million of the loan will be available to the child if the loan is secured by a mortgage on a child's residence, and the loan to the child is made in connection with either the "purchase or improvement" (or both) of such residence. In addition to the deduction of interest on such $1 million borrowing, interest on another $100,000 mortgage on the child's residence, which secures the parents' loan, will be deductible to the child.

The child's interest expense will be deductible as "investment interest" in an amount up to the child's "investment income," to the extent the proceeds of the loan are utilized to acquire property held "for investment," generally, property that is held by the child for profit and is not a "passive activity." A passive activity is broadly defined as a trade or business activity in which the child does not materially participate, and rental activities. (The deduction for any interest expense attributable to a passive activity is subject to special limitations on passive loss deductions.) Interest expense that relates to noninvestment activity of the child may not be deductible.

Pursuant to regulations promulgated by the Internal Revenue Service, special tracing rules are employed to identify the actual investment use of the loan proceeds, and thus to determine the deductibility of the interest on the loan, in cases where such proceeds are commingled with other funds of the child. The administrative difficulties of complying with these tracing rules are avoided if the loan proceeds are segregated in an account of the child that is used solely for investment activities.

GRITs

A GRIT in tax-planning jargon is not a Southern food but a grantor retained income trust. During the 1980s, GRITs of cash, closely held securities, and art were an extraordinarily effective estate planning device.

As a result of a change in the federal estate tax law in late 1990, GRITs can now mostly be used only with respect to personal residences. However, a personal residence GRIT, commonly known as a "house GRIT" or simply a "personal residence trust," has become one of the more effective estate planning vehicles currently available. Here is an example of how it works:

G transfers his house worth $900,000 to a trust (the GRIT). G lives in the house for fifteen years. Then the house, while still owned by the GRIT or by G's children, as he determines, is rented by G for his lifetime and, if so desired, for the lifetime of G's spouse. A gift of the house is not its $900,000 fair market value, but a much smaller value because of the discount for G's retained use of the house for fifteen years.

To create a house GRIT, the grantor transfers title to his personal residence to a trust (the GRIT), but he retains the exclusive right to live in it for a term of years. After the specified number of years expires, the house can either be held in further trust for the grantor's wife and children (or only the children) or be distributed to the children outright. If the grantor survives the trust term, the house, including all appreciation in its value, will pass to the grantor's children free of all estate and gift taxes.* This trust gift to the children does not mean the grantor will lose the use of the residence — that can be assured in several ways, as discussed hereafter.

By creating a house GRIT, the grantor will make a taxable gift equal to the present value of the remainder interest in the trust property, i.e., the value of the house minus the value of the grantor's right to live in it for the specified term of years. These values are determined

---

* It is assumed, as explained below, that no federal gift taxes will be paid because the grantor's $600,000 exemption will be used.

by reference to actuarial tables issued by the IRS, which fluctuate monthly based on prevailing interest rates. The actual amount of the gift will depend on the age of the grantor, the term of the grantor's retained interest, and the value of the house.

As previously explained (pp. 36–39), everyone who can do so should utilize his or her $600,000 exemption now, because it may soon disappear, and in any event, it is advisable to lock in these exemptions from estate taxes, as their value should grow during the rest of the lifetimes of two spouses. The major benefit of the house GRIT is that it permits the creator of it to enlarge or leverage his exemption—the amount (currently $600,000) that can pass free of federal estate or gift taxes to any recipient. For example, assume a 65-year-old grantor transfers a $1.75 million home to a ten-year house GRIT. Using recent IRS actuarial tables, the value of the gift will be only $544,500, because the value of the ten-year retained use for a 65-year-old person will be $1,205,500. Since this $544,500 will be sheltered by the grantor's $600,000 credit, no federal gift tax will be due at the time the GRIT is created, and no estate tax will be due when the grantor dies, since the home will no longer be an asset of his estate. The result is that $1.75 million in actual value has been passed on to the grantor's descendants at no federal gift or estate tax cost. Furthermore, if the house appreciates during the ten-year trust term, that appreciation will also pass free of gift and estate taxes. If, on the other hand, the grantor had not created the GRIT and had retained the house until his death, it would ultimately be subject to a 55% federal estate tax.*

The principal risk of a GRIT is that a grantor may die during the term of the trust. If that happens, the entire value of the house will be included in the grantor's estate for estate tax purposes. Of course, if the grantor had not created the GRIT, that would have been the result anyway, so nothing has really been lost, except the expenses of creating and maintaining the GRIT, which are not large. In the event of a

---

* This assumes that the grantor's taxable estate is in excess of $3 million. It is important to note that if the grantor survives the trust term, the tax basis in the assets held by the GRIT will not be "stepped up" to fair market value at the time of the grantor's death. Rather, the trust remaindermen (the beneficiaries of the trust after the grantor's retained interest expires) will have the same basis as the grantor originally had.

premature death, any portion of the grantor's unified credit used at the time the GRIT was created will be restored to the grantor's estate.

After the trust term, how can the grantor and his spouse make certain that they will be able to continue living in the residence transferred to the GRIT? This potential problem can be circumvented in two different ways. First, the house, as previously indicated, can continue to be held in trust (the GRIT) for the grantor's spouse and children, or just his children, and the grantor could rent it from the trust for its fair rental value. In that way, the grantor could transfer additional assets (the rent) to his children free of gift tax. Second, shortly before the end of the GRIT term, the grantor could buy the house back from the trust at its then value. This alternative is especially attractive if the GRIT is a so-called grantor trust for income tax purposes, since, in that event, no capital gain will be recognized on the transfer back to the grantor. (Simply put, a grantor trust is a trust under which the grantor—the creator of the trust—remains taxable for income purposes but not for estate and gift tax purposes. Thus, the sale by the trust back to the grantor is considered a nonevent for tax purposes.) As a result of the buyback, the grantor regains full ownership of his residence, and the trust has cash to invest and use for the children. Furthermore, since the grantor again owns the house, at his death the house will gain a "stepped-up" basis equal to its date-of-death value. Accordingly, if the heirs sell the house after death there will be no gain on the difference between the house's original cost and its date-of-death value, since the latter becomes the tax basis for post-death sales purposes.

The Treasury Department has issued final regulations establishing a variety of technical requirements that must be met in setting up a house GRIT. Some of these requirements are discussed below.

Personal Residence

The grantor is limited to two house GRITs, and if two are created, one of them must consist of the grantor's *principal* residence. A vacation home will qualify as long as the grantor uses it at least two weeks each year. A condominium or cooperative apartment will also qualify. If a couple has more than two residences, they together can create three house GRITs, each of them contributing one-half of the principal residence, and each of them also creating a GRIT of one of their separate residences.

Even if the couple are doing one house GRIT, it may be advisable to do it jointly — each contributing an undivided one-half interest — because it seems the value of each half is less than the whole, so a smaller gift will be made. For example, the husband owns a $1 million residence. If he puts it in a GRIT the value of the gift will be $1 million minus his retained interest. If he and his wife own it equally and they each put in one-half, then it seems that the total value of the gift may be discounted to, say, $800,000 to $850,000 (before subtracting the retained interests), because no one would pay $500,000 for either the husband's or the wife's one-half interest.

Expenses

During the trust term, the grantor is permitted to pay the expenses of the house (including mortgage payments), and may do so either directly or by contributing additional funds to the trust. In the latter event, the grantor is only permitted to contribute an amount necessary to pay the trust's expenses for the next six months. Any excess cash held in the trust at the end of the trust term must be returned to the grantor.

Although the Treasury regulations do not address this issue, in some instances the grantor's payment of the house expenses may constitute additional taxable gifts by the grantor. This result will depend on whether the payment is primarily for the benefit of the grantor or the remaindermen. For example, while the amortization component of a mortgage payment primarily benefits the trust remaindermen, the interest component, as a short-term obligation, mostly benefits the grantor. Accordingly, the former should be a gift and the latter should not be. The same distinction can be made between ordinary repairs, which are for the grantor's benefit and thus not a gift, and capital improvements, which are for the benefit of the remaindermen. To the extent that an additional gift is made, its value will be based on the actuarial value of the amount contributed, which, in turn, will depend on the length of time remaining in the original trust term.

Sales and Insurance Proceeds

If the house in the GRIT is sold, the trustees will have two years in which to reinvest the proceeds in another house. The same is true if the house is destroyed and insurance proceeds are recovered. If the trustees do not reinvest the proceeds within this time period, the GRIT must be converted into a grantor retained annuity trust, or GRAT, discussed in more detail later in the next section of this chapter. With a GRAT, a guaranteed amount, based on the actuarial value of the grantor's original retained interest in the trust, must be paid to the grantor each year. The obligation to pay this amount will relate back to the date of sale or destruction and could reduce the benefit of creating the house GRIT. For example, consider once again the 65-year-old grantor who transfers a $1.75 million house to a ten-year GRIT. If the house is sold on the fifth anniversary of the creation of the GRIT and the trustees do not reinvest the sale proceeds in another house, the grantor, according to the IRS tables, must receive an annual payment of $209,270 for the last five years of the trust.

This conversion requirement will also apply to any excess cash held in the trust if the trustees reinvest the sale or insurance proceeds in a house that is less costly. The same will be true if the house in the GRIT ceases to be the personal residence of the grantor for any reason unrelated to sale or destruction. This result could occur, for example, if the house is rented out full-time.

A house GRIT can be an extremely valuable estate planning device, especially in times of depressed real estate values. By using a house GRIT, any appreciation resulting from an upturn in the market can be passed on to future generations tax-free.

Common-Law GRITs for Unrelated Beneficiaries

The principal drawback of a house GRIT is that it can be used only with residential property. The traditional common-law GRIT, from which the house GRIT derives, was far more flexible, because it could be funded with any assets, such as growth stocks, closely held stock, partnership interests, or even art. With a common-law GRIT, the grantor retains the right to receive all trust income (i.e., dividends, interest, rents, etc.) during the trust term no matter how small or large such income may be. The trust lasts for a specified number of years, after which the assets held in the trust pass to the grantor's intended beneficiaries, either outright or in further trust.

If the grantor survives the trust term, the trust property, including all appreciation in its value subsequent to the creation of the trust, will pass to the trust beneficiaries free of federal estate and gift taxes. The common-law GRIT is, therefore, especially useful for assets with high potential for appreciation. If the grantor dies during the income term, the entire trust will be included in his estate for estate tax purposes.

Because of its flexibility, the common-law GRIT was perhaps the most widely used estate planning device in the late 1980s. Unfortunately, as is all too common, once Congress became aware of the substantial tax benefits of a GRIT, it essentially repealed the use of this device in a family context. However, the common-law GRIT is still available for those individuals who are interested in making tax-free gifts to persons outside of their immediate families, such as nieces, nephews, friends, lovers, etc. "Immediate family" is defined as the grantor's spouse and lineal descendants and spouses of such descendants.

GRATs

For many individuals, a GRAT, or grantor retained annuity trust, is a highly useful method of transferring wealth to their descendants without incurring a federal gift or estate tax.

Trust Terms

A grantor retained annuity trust is a relatively new estate planning device that is ideally suited to those individuals who are capable of generating consistently high returns on their investments or expect an asset to appreciate significantly in the short term.

A GRAT is a trust in which the grantor (i.e., the creator of the trust) retains the right to receive a fixed annual dollar amount (the "annuity") for a specified number of years. The annuity is typically expressed as a percentage of the initial value of the property transferred to the trust. After the specified annuity term elapses, the property held in the GRAT will pass to the grantor's designated beneficiaries in whatever form he or she provides in the trust instrument. For example, it could be held in further trust for the grantor's spouse and children, held in trust exclusively for the children, or distributed to the children outright.

If the grantor survives the annuity term, the grantor's beneficiaries will receive the property held in the GRAT, including all appreciation in its value, free of all estate and gift taxes. The GRAT should therefore be funded with assets that have the greatest potential for appreciation.

Since the grantor's annuity is fixed, any income earned by the GRAT in a given year that exceeds the annuity amount will be added to principal for eventual distribution to the grantor's children free of estate and gift taxes. Conversely, if the trust's annual income is insufficient to pay the annuity, the trust principal will have to be invaded to make up the difference. In that event, the trustee will have three options:

- The trustee can make an in-kind distribution of trust assets to the grantor.

- The trustee can sell trust assets to generate the necessary cash to cover the shortfall.

- The trustee can borrow the necessary funds from the grantor or anyone else, as long as the trust pays a market level interest rate to the lender.

During the annuity term, the grantor can act as the sole trustee. Afterward, if the trust property continues to be held in trust for the grantor's family, the grantor can still act as trustee for investment purposes but can have no discretionary authority with respect to distributions of trust income and principal.

Estate and Gift Tax Consequences

Upon creating a GRAT, the grantor will make a taxable gift equal to the initial value of the trust property reduced by the present value of all annuity amounts payable to the grantor during the trust term. This present-value computation is made by reference to the actuarial tables issued by the IRS, which fluctuate monthly based on prevailing interest rates. The actual amount of the gift will depend on

- the size of the grantor's retained annuity
- the term for which the annuity is payable to the grantor
- the value of the initial trust property
- the age of the grantor

If the grantor dies during the annuity term, that portion of the trust property necessary to produce the annuity payment will be included in the grantor's gross estate. This amount will be determined under the IRS actuarial tables in effect at the time of the grantor's death. Thus, if the annuity is $100,000, the value of the trust at the grantor's death is $1.5 million, and the IRS assumed interest rate is then 10%, and the amount includable in the grantor's estate would be $1 million.

In order to take maximum advantage of the estate plan implemented in the grantor's will, the trust will provide that any portion of the trust principal included in the grantor's taxable estate will be paid over to his estate and pass under his will. This protective clause will enable a grantor who is married at his death to defer estate taxes through use of the estate tax marital deduction.

Estate Planning Benefits

The estate planning benefit of the GRAT derives from the grantor's ability to generate a higher return from the GRAT's assets than the assumed interest rate upon which the IRS's actuarial tables are based.

For successful investors, this will often not be terribly difficult to accomplish, since the IRS assumes that assets will grow, through a combination of both income and appreciation, at only 120% of the "applicable federal midterm rate" for the month in which the GRAT is created. For February 1994, this 120% assumed rate of return was only 6.4%. Thus, if the grantor is capable of outperforming that rate over the annuity term, the IRS will have undervalued the amount of the original gift and the grantor will have succeeded in transferring a greater amount to his children tax-free.

Consider the following example:

In February 1994, a 50-year-old grantor transferred $1 million in marketable securities to a fifteen-year GRAT and retained the right to receive a 7% annuity, or $70,000 per year. Assuming the grantor survives the annuity term, he would receive a total of $1,050,000 (i.e., fifteen payments of $70,000). Under the IRS tables, the present value of the grantor's interest was approximately $627,000, leaving a taxable gift of $373,000. To the extent the grantor had not used his unified credit, i.e., the amount (currently $600,000) that can pass free of federal gift and estate taxes to any individual, no federal gift tax would actually be owed.

Now assume that as a result of the grantor's investment acumen he obtains a total average return on the GRAT's assets of 20% per year. At the end of the fifteen-year term, the $1 million originally put in the GRAT will have grown to over $10 million, which will pass to the grantor's children free of estate tax. Thus, by using only $373,000 of his unified credit, the grantor will have successfully removed over $10 million from his estate. Had he not created the GRAT, this property would have been subject to as much as a 55% federal and state death tax rate at the grantor's death.

In essence, the GRAT permits the grantor to leverage the use of his unified credit. Thus, the more of his unified credit that the grantor uses, the greater the estate tax benefit that he will achieve. The following table illustrates the maximum amount 45- and 55-year-old grantors could have transferred tax-free in February 1994 to 7% GRATs of varying terms by using their entire $600,000 unified credits. If the grantor's spouse chooses to join in the transfer, these amounts can be doubled.

GRAT term*	Maximum amount that a 45-year-old grantor can transfer tax-free	Maximum amount that a 55-year-old grantor can transfer tax-free
5 years	$ 843,701	$ 839,011
10 years	1,187,620	1,154,725
15 years	1,663,801	1,539,073
20 years	2,295,561	1,949,242

* These figures are actually for annuity terms of the specified number of years or until the grantor's death, whichever occurs first.

A 7% annuity is used for illustration purposes only. If the grantor wished to retain a higher annuity, the amount of his retained interest would be greater in each case and, conversely, the amount of the gift would be less.

The Zero Gift GRAT

The one real risk associated with a GRAT is that if the GRAT assets underperform the IRS assumed rate of return, the initial gift will have been overvalued, and thus the grantor will have wasted his unified credit to that extent. Furthermore, there are many individuals who no longer have their unified credits available to them or who wish to use their credits for other estate planning devices, such as the previously discussed house GRIT. The solution to both these situations is to create a zero gift GRAT—i.e., a GRAT that pays such a high annuity that, under the IRS tables, the grantor is considered to have retained the entire actuarial value of the property transferred and thus made no gift.* In February 1994, the required return for a zero gift GRAT created by 45- and 55-year-old grantors, respectively, was as follows:

* The IRS takes the position, which many practitioners do not accept, that a true zero gift GRAT is not permissible. Choosing an annuity that results in a *de minimus* gift seems advisable until this issue is resolved.

GRAT term*	Required annuity for a 45-year-old grantor	Required annuity for a 55-year-old grantor
5 years	24.24%	24.58%
10 years	14.15	14.58
15 years	10.95	11.48
20 years	9.48	10.12

* These figures are actually for GRAT terms of the specified number of years or the grantor's death, whichever occurs first.

For the investor who is capable of generating consistently high returns, the zero gift GRAT is literally a no-risk proposition. For example, assume a grantor creates a five-year GRAT with the required 24.24% return and funds it with $1 million. If he is able to earn an average annual total return equal to the annuity amount, he will have successfully transferred $1 million to his children tax-free without using any portion of his unified credit. If, on the other hand, he is incapable of generating such a high return and is required to invade the trust principal to a limited extent to pay his annuity, whatever remains in the GRAT at the end of the term will still represent a tax-free gift to his children. Moreover, even if there is nothing left in the GRAT at the end of the term, the grantor will essentially be no worse off than if he had not created the trust in the first place, except for the expenses of creating and administering the GRAT.

For individuals who invest in many different types of speculative ventures, a series of zero gift GRATs, each of which holds an interest in only one such venture, should be considered. That way, if one of the ventures is highly successful and another is a total bust, the children will receive the full benefit of the successful investment. Had the two been held in the same GRAT, the benefits of the first might have been wiped out by the second and the children would have received nothing.

Closely Held Stock and Limited Partnership Interests

By funding a GRAT with closely held stock (including Subchapter S stock) or limited partnership interests, additional amounts can be transferred to the grantor's children tax-free. These additional transfers can be made because for gift tax purposes the value of such assets can be discounted to reflect their lack of marketability and, when appropriate, their minority position. Accordingly, when a grantor transfers such an asset to a GRAT, the amount of the initial transfer, and thus the gift, may be valued at less than the interest's true liquidation value. At the end of the annuity term, however, the grantor's children receive the undiscounted value of the interest, which results in the amount of the original discount passing to the children tax-free.

One further benefit in using such assets is that the discount will lower the annuity that is required to zero out the gift. For example:

Assume a 45-year-old grantor transfers a 10% limited partnership interest with a liquidation value of $1 million to a ten-year zero gift GRAT. After applying a 30% discount, the amount of the initial transfer will be valued for gift tax purposes at $700,000. In order to zero out the gift, a 14.15% annuity (see the table on p. 122) will be required. However, this percentage is based on the $700,000 gift tax value, not the $1 million liquidation value. The result is an annuity of $99,050, which is only 9.90% of the partnership interest's actual value.

Income Tax Considerations

In most cases, a GRAT will be a grantor trust for all purposes. This classification means that during the annuity term, all income, whether ordinary or capital gain, will be taxed to the grantor. The GRAT's status as a grantor trust for capital gains purposes presents an additional tax savings opportunity. If an asset is sold at a gain in the GRAT, the sale proceeds will belong to the trust and the tax on the gain will be paid by the grantor. By paying the tax out of his or her other assets, the grantor will essentially be making an additional tax-free gift to his or her children, since they will then receive the gross sales proceeds unreduced by any tax.

One drawback of a GRAT is that if the grantor survives the annuity term, the income tax basis in the assets held by the GRAT will not be "stepped up" to the fair market value of the GRAT assets at the time of the grantor's death. To avoid the disadvantage of the loss of basis increases, the grantor can purchase the GRAT assets immediately before the termination of the GRAT. This purchase can be made without income tax consequences to the grantor or to the trust. The grantor receives the assets back and the trust (the GRAT) receives cash. When the grantor dies, the income tax basis of the asset will be increased to its fair market value at that time.

LIFE INSURANCE TRUSTS

One traditional and valuable estate tax shelter untouched by Congress (thus far) is the irrevocable life insurance trust. It remains among the safest and most effective means of leaving substantial funds to children and more remote descendants free of all death taxes, which is why these trusts are often called "wealth replacement trusts."

While you can leave an unlimited amount of insurance proceeds (or any other asset) to your spouse tax-free, this does not avoid death taxes. It only defers them, since the amount received will be taxed in the surviving spouse's estate unless he or she has spent it.

The primary purpose of a life insurance trust is to avoid an estate tax in both spouses' estates and thus leave the insurance proceeds to younger generations tax-free. Of course, a surviving spouse also can be a beneficiary without causing the insurance proceeds to be taxable in that person's estate.

A federal estate tax is imposed on life insurance proceeds payable to anyone other than a spouse if the insured has certain ownership rights, referred to as "incidents of ownership," in the policy at the time of his or her death. These include the right to change the beneficiary, the right to borrow against the policy or pledge it as collateral, and other similar interests. When you create a life insurance trust, you can assign the ownership of the policy, and all attendant incidents of ownership, to the trust; or the trustees can buy the policy, which is preferable for tax purposes. In either event, the trust becomes the owner of the policy. The insured has no ownership rights in the policy at his death, which allows the proceeds to pass to the trust estate tax-free.

In a typical insurance trust, after the death of the insured, the proceeds are held for the benefit of the insured's spouse ("spouse" should be defined to cover divorces and deaths that might occur after the nonamendable, irrevocable trust is created) and issue.

The trustee is given the discretion to distribute as much, or as little, of the trust income and principal to any one or more of the beneficiaries the trustee deems advisable. When the insured's spouse dies, the trust assets pass to the children, either outright or in further trust, tax-free. Money for the premiums is paid into the trust by the insured, utilizing an estate-planning device called a Crummey power, which results in no gift tax.

An insurance trust also can be used in conjunction with a charitable remainder trust (CRAT or CRUT see pp. 155–158) to "replace" the assets that will be distributed to charity, so your children's inheritance will not be any the less and could be more, depending on the amount of insurance purchased. In fact, in many cases, the annual insurance premiums can be paid from the additional income you receive from your CRAT or CRUT.

An additional benefit of a life insurance trust is that it provides a means of passing literally millions of dollars to grandchildren and more remote descendants free not only of estate taxes but also of the relatively new and confiscatory GST (generation-skipping tax) (which in the highest brackets can almost double the death taxes for direct bequests made to one's grandchildren).

I should make one additional point concerning the type of insurance to put in a trust. Life insurance serves two basic purposes: it provides funds that can generate income to the insured's family to maintain its standard of living; and it provides a fund with which to pay estate taxes.

If the insured's spouse is adequately provided for by other assets, the first purpose becomes irrelevant. In such cases, there is little sense in purchasing a traditional life insurance policy payable at the insured's death. Instead, the insured and the spouse probably should purchase a so-called second-to-die policy payable on the death of the survivor. Such policies are cheaper than traditional policies, since the premiums are based on two life expectancies, not one. And, as with a traditional policy, a second-to-die policy can be put in an insurance trust so the proceeds themselves pass estate tax-free to the beneficiaries.

Creating a life insurance trust is essentially irreversible. However, if the insurance trust ever became inadvisable or if you were no longer happy with the terms of the trust, the policy could be cashed in for its cash surrender value, and this amount would belong to the trust for distribution to the beneficiaries, usually your spouse and children. Alternatively, the policy could be distributed in kind to the trust beneficiaries. In either event, if you wished, you could then create a new insurance trust (funded with a new policy) to replace the old one.

One way to avoid the irrevocability of an insurance trust and all gift tax consequences of large insurance premium payments is to use the "just in time" approach. Under this method of insurance ownership, you and your spouse would each own individually a policy on the other's life and would pay all premiums. If the owner-spouse does not have sufficient funds to make the premium payments, the insured-spouse may transfer funds to the owner-spouse for this purpose that would qualify for the marital deduction. Thus there would be no gift taxes owed with respect to any premium payments. Furthermore, the $20,000 annual gift tax exemption amount for each of your children and grandchildren would be available for other purposes (e.g., to give highly appreciating assets to a trust for their benefit).

Under this ownership approach, once the owner-spouse becomes aware that the insured-spouse is about to die, the owner-spouse will transfer ownership of the policy to the children, or trusts for their benefit. Although the cash value of the policy at that time would constitute a taxable gift, this is considerably less than the face value of the policy. Since the insured-spouse has no "incidents of ownership" in the policy, it will not be included in his or her estate. In addition, since the owner-spouse is not the insured, the face value of the policy is not includable in his or her estate, and no three-year rule applies, so it does not matter how soon after this transfer the insured dies. Thus, under this scenario, the owner-spouse will transfer ownership of the policy "just in time" to avoid having the full face value of the policy includable in either spouse's estate.

On the other hand, if the owner-spouse dies first, ownership of the policy can pass under his or her will to the children (or trusts for their benefit) and only the cash value of the policy will be included in the owner-spouse's estate. Thereafter, the children (or the trusts) will be responsible for paying the premiums.

A variation on this is to have *each* spouse own a second-to-die insurance policy on the lives of both of them. In particular, the policy selected would be one that does not have a significant increase in cash value upon the death of the first spouse. The owner-spouse would make all premium payments until the death of the first spouse and no gift taxes would be due upon the payment of the premiums, as explained in the above scenario. Upon the death of the first spouse, two things would happen. First, the surviving spouse would transfer the policy owned by him or her to the children or a trust for their benefit (thereby making a taxable gift of the cash value of the policy at that time). Assuming that the surviving spouse did not die within three years of the transfer, the policy would not be includable in either spouse's estate for tax purposes. Second, the policy owned by the deceased spouse would pass under his or her will to the children (or trusts for their benefit). Only the cash value of the policy at the first spouse's death would be includable in the deceased spouse's estate because the other spouse is still alive. Thereafter, the children (or the trusts) would pay the premiums on the policies.

One disadvantage of both of these methods of insurance ownership (i.e., those other than ownership by an irrevocable insurance trust) is that if both spouses die together or within a very short time, no estate tax savings is achieved, because the transfers to children (or trusts for thier benefit) cannot be completed before the death of the second spouse. For this reason, you may wish to consider combining these techniques with the use of an immediate insurance trust. This combination would mean putting some insurance in an irrevocable trust (thereby guaranteeing the exclusion from both your and your spouse's estates of the policy proceeds) and owning additional insurance through the methods described above.

Closely held companies provide additional opportunities for effective life insurance planning, because of a type of life insurance product known as split-dollar insurance that is available to businesses. Split-dollar is essentially the only remaining form of interest-free loan available. Basically, with split-dollar, the premiums are paid by the insured's company, and at the insured's death, the company recovers the aggregate amount it paid in premiums. The death benefit, however, passes to the insured's estate or to an irrevocable insurance trust.

The insured, who is generally an executive of the company, has taxable income for a small portion of the premium paid, known as the P.S. 58 cost. Significantly, this P.S. 58 amount also represents the amount of the gift the insured makes if the policy is held by an insurance trust. Here is where the real benefit lies. Consider a matter on which I'm working right now.

A client of ours is considering purchasing a new $50 million life insurance policy, on which annual premiums average approximately $2 million per year for ten years. We have recommended that the policy be put into an irrevocable insurance trust, which means that if he paid the full premium, he would owe a gift tax of more than $1 million each year. However, because the policy is a split-dollar policy, only the P.S. 58 cost is taxed as a gift, and this is a minuscule portion of the actual premium payment. Thus, in year one, instead of making a $2 million gift, he would only make a gift of $76,000, which could presumably be covered by his annual gift tax exclusions. In subsequent years, the P.S. 58 cost increases slightly each year. The result is almost a $50 million tax-free transfer to the children. Such a transfer would not have been possible without a split-dollar arrangement. Second-to-die policies can also be used in split-dollar arrangements with the right set of facts.

There are a few other points to keep in mind with insurance:

1. A careful evaluation of the financial strength of the insurance company or companies selected is even more needed these days than in the past.

2. A second opinion regarding the product, structure, and pricing of an insurance program is often prudent. An independent opinion may also provide a different strategy to achieve the goal either through a different policy form or a potentially different payment and ownership arrangement.

3. High net-worth individuals are concerned with the confidentiality of their personal affairs. The individual involved in the life

insurance transaction wants to preserve confidentiality regarding medical conditions and financial worth. Normal channels for insurance processing may alert a small community if a large insurance transaction is taking place. There are occasions where nonlocal professionals (both insurance agents and lawyers) may be able to maintain a higher degree of confidentiality than local professionals.

Finally, the most exciting development in insurance is, in my opinion, the new variable life products that are developing, whereby the insurance owner can not only have his premium money grow income tax-free but select sophisticated money managers to invest it with all of the proceeds eventually passing estate tax–free to the insured's family.

FREEZES

One of the most popular techniques that many of us have used over the last twenty years or more is called an estate freeze. It was an effective device to reduce death taxes substantially in order to pass family-owned businesses on from generation to generation without forced sales of the business.

In a typical freeze, the owner of a business recapitalizes it into preferred and common stock. Nearly all of the current value is allocated to the preferred stock retained by the older family member or members, and the common stock is either given or sold to the children or to trusts for their benefit. (The same thing could be done with a partnership, by dividing it into frozen and nonfrozen interests.)

Suppose Bountiful Co. is worth $30 million. Bountiful's founder-owner wants his children to take over the company, but he wants to spare the firm and his children the burden of buying out his entire equity at once. So he "freezes" the value of his stock by recapitalizing the company.

He splits the $30 million total equity value into preferred stock worth, say, $26 million and common stock worth $4 million. He keeps the preferred and gives his children the common, paying the appropriate gift taxes. The preferred also pays an appropriate dividend and is also a voting security, so that the founder can retain control.

If the business prospers after the recapitalization, the founder's preferred will not appreciate (it is frozen in value), but the children's common stock will reap all the future appreciation. As a result, when the founder dies, it will be easier for the children and the firm to buy the founder's stock from his estate: the preferred stock will account for a smaller chunk of the company's equity. The founder's estate taxes (55% of $26 million) will also have been locked in by the freeze.

Without estate freezes, a founder might die and leave so much valuable equity in his estate that the children could never raise the money to buy it or to pay estate taxes. Then the only practical solution would be to sell the company to pay the death taxes.

Were freezes abusive? Certain staff members of the Congress's Joint Tax Committee didn't like the technique, largely because of the difficulties involved in accurately valuing private enterprises' securities. The IRS assumed that any time a parent sells or gives anything to children or grandchildren, the assets will be undervalued so as to reduce the parent's estate. Congress, therefore, pushed through a new law in 1987 that effectively destroyed estate freezes and, with typical overkill, managed to throw the baby out with the bath water.

Under the 1987 law, these previously established intrafamily estate-freezing transfers were treated as if they had never existed. If a business happened to have grown between the time the estate was frozen and the death of the founder, all of that subsequent appreciation was thrown back into the founder's estate and taxed, at federal rates up to 55%.

To return to our hypothetical example, suppose that when the founder dies, the value of the common stock has grown to $40 million from $4 million. Under the pre-1987 law, that $36 million of appreciation would have belonged to the children and not be in their father's estate.

Under the 1987 law, the appreciation would have been taxed in the founder's estate, which would pay as much as $34.1 million in estate taxes (55% of $36 million of common stock and of $26 million of preferred), as opposed to $14.3 million (55% of $26 million) under the old law.

As might be expected, the public outcry against this new law from small businessmen throughout the nation was ear-shattering. They viewed it as unnecessarily complex and hopelessly overbroad. In fact, many of us in the estate tax field felt that the law was so poorly drafted that it could be interpreted to apply to a transaction as simple as the sale of a house from parent to child.

One business executive upset over the law was Jack Miller. Miller and his two brothers own and run Quill Corp., based in Lincolnshire, Illinois. Started in 1956, Quill, the L.L. Bean of office supplies, grosses over $200 million annually from mail-order sales of paper clips, stationery, and microcomputers.

Miller and his siblings have five children working at Quill. He wanted to give some nonvoting stock in Quill to his two children. But the 1987 law would have kicked any appreciation on this stock back into his estate — unless he gave both regular common and voting common in the same proportions in which he owned them. But that would have changed the balance of ownership between him and his brothers.

"The government is absolutely crazy," said Jack Miller. "If you work hard and build a successful private business, it's almost impossible to keep it in the family. Maybe the Japanese will buy us all out."

Under intense pressure from irate citizens like Jack Miller and from the Small Business Administration, the American Bar Association, and other legal organizations, Congress finally recognized the error of its ways in October 1990 and repealed the 1987 law. Senator Lloyd Bentsen said: "The 'cure' three years ago turned out to be worse than the disease. The complexity, breadth, and vagueness of the new rules have posed an unreasonable impediment to the transfer of family businesses. As a result, many taxpayers, uncertain about the scope of current law, have refrained from making legitimate transactions."

In its stead, Congress enacted a new law that doesn't automatically assume every intrafamily transfer is tax-motivated but rather focuses on the value of the common stock being transferred to the younger generation. At a minimum, no matter how many special financial accoutrements adorn the preferred stock, the common stock will be considered to be worth at least 10% of the value of the company. In addition, the preferred must be *true* preferred in that it must receive a market-level dividend. If it doesn't, the IRS will assume it does anyway and impose a gift tax on it with interest.

Although highly technical, the new law represents a major step forward from the 1987 law. Among other things, it has eliminated the huge excesses of the 1987 law and more narrowly confined its scope. Thus, some valid intrafamily transfers that were unwittingly caught in the 1987 law's web may now pass muster. On the other hand, because of the many restrictions in the new law, many estate freezes, for both corporations and partnerships, that were once viable will still no longer be economically feasible. At this point, it seems that the only family businesses that should undertake a freeze are those that can afford to pay a substantial dividend and are reasonably certain to grow in value, even after the dividend is paid.

FAMILY PARTNERSHIPS

The family partnership has always been an effective means of allowing children to share in their parents' investments while at the same time allowing the parents to maintain control over those investments.

Recently family partnerships are, with GRITs and GRATs, the hottest technique being used by estate planners as a means of transferring property to children and other family members in order to discount substantially the value of such property for gift and estate tax purposes. These discounts are because of the various restrictions that accompany a limited partnership interest, such as lack of control over it due to minority ownership and the inability to sell it, referred to as a lack of marketability. Marshall S. Cogan, a very successful entrepreneur and owner of, among many businesses, the famous "21" Club in New York City, has said that "the family limited partnership has proven to be a most efficacious method for me to get a part of my business enterprises to my children at lower gift tax rates, and without the loss of any control."

Crucial to the utility of giving away family partnership interests is a 1993 revenue ruling (93-12) in which the Internal Revenue Service abandoned its past views and allowed a substantial discount on a gift of a minority interest in a family partnership even though all interests in the partnership were controlled by members of the same family. Before this ruling, the IRS position was that if family members owned all the interests of an enterprise the family control meant no discount was allowable.

This ruling opened the floodgates and in rushed a tidal wave of family (a/k/a "discount") partnerships, often integrated into a myriad of other estate planning techniques.

In a typical family partnership, a corporation owned by the parents has a 1% general partnership interest and the parents initially share the 99% limited partnership interest. The general partner has complete control over all aspects of the business, including the purchase or sale of partnership assets, what distributions of income should be made, if any, and whether or not to continue the partnership. During the term of the partnership, a limited partner cannot demand a distribution or a return of his or her capital account.

The partnership can be funded with a family business, real estate, or even marketable securities. There is some dispute whether you can put one publicly traded stock, say Toys "R" Us, into a family partnership, then, in effect, give away pieces of that stock and take the quite usual discount of 30%. Most experts think an investment portfolio (or a pro rata portion thereof) is a suitable and IRS-acceptable asset for a family "discount" partnership.

Once the partnership is in place, one or both of the parents make gifts of minority limited partnership interests to their children or to trusts for their benefit. In valuing the gifted interest, the usual test applies, that is, what an unrelated individual would pay for the interest in a true arm's-length transaction. The answer is quite a bit less than the value of the underlying property represented by the interest, because there is very little one can do with a limited partnership interest. It can't be sold, because, apart from the family, there is probably no market for it. It can't be liquidated in order to obtain the underlying property, because the general partner must consent to such a liquidation. It may not even throw off any income, because, again, the general partner makes all decisions with respect to partnership distributions.

For all of these reasons, the gifted interest may be discounted for gift tax purposes, and an appropriate discount is available for *each* of these restrictions. Thus, depending on the nature of the partnership's assets, aggregate discounts ranging from 25% to over 50% may be available to reflect the interest's illiquidity (lack of marketability) and lack of control due to its minority position. As these partnerships have proliferated, many tax advisers have become more aggressive on the size of the discounts. Discounts of 20% to 35% are quite common, but some valuation experts will support 50% to 60% discounts regardless of the underlying property. (A case decided in 1993, involving wealthy New York City real estate developer Samuel LeFrak, allowed 30% discounts on gifts of interests in twenty New York City buildings, even though the IRS successfully argued that these were not gifts of partnership interests but of undivided interests in the buildings themselves.)

To better understand how a limited partnership operates, consider the following situation I recently implemented. Some years ago, a woman had inherited a New York City building that is currently worth $14 million and has a yearly 10% cash flow, i.e., $1,400,000. She wanted to start transferring her interest in the building to her children for estate planning purposes. So we put the building into a limited partnership, with a corporation owning the 1% general partnership interest in such partnership, the mother-donor owning 89% of the limited partnership interest, and her husband owning the remaining 10% limited partnership interest.

At first, we considered simply making outright distributions of minority limited partnership interests to the children. Had we done that, we would, under all the circumstances of that case, have discounted the interests by 30% for gift tax purposes. However, the mother-donor was concerned about decreasing her cash flow, and thus her income, over the short term. So, instead of having her make an outright gift, we decided to have her transfer the limited partnership interest to a ten-year GRAT that would pay her a 9.5% annuity.

As illustrated below, this annuity is stated as a fixed dollar amount equal to 9.5% of the value of the initial property put into the GRAT.

Here, the mother-donor wanted to transfer 11% of her limited partnership interest, which, on an undiscounted basis, was worth $1,500,000 based on the $14 million total value for the building. However, because it was a limited partnership interest that was being transferred, we felt a 30% discount was appropriate. Thus, for gift tax purposes and for purposes of determining the annuity, the value of the interest was only $1,050,000 ($1,500,000 minus $450,000, i.e., 30% of $1,500,000) and the annuity was $100,000 (9.5% of $1,050,000). Under the then applicable IRS actuarial tables, a ten-year GRAT with a $100,000 annuity will result in a taxable gift of 40% of the trust property or, in this case, $420,000 (40% of $1,050,000). Thus, the mother-donor successfully transferred $1,500,000 worth of property by only making a gift of $420,000. And no federal gift tax was paid since the entire gift was covered by her $600,000 unified credit. Furthermore, if the building appreciates in value over the ten-year GRAT term, all of the appreciation attributable to the gifted interest will pass to the children transfer—tax free. Thus, assume the building is sold for $16,500,000 in twelve years. The children will receive 11% of the sale proceeds or $1,815,000, all of which derived from only a $420,000 gift.

To summarize the major advantages of the family partnership:

1. There are very substantial discounts on gifts of the limited partnership interests to younger members of the family. (Similarly, such interests will have lower, discounted values for estate tax purposes if they pass by will to younger family members.)

2. Control of the entire partnership is retained by the senior family members, without such retained control bringing the transferred partnership interests back into the estates of the senior family members as is the usual case with a family-controlled corporation.

3. Senior family members have the power to control all distributions (income and principal) from the partnership.

4. Consolidation of family assets may generate substantial operational cost advantages.

5. Annual distribution of diverse assets by gifts of family partnership interests — e.g., ranch land, closely held business interests, etc. — is simplified.

6. Protection of family assets from future creditors is enhanced. Family partnerships may also provide asset protection against claims of nonfamily members (in-laws who become "outlaws" by divorce) in failed marriage situations.

7. There is added flexibility. For example, a family partnership is easier to amend or to terminate than an irrevocable trust.

8. Partnerships can require family disputes to be arbitrated rather than resolved in the courts. Also, it can assess all arbitration costs against a family member who institutes a nonmeritorious claim.

9. Family partnerships can save legal and other costs of out-of-state probate.

10. Family partnerships allow the senior family members (general partners) to follow modern portfolio theory in investing the family assets.

But beware! The limited family partnership may seem to be too good to be true. Several tax commentators have recently pointed out that very high on the Internal Revenue Service wish list is a desire for congressional action to limit discounts for transfers of minority interests among family members.

INTENTIONALLY DEFECTIVE TRUSTS

There is one thing almost every middle-class American who can afford it wants to do: make gifts to children and grandchildren without having to pay gift taxes. Once you have used up your annual exclusion of $10,000 per child ($20,000 if from a married couple) and your present lifetime exclusion of $600,000 plus paying for medical and educational costs, what can be done?

There is a little-known, somewhat complicated, but still remarkably effective device that works. It is called a "defective grantor trust." What it does is allow the creator (grantor) of the trust to pay income taxes on both the ordinary income and the capital gains of the trust even though all of such income and capital gains is going to the grantor's children and not to the grantor. The payment of such taxes is, of course, an indirect gift to the children that under present law does not cause any gift tax on the parent-grantor. Depending on the size of the trust and its income and capital gains, this can result in the gift-tax-free transfer of substantial monies to children and grandchildren.

A variation of this extraordinary but legitimate device was used by Aristotle Onassis to provide income for Jackie Kennedy Onassis during their marriage without either of them having to pay U.S. income or gift tax. How did he do it? By means of an intentionally defective trust that he created as grantor for her benefit, with Jackie as the sole beneficiary of the trust income. This income was taxed to him under the relevant grantor trust rules although received by Jackie, and, as a nonresident alien, Onassis was subject to neither U.S. income taxes nor gift taxes on it.

What exactly is a defective grantor trust? In a nutshell, it is an irrevocable trust that will *not* be includable in the grantor's (creator's) estate at his or her death but whose ordinary income (interest, dividends and the like) and capital gains, or in some cases only its ordinary income, remain taxable to the grantor even though it is paid over to others, usually the grantor's children.

There are various ways in which a trust can be made intentionally defective. Three of the most common methods will be discussed in turn.

First, a grantor will be treated as the owner of a "sprinkle" trust (that is, a trust the income and principal of which can be distributed among a group of beneficiaries in the unrestricted discretion of the trustees) if more than one-half of the trustees are "related or subordinate parties" to the grantor. Related or subordinate parties include certain members of the grantor's family, i.e., spouses, parents, descendants, and siblings, and certain persons who conduct business with the grantor, all of whom are treated as being subservient to the grantor. An advantage of this type of grantor trust is its tax malleability—thus, if it becomes inadvisable for the grantor to remain taxable on the ordinary income and capital gains of the trust, the subservient trustees can be replaced with independent trustees, and once one-half or more of the trustees are independent, the trust ceases to be a grantor trust.

Second, a grantor will also be treated as the owner of a trust if the grantor or a third party retains, in a nonfiduciary capacity (i.e., not as trustee), the power to reacquire the trust principal by substituting other property of an equivalent value. Again, this power can be waived by a grantor in order to change the tax status of the trust opportunistically.

In addition, the grantor will be treated as the owner of a trust if the trust income can be distributed to the grantor's spouse. Accordingly, the grantor will be treated as the owner of a "sprinkle" trust for the benefit of the grantor's spouse and descendants, even if no distributions are ever made to the spouse and the entire trust is preserved and used for the grantor's descendants.

Besides the gift-tax-free transfer of the trust's income taxes to other family members, there are other benefits to grantor trust status. In the case of a house GRIT, as previously discussed (p. 114), the grantor can buy back the residence during the GRIT term without recognition of gain. Alternatively, if the residence is sold in the trust to a third party, the benefits of both the deferral of gain on the sale of a principal residence replaced with a new residence and the exclusion of up to $125,000 of gain on the sale of a residence by a taxpayer age 55 or over remain available to the grantor. Lastly, the grantor will be entitled to deduct all real estate taxes and mortgage interest paid by the trust.

With a GRAT (pp. 117–124), grantor trust status is desirable if, for example, the grantor wishes to fund the GRAT with Subchapter S stock. Only certain types of trusts are permitted to be Subchapter S stock shareholders without jeopardizing the corporation's favorable tax treatment. One type of trust eligible to hold Subchapter S stock is a grantor trust. Thus, if the GRAT is a grantor trust and holds Subchapter S stock, the tax advantages of Subchapter S corporation status will be preserved while the substantial tax benefits of a GRAT are also obtained.

Usually for tax mavens something defective is to be avoided, but that is not so with the intentionally defective trust. It is an extraordinary technique for making tax-free gifts—while it lasts!

IX

'Tis Better to Give
Than to Receive

A BRIEF HISTORY OF PHILANTHROPY

Perhaps the oldest record of giving is the Egyptian *Book of the Dead*, the collective title given to about two thousand papyrus rolls dating from 2600 B.C. Found in the tombs of the then rich and famous, those rolls were purchased from priests to assure the acquirers a happy afterlife and contained, among other things, self-serving statements of acts of charity toward the poor and needy. (Interestingly enough, at least to me as an estate planning lawyer, the oldest copy of a testament is also Egyptian, the will of Uah, dated 2548 B.C.)

Charity, of course, owes much to the great religions, all of which encourage giving to the needy. Buddha decreed benevolence as one of the five ways a follower should do good, and charity is one of the five "pillars" or obligatory duties of Islam. Jesus asked his followers to "love thy neighbors as thyself" and proclaimed, "It is more blessed to give than to receive" (Acts 20:35).

The word "philanthropy," which is derived from Greek words meaning "love of mankind," was not commonly used before the eighteenth century. (The first recorded use was in a sermon delivered in London in 1650 by Jeremy Taylor, an English cleric who was chaplain to King Charles I.) The word "charity," whose etymology includes connotations of love, has a venerable pedigree going back to the early Christian era. I shall use the words interchangeably. The acts they encompass, of course, are as old as society itself.

The great Code of Hammurabi, inscribed on a seven-foot column about 2000 B.C., directed Babylonians to see that "justice be done to widows, orphans, and the poor." Early Greeks and Romans generally gave to enrich the community as a whole, creating parks and gardens and municipal games as well as schools and other institutions.

Judaism developed the concept of tithing—giving literally one-tenth of one's income (in biblical times, usually crops). Some say the custom of giving a tithe was originated by Moses, but it probably began somewhat earlier with Abraham's gifts to the priest-king Melchizedek. The Mosaic code of laws also provided that a portion of one's field be left for the poor to harvest. To Jews, giving is an obligation—a duty to one's fellow person. Thus Jews do not have a word for charity; the Hebrew word used for it is *tsedaka*, which means justice or righteousness.

To Jews, some forms of giving are more praiseworthy than others. About A.D. 1180, the great Jewish theologian Maimonides stated eight "degrees of charity," which he ranked in the following descending order of desirability:

1. To take hold of a [person] who has been crushed and to give him a gift or a loan, or to enter into partnership with him, or to find work for him, and thus to put him on his feet so that he will not be dependent on others.

2. One who gives charity to the poor, but does not know to whom it is given, nor does the poor man know from whom it is received. [In other words, when the gift is completely anonymous from every point of view.]

3. When the giver knows to whom he or she gives, but the poor does not know from whom he or she receives.

4. When the poor knows from whom the gift is received but the giver does not know to whom it is given.

5. When one gives even before being asked.

6. When one gives after having been asked.

7. When one gives less than one should but graciously.

8. When one gives grudgingly.

PHILANTHROPY IN THE UNITED STATES

In our society, private philanthropy of the rich regularly makes big news.

For example, in 1992, Henry M. Rowan gave $100 million to Glassboro State College in New Jersey, the largest individual gift ever to a public educational institution and second only at that time to a $105 million gift given in 1979 to Emory University, a private school in Atlanta, by the late Coca-Cola magnate Robert M. Woodruff. Mr. Rowan heads Inductotherm Industries Inc., a leading maker of industrial furnaces. School officials decided to rename the institution Rowan State College in his honor.

Mr. Rowan, a graduate of MIT, decided to make the gift to repay the debt that he felt to the people and the area that helped make his business a success. The Rowans' business and residence is located in Rancocas, New Jersey, a village about twenty-five miles from Glassboro.

The Rowan endowment cannot be used for operating expenses or capital projects. It is to be used to start a school of engineering, to create visiting professorships, and to establish a scholarship fund for children of Inductotherm employees to attend Rowan (the former Glassboro) for free. This college has an enrollment of about ten thousand students with majors in twenty-five academic disciplines.

Not long after Mr. Rowan's very substantial gift, billionaire Walter

Annenberg, whose fortune derives (with a Balzacian overtone from his father), from *TV Guide*, the *Daily Racing Form*, *The Philadelphia Inquirer*, and the Philadelphia *Daily News*, made the largest onetime gift to private education — $365 million in cash. The money, coming out of the Annenberg Family Foundation, which he apparently controls and which has assets of $1.55 billion, is to be distributed this way: $25 million to Harvard College, $100 million to Peddie School (a little-known prep school in Hightstown, New Jersey, which Mr. Annenberg, a former ambassador to Great Britain, attended), and $120 million each to the communications programs at the University of Southern California and the University of Pennsylvania. Individually, the grants to Peddie, USC, and Penn are the largest cash gifts ever made to either a preparatory school or a university. All were to be paid by the end of the year, rather than gradually and in staggered sums. In contrast, the record contribution to one university — $125 million in cash, stocks, and bonds from C. B. Pennington, who made his fortune in the oil business, to Louisiana State University in 1980 — was a pledge, kept in trust, and less than half of the money has been released so far. See the accompanying chart. Recently the Pennington gift may have been eclipsed by a gift from Sir Harold Acton, a British historian and art collector, to New York University. Sir Harold, who died in February 1994, in his will gave his magnificent estate, La Pietra, which overlooks Florence, his art collection, and $25 million to NYU. The estimated value of the Acton bequest is between $100 and $500 million.

In December 1993, Walter Annenberg announced his foundation would give grants totaling $500 million to public education, the largest such gift ever. Asked his motivation for his huge gifts, Mr. Annenberg said: "Why? Because I wanted to. I'm interested in sending word to others who have sizable foundations that now is the time to stop talking and act. If anybody objects to that, well, I'm sorry."

Very good advice! I have often wondered why so many wealthy persons so often postpone really substantial giving until their deaths. I hope Mr. Annenberg will do even more by encouraging his friends to follow his example. In any event, Mr. Annenberg's very much publicized gifts may at the least make many realize that it is better to give

LARGE GIFTS TO HIGHER LEARNING

Recipient(s)	Donor	Amount*	Date
University of Southern California, University of Pennsylvania, Harvard University	Walter H. Annenberg	$265 million	1993
Louisiana State University	C. B. Pennington	125 million	1980
Emory University	Robert W. Woodruff	105 million	1979
Rowan College of New Jersey	Henry M. and Betty Rowan	100 million	1992
Stanford University	David Packard	70 million	1986
Columbia University	John W. Kluge	60 million	1993
University of Miami	James L. Knight	56 million	1986
Texas A&M University	Dwight Look	52 million	1992
University of Houston	John and Rebecca Moores	51.4 million	1991

* Most gifts are cash and negotiable securities except for Mr. Look's, which is real estate.
Source: *The Chronicle of Higher Education*

while you are alive — to see the effects of gifts, to implement wisely their use, and, in many cases, to have the pleasure of working with and getting to know the actual persons to be benefited.

As large as the Rowan and Annenberg gifts are, we should note that Paul Mellon gave Yale University $15 million in 1958, which in 1994 dollars could be worth about $122 million. Paul Mellon's total charitable gifts to the present time exceed $670,000,000. (John D. Rockefeller founded the University of Chicago in the 1930s with gifts whose present value would probably approximate over $1 billion.)

Philanthropy in the United States often creates headlines, partly because we seem to have more of it here than in any other country in the history of the world. Why is that so? Why do people give large sums for charitable purposes? How do they give it? What are the most efficacious tax methods of giving? Who should have a CRAT (charitable remainder annuity trust) or a CRUT (charitable remainder unitrust)? How should you give art to charity? How should you give a personal residence to charity? Is a CLAT (charitable lead annuity trust) or a CLUT (charitable lead unitrust) advisable? Why might every American family of financial substance, in due course, be well advised to have its own private foundation?

As a lawyer who has specialized in advising private donors and their eleemosynary entities and has served on the boards of many, I have developed rather strong views on many of these questions and related issues, which I shall discuss in this chapter.

WHY THE RICH GIVE TO CHARITY

Although countless institutions, both cultural and educational, are appropriately named for their donors, some donors have what I call an "Edifice" (or perhaps I should say "Ediface") Complex, giving *only* if the result of the gift — a building, sports facility, room, or whatever nook or even cranny — has their names prominently displayed.

Billionaire William Gates III, chairman of Microsoft Corp. and Harvard's most economically successful dropout, gave $6 million to Stanford for a new information sciences building. Although the building cost $26.1 million, it will be named the Gates Information Sciences Building. Perhaps being eponymous was not his main concern; other more practical reasons may have been the motivation, for as Gates himself stated forthrightly: "I want to invest in the future of the industry and Stanford is one of the five best computer science schools in the country." Let the other four take notice, as there is plenty more from where this $6 million came from — Gates who, according to *Forbes* in October of 1994, is the richest man in America with an estimated net worth of over $9 billion.

Many benefactors have negotiated in a "hardball" way with major cultural and educational institutions (e.g., Mt. Sinai Hospital in New

York, several Ivy League schools, and the Metropolitan Museum of Art) for a named building or wing or whatever, sometimes perpetuating their names while leaving the institution with a great financial burden of providing the money to complete the project or for its subsequent maintenance and care. An offshoot of this kind of problem is the case of the late André Meyer, the legendary financier who headed the investment banking firm Lazard Frères for many years. He gave money to the Metropolitan Museum, which named a wing after him while he was alive to house nineteenth-century European paintings. Apparently it was thought that some if not all of his vast art collection would end up in that wing. However, when he died, his art was sold at auction, with the proceeds going to his heirs and not to the museum — again proving the need for clear contracts and understandings for the benefit of substantial donors and the recipients of their art.

One well-known New York City businessperson offered the Metropolitan Opera a substantial sum (although not all *that* substantial) for the simple quid pro quo of renaming the Opera House after him — an immodest proposal, promptly and properly rejected. Other institutions have faced this issue, and rightfully protected a cultural institution's name by rejecting substantial money for a name change. Intelligent, substantial donors to such institutions should consider the advisability of helping them by conditioning their own gifts on the proviso that the name of an established institution to which they are giving, e.g., the Smithsonian or the Metropolitan Museum of Art, never be changed. This condition could help your favorite institution say no to would-be eponyms without directly offending them.

Sometimes the use of a name can lead to a humorous misunderstanding. When the then mayor of Jerusalem Teddy Kolleck was showing the city to Willy Brandt, then chancellor of West Germany, they came to a beautiful building named the Mann Library. Brandt said to Kolleck: "I did not realize that you had named your library after one of my country's greatest writers." "Oh, no," said Kolleck, "it is named after Freddy Mann of Philadelphia." "Really," said Brandt. "Well, what did he write?" Kolleck replied: "He wrote the check!" Proving again that money does talk, and in this case gave a nonliterary creator his own kind of earned immortality.

Do Americans often give for tax reasons? Undoubtedly. If there ever were any doubt about that, a change in the 1986 tax reform law proved the point. Under that 1986 law, wealthy donors of art lost the benefit of deducting for income tax purposes the market value of the gifted property, e.g., of a painting that was purchased for $10,000 but was worth $100,000 when donated. A so-called alternative minimum tax could be assessed against the donor on the $90,000 of appreciation in such gift.

A 1989 survey showed that within a year of the act, the value of donations dropped one-third. Another study found a two-thirds decline. Contributions increased when Congress restored the tax benefit for gifts of tangible personal property for eighteen months in 1991 and 1992. When the window closed, the giving dried up. In December 1991 the Art Institute of Chicago received a record 1,895 gifts. In December 1992, after the window closed, it received five gifts. The National Gallery received 1,870 gifts in 1986, but the number fell to 247 the next year after the law had changed. During the window period the number jumped to 2,444.

The most dramatic example of the loss of a gift of art during this period was the sale of a splendid van Gogh, rather than the expected gift of it to the Metropolitan Museum, where it had been on loan by the heirs of Siegfried Kramarsky, a New York banker and philanthropist. The painting, a portrait of van Gogh's friend and physician Paul-Ferdinand Gachet, was sold to a Japanese collector, Ryoei Saito, at auction for $82.5 million.

Thanks in large part to Senator Daniel Patrick Moynihan, the 1993 tax law reinstated the full income tax deduction for the market value of art and other assets donated to museums and other charitable organizations.

There can, of course, be purely prudential reasons to give to charity. The story is told of the jet-set couple whose yacht runs amok in the Pacific. They leave their yacht and take their small boat to a nearby isolated island, where they appear to be totally stranded. The wife asks her husband: "Darling, did you pay our pledge to Federation this year?" "No," he answers. "Thank God," she said, "they'll find us!"

One of the primary motivations for giving money to charity is to alleviate guilt. The guilt, as might be expected, takes many forms. Many benefactors have felt they must atone for their actions or those of their family. One of the most famous benefactions is that of the German Thyssen family, whose patriarch was convicted of war crimes at Nuremberg. After World War II his widow created a substantial charitable foundation to do good works with money made in large part from the production of munitions to fuel the Nazi war machine.

Personal tragedies or afflictions are quite different motivators that often lead to the formation of charitable entities to combat or eliminate them. There are many, many examples. Beverly Sills now chairs the March of Dimes, an activity prompted in part by her own children's afflictions with birth defects. The Kennedy family has long supported the Special Olympics and aid for the mentally retarded, motivated by the plight of Rosemary Kennedy, the late president's retarded sister. The Huntington's Disease Society of America was founded by Marjorie Guthrie, wife of folk singer Woody Guthrie, who died of the degenerative disease in 1967. (A recent discovery of the defective gene in persons with this disease may ultimately lead to a cure.)

Princess Yasmin Aga Khan has supported efforts to find a cure for Alzheimer's disease, from which her mother, Rita Hayworth, tragically suffered.

Gordon Gund was blinded by an incurable, little-known disease called retinitis pigmentosa. Today his RP Foundation Fighting Blindness has fifty-five chapters nationwide and seems to be achieving progress in its medical research. His late father, George Gund II, created the family fortune out of a decaffeinated coffee company, which later became today's Sanka division of the General Foods Corporation.

When all is said and done, which donors deserve special commendation? A friend of mine who heads an outstanding educational institution says only those whose net worths are substantially reduced by their charitable giving while they are alive (or perhaps after death, even though in those cases our government pays for 55% or more of the gift because of its deductibility for estate tax purposes).

That may be a harsh test. I know of very few persons who have met it. Henri Dunant, a wealthy Swiss banker and the founder of the

International Red Cross, was eventually led into bankruptcy by his efforts on behalf of the abolitionists, the creation of a state for the Jews, and numerous other causes.

Perhaps the paradigm of a charitable donor is the person who gives anonymously, even if Maimonides puts such giving in second place on his list. There are cases — again, very few, I think — of large anonymous gifts. Two, of particular note, come to mind, a 1983 $50 million gift to the Cornell Medical Center and a 1961 $35 million gift to the Woodrow Wilson School of Public and International Affairs at Princeton University.

The Cornell donor remains known only to a few Big Red cognoscenti. More than ten years after the Princeton gift, following the death of one of the two donors and allegations that the money had come from the CIA, it was disclosed, with reluctance by the surviving donor, a successful investment banker, Charles S. Robertson (Princeton Class of 1926), that he and his wife, Marie Louise Hoffman, an A&P heiress, had made the gift.

The motives of the richest donors are often mixed, unstated, or ambivalent, and it may serve no useful service to speculate about them. The results may be more important than the reasons; the deeds more meaningful than the words. John Steinbeck caustically stated

Perhaps the most overrated virtue in our list of shoddy virtues is that of giving. Giving builds up the ego of the giver, makes him superior and higher and larger than the receiver. Nearly always, giving is selfish pleasure, and in many cases is a downright destructive and evil thing. One has only to remember some of the wolfish financiers who spend two thirds of their lives clawing a fortune out of the guts of society and the latter third pushing it back. It is not enough to suppose that their philanthropy is a kind of frightened restitution, or that their natures change when they have enough. Such a nature never has enough and natures do not change that readily. I think that the impulse is the same in both cases. For giving can bring the same sense of superiority as getting does, and philanthropy may be another kind of spiritual avarice.

Louis Auchincloss, an astute observer of the upper class, has observed that the very rich have few options for the use of their great wealth. They can hoard it, try to establish a family dynasty, collect art, go into politics (often via one's son or sons, like Joe Kennedy), or give it away. Auchincloss concludes: "One keeps coming back to the conclusion that the only present practical, dignified alternative to conspicuous consumption seems to be plain charity. Would Veblen have called that the most conspicuous consumption of all? I am afraid he would."

The "Golden Donors" of our major foundations include many famous American entrepreneurs (often the richest of the then rich), including Andrew Carnegie, John D. Rockefeller, Henry Ford, Andrew Mellon, Alfred Sloan of General Motors, James Buchanan Duke, John D. MacArthur, Robert Wood Johnson, William Randolph Hearst, Charles Stewart Mott, and Conrad Hilton. Some names are conspicuously absent, such as J. P. Morgan, H. L. Hunt, and the Du Ponts. The best analysis of the then thirty-six largest U.S. private foundations is Waldemar A. Nielsen's *The Golden Donors* (E. P. Dutton, 1985).

Private foundations have existed in one form or another in ancient Greece and Rome, the Anglo-Saxon kingdoms, Renaissance Europe, and preindustrial England. In their present form they are primarily the product of the modern industrial society and the large fortunes accumulated in the nineteenth and early twentieth centuries. The United States has far more private philanthropic foundations disposing of far greater wealth than any other democratic society. Their ranks keep growing — eleven thousand of them since 1980. In 1993 there were 35,765 grant-making foundations in the United States, with assets of approximately $177 billion.

To avoid inheritance taxes and keep control of a family business in the family were motivations for the creation of our largest private charitable foundation — the Ford Foundation. Thus the noncharitable, if not misogynistic, Henry Ford and later his son, Edsel, bequeathed in their wills 90% of their stock (in a nonvoting form) to the foundation, enabling their heirs to avoid over $300 million in death taxes while leaving 10% (with all the voting powers and thus control of the company) in the hands of the family. (Similar motivations were crucial to the creation of other major foundations — Hearst, Lilly, Keck, Kellogg, Moody, Gannett, and Duke.)

Such perpetuation of control of a family company through the use of a private foundation has been effectively eliminated by changes in our tax laws, mainly the 1969 Tax Act.

Others try to achieve a different kind of corporate immortality. For example, the Bernard van Leer Foundation in Holland received the founder's immense business interests to avoid "the disadvantage of eventual inexpert family control." The Tata charitable trusts in India own more than 80% of the stock in the parent firm, Tata Sons, of which Tata Industries, the largest industrial group in India, is a 100% subsidiary. The Wellcome Trust in England was created by the will of Sir Henry Wellcome, who at the time of his death was the sole proprietor of the worldwide pharmaceutical business Burroughs Wellcome. Under the terms of his will, all of the assets of the company were vested in the trustees of the foundation, who were to use the profits for specified charitable purposes. In Denmark, J. C. Jacobsen, who established the Carlsberg Brewery, bequeathed his business to the Carlsberg Foundation. In effect, those donors were preserving the stability and continuance of their businesses without decimating tax payments to their governments.

Some donors had a religious sense of a charitable duty, like Rockefeller and Pew, or felt a social obligation to their fellow man, like Carnegie, Mott, and the Mellon heirs. Others, like Henry Ford and John MacArthur, seem to have had no charitable purpose whatsoever in mind. MacArthur said, "I'll make the money — you guys will have to figure out how to spend it." (Fortunately for society, the "guys," with their creation of the MacArthur Foundation genius fellowships and other endeavors, seem to be doing a very good job of charitable giving that never interested Mr. MacArthur.)

Nielsen concludes that "on the whole, therefore, what the donors gave their foundations was a mass of resources and little else — in half the cases or more the donors endowed their foundations simply because they were running out of time [their lifetimes], were drowning in money, and were unable to think of anything better to do with it." Aristotle stated the problem succinctly:

> To give away money is an easy matter and in any man's power. But to decide to whom to give it, and how large and when, and for what

purpose and how, is neither in every man's power — nor an easy matter. Hence it is that such excellence is rare, praiseworthy, and noble.

A recent example of how not to provide for one's personal philanthropy is the case of Doris Duke. Miss Duke died on October 28, 1993, at the age of 80, and she left her estate, estimated at between $1.5 and $2 billion, in the almost total control of one man, Bernard Lafferty, her butler for the six years before her death.

Most of her estate will go to a new Doris Duke Charitable Foundation. It is "dedicated to improvement of humanity through supporting the arts, medical research, education, the environment, and the prevention of cruelty to children and animals."

Lafferty will control the foundation, which will be one of the largest in the United States. The will also named a longtime friend, Marian Oates Charles, as a trustee, but Lafferty alone can appoint three other trustees of the foundation. Of even greater importance, Lafferty can establish new tax-exempt foundations and, if he chooses, terminate the mother foundation in favor of his new foundations.

According to Nielsen, who is now director of the New York–based Program for the Advancement of Philanthropy (an arm of the Aspen Institute in Washington), Duke "in effect cast her money to the winds . . . she abandoned this enormous fortune of hers to philanthropy with only the most general idea of where she intended it to function. And she left it to a minimal board and gave it the widest discretion to define its eventual program."

On the other hand, her father, James Duke, carefully and thoughtfully planned the Duke Endowment while he was alive and appointed colleagues and persons of substance whom he knew well to run it.

Little is known about Doris Duke's butler. He is 48 and a native of County Donegal in Ireland. He had been employed by Nelson Peltz, the wealthy businessman and brother-in-law of Chandi Heffner, the adopted daughter of Doris Duke, who is suing her estate. Like Doris Duke, Lafferty was orphaned as a teenager. He came to the United States twenty years ago and worked in hotel, restaurant, and entertainment businesses, and for a time as a kind of majordomo for Peggy Lee.

Nielsen says that Doris Duke's case proves the need to start your philanthropy "in the years when you've still got your marbles. Start early, learn the trade." Of most importance, develop early the mission for your personal philanthropy and select and cultivate the people to carry it out.

Doing that will allow a philanthropist to turn over a foundation to a group of persons with confidence that they will carry out the philanthropy in a responsible way, truly reflecting the purposes of the foundation's creator.

In contrast to Doris Duke, George Soros, a U.S. citizen of Hungarian origin, has shown the same creativity, foresight, imagination, and risk-taking in his giving as he has in creating his wealth. Considered by many to be the "world's greatest money manager" (*Financial World* estimated his 1993 income to be $1.1 billion), George Soros has done more than any private citizen to advance the cause of freedom and democracy in Eastern Europe, acting in a sense as a one-man Marshall Plan. His philanthropy helped attain freedom for Eastern European societies, most notably Hungary, Czechoslovakia, and the former Soviet Union, long before it was either safe or fashionable to do so.

Guided by his own *Weltanschauung*, springing from philosopher Karl Popper's concept of an "open society," which influenced him while he was a student at the London School of Economics, he spent millions, starting in 1979, when each dollar was of immense value to the brave Eastern and Central Europeans willing to put their lives on the line for liberty. For example, in 1985 he gave hundreds of photocopiers to Hungarian libraries on the condition that they not be subject to government control. The government was eager to accept, because it could not afford to buy such machines with its shrinking reserves of hard currency. Soon the secret service stopped patrolling all copy machines, and the underground press was helped tremendously, as, of course, was the cause of freedom in Hungary.

George Soros now has a network of foundations operating in twenty-six countries (including nineteen former Communist nations), mostly in Central and Eastern Europe, and the former Soviet Union, but also in South Africa. He has set forth the goal of his philanthropy:

The goal of the foundation network is to promote an open society. The concept of open society is based on the recognition that people act on the basis of imperfect knowledge and nobody is in possession of the ultimate truth. This leads to a respect for the rule of law, to a society which is not dominated by the state, to the existence of democratic government, to a market economy, and, above all, to respect for minorities and minority opinions. The key point that needs to be recognized is that an open society is more complex, more sophisticated, than a closed society. A closed society expends most of its energies in preserving the existing order, whereas an open society takes law and order as its starting point and creates progress and prosperity from that base. That means that an open society is a more desirable but also a vulnerable structure.

The Soviet system represented a universal closed society because Communism was a universal dogma. But Communism as a dogma is now well and truly dead. There was an opportunity to make the transition to a universal open society, but that opportunity was lost because the free world failed to rise to the challenge. Now the danger is that what was a universal closed society is going to be reshaped into territorially separate closed societies based on an ideology of ethnic nationalism. To mobilize society on the basis of ethnic nationalism, you need an enemy. If you do not have an enemy, you need to invent one. Therefore, ethnic nationalism is a threat, not only to the countries concerned, but also to their neighbors. Where violence prevails, open society perishes.

In the past two years, Mr. Soros has given $500 million and made commitments to give another $500 million. The *Chronicle of Philanthropy* has indicated that in 1994 this "modern Carnegie" gave away more money ($330 million) than did the Ford Foundation ($307 million), America's largest private foundation, while at the same time spending ten times the estimated amount spent in former Soviet-bloc countries by all U.S. foundations combined. The two largest gifts have been $250 million for educational programs in Russia and $220 million to build and sustain the Central European University that he created in Prague and Budapest. The Central European University is an international educational institution providing postgraduate programs in the social sciences, environmental sciences, and humanities. And it seems to have a broader agenda: by organizing a university network of the leading institutions of the region through research collaboration, information sharing, and library cooperation, the Central European University promotes lasting regional harmony and diffuses ethnic and national divisiveness and conflict. Also, in 1992 Soros personally committed $50 million for humanitarian relief in Bosnia and other parts of the former Yugoslavia. This aid, among other things, made it possible for the besieged Bosnians in Sarajevo to have fresh drinking water as well as an important satellite telephone system.

Most noteworthy is that although George Soros commits so much money, as well as most of his time, and his Herculean energy, and brainpower, to working actively to create a universal open society, it is always with a skeptical eye toward philanthropy. He has said

> In my opinion, philanthropy goes against the grain because our civilization is built upon the pursuit of self-interest, not on any preoccupation with the interests of others. As a consequence, philanthropy is often hypocritical and always paradoxical. . . . There is a basic paradox to charity: it turns the recipients of charity into objects of charity.

While it is beyond the scope of this book to reach conclusions about the charitable motives of the rich, I can say, without qualification, that there are today eminently sound tax reasons in the United States why the rich give to charity — and about those reasons I know quite a lot. Without moralizing, let's consider some of the tax techniques that the rich now use to give wisely, bearing in mind that tax avoidance (not evasion) is the right of every citizen of a free society. In the words of Judge Learned Hand, considered by most lawyers to be the greatest U.S. judge never to be appointed to the Supreme Court:

> There is nothing sinister in so arranging one's affairs as to keep taxes as low as possible. Everybody does so, rich or poor; and all do right,

for nobody owes any public duty to pay more than the law demands; taxes are enforced exactions, not voluntary contributions. To demand more in the name of morals is mere cant.

HOW THE RICH GIVE TO CHARITY

The very rich, like Walter Annenberg, often give to charity directly or from family foundations that they control. But they also sometimes use tax techniques, which are usable by any middle-class person for his or her benefit. Let's consider a few of these techniques.

CRATs and CRUTs

The charitable remainder annuity trust, or CRAT, is a technique that should interest everyone who plans to leave money in his or her will to any charitable institution. Instead of bequeathing by will, it makes much more economic and tax sense to create a CRAT or a CRUT to get several important lifetime financial benefits while still making the same charitable gift at death.

A CRAT is a trust that pays a fixed rate of income to one or more individuals for life or a specified term of years, and then passes outright to charity — either to a private family charitable foundation or to designated public charities. Let's take an example:

Mrs. Ellie Mosynary, age 64, has a highly appreciated asset worth $500,000 for which she paid only $75,000. She would like to sell this asset without incurring a capital gains tax, and she also would like to increase her income, as she is nearing retirement.

The solution to Mrs. Mosynary's problem is not complicated. She can create a CRAT, reserving a fixed income for her life (and, if she wishes, for the lifetime of her spouse). She transfers her appreciated asset to the CRAT, which then sells it. There will be no capital gains tax, because the charitable trust (the CRAT) sold it. Thus, her income can be increased by having the trust invest the entire proceeds of the sale unreduced by income taxes on the appreciation in the sold asset.

At her death (or her spouse's), the remaining property in the trust will pass to her designated charity free of death taxes. As a bonus, she gets a current income tax deduction for the value of her future gift to charity. If she wants an additional amount equal to the trust principal to go to her children at her death, she can easily do so by insurance, which can be paid for from her increased income and, with appropriate estate planning, can also be made excludable from her taxable estate. (See the earlier discussion of life insurance trusts, pp. 124–129.)

The CRAT provides a fixed income that must be no less than 5% of the initial value of the trust but, of course, can be more (for example, 8%). Therefore, in the case of Mrs. Mosynary, whose CRAT would get $500,000 on the sale, her lifetime income from this CRAT could be either the minimum of $25,000 per year (5% of $500,000) or something higher like $40,000 per year (8% of $500,000). That amount must be paid to her even if the actual trust income is less. If so, trust principal must be invaded to cover the annual payments.

Another example:

An older gentleman, a widower, inherits a group of fine paintings from a trust created by a long-deceased grandfather. His tax basis is practically zero, as he inherits such basis (the original cost of the paintings) from the trust, which has now terminated as a result of the death of his uncle, who was the income beneficiary of the trust.

If he puts all or a substantial portion of the paintings in a CRAT, he can sell them without any tax, reinvest all of the proceeds to create income for the balance of his life, and leave the proceeds at his death to a new family foundation to carry out his own charitable intentions and provide funds for his children to meet their charitable obligations for their lifetimes. However, in the case of paintings, he would not obtain an income tax charitable deduction.

The CRUT (charitable remainder unitrust) is essentially the same as the CRAT except that the income fluctuates, since it is a percentage (not less than 5%) of the *changing* value of the trust, determined yearly. Also, once established, additional contributions can be made to a CRUT, which is not permissible with a CRAT. Younger donors seem to prefer the CRUT to the CRAT in part because in times of inflation their income will rise as the value of the CRUT goes up each year instead of remaining at a fixed amount for their lifetimes as is the case with a CRAT.

In addition, a CRUT, unlike a CRAT, may include a "net income" provision that permits the trustee to pay out the lesser of net income or the percentage amount even though this results in a payment that is less than 5% of the fair market value of the assets, valued annually. This alternative payment technique makes the unitrust the ideal vehicle for holding either appreciated closely held stock or real estate that has little or no income yield. (If the net income should exceed the percentage amount — i.e., 5% or above — the distribution is limited to the percentage amount.)

However, a CRUT has an even better known ingenious use as a provider of retirement income, with its own acronym, namely, NIM-CRUT,* which stands for "net income with makeup charitable remainder unitrust." (It has also been dubbed a "private retirement trust" by the Chase Manhattan Bank, N.A., and a "charitable deferred income trust" by the Morgan Guaranty Trust Company of New York.) The "makeup" provision provides for income earned in excess of the percentage amount to be paid out in later years to the extent that income paid in prior years was less than the percentage amount. Accordingly, in using a NIM-CRUT one invests for growth while earning little or no income. Then on retirement, the investments are changed to high-yield assets to have abundant income to make up the prior deficits. For example, zero coupon bonds can be very useful in a NIM-CRUT. While an individual holder of such bonds has taxable income each year, the IRS has ruled that the CRUT does not have to treat the bonds' yearly appreciation as trust income until the trust redeems the bonds. A commercial deferred annuity may be another good asset to use with a NIM-CRUT.

Consider this example:

Sally Salient is a business executive, age 55, with an income that puts her well into the highest tax bracket. She establishes a CRUT for her own benefit with a 6% payout and funds it with $150,000 of highly appreciated securities. The CRUT is drawn as a net-income unitrust with a makeup provision.

Assume the gift to the unitrust will generate a charitable income tax deduction of $45,753 and she will pay no tax on the unrealized

---

* Coined by Conrad Teitell, Esq., a leading expert on taxwise charitable giving.

appreciation in the securities, even when the trust sells the securities and reinvests the sale proceeds.

If the trustee invests the proceeds of the securities in growth stocks that increase in value at the rate of 10% per year but that pay no current dividends, by the time Sally reaches age 65 the trust assets will be worth $389,061. The trust will have developed a deficit due Sally of $157,781, representing the percentage amount that would have been paid out but for the net income limitation minus the amount that was actually paid out (in this case zero).

If, at that point, the trustee sells the growth stocks and invests the proceeds in securities with an 8% rate of return, the trust will produce income of $31,125 per year, and, although the trust calls for a 6% payout, the makeup provision requires the full $31,125 to be paid out to Sally until the "balance due" is worked off, thereby providing Sally with a retirement income of $31,125 per year for approximately twenty-seven years and a 6% payout thereafter.

CLATs and CLUTs

A charitable lead annuity trust (CLAT) permits persons to confer an immediate economic benefit on charity while still providing for their families' financial future.

Under the terms of a CLAT, a fixed dollar amount (annuity) is paid each year to charity for the duration of the charitable term, usually a fixed number of years. At the end of the charitable term, the remaining trust principal is paid to noncharitable beneficiaries — usually members of the trust creator's family, either outright or in further trust.

If you create a CLAT during your lifetime, you get a gift tax charitable deduction at that time equal to the present value of the annuity that the trust will pay to charity during the term. The present value of the annuity is based on two factors: the annuity amount and the length of the charitable term. The greater these factors, the larger the amount of the charitable deduction. Another factor, of course, is the applicable IRS interest rates at the time of a transfer.

If the trust income happens to exceed the annuity amount in a given year, the excess is added to principal, which eventually will pass to the family, as will all appreciation in the value of the trust assets.

Assume that Mrs. Mosynary places $1 million in an eleven-year charitable lead trust. She has not used her lifetime exemption from gift tax of $600,000, even though she has been warned it may at any time be repealed or reduced by Congress. The $1 million charitable lead trust is to pay $50,000 (5% of $1 million) to Princeton for eleven years. At the end of the eleven years, the property is to go to her children. Results:

Total gift	$1,000,000
Gift tax charitable deduction	(403,100)
Taxable gift	596,900
Federal gift tax	0
Charitable payments	550,000
Distribution to children in 11 years	$1,918,191
(assumes 3% income/7% growth)	

As mentioned, at the end of eleven years, the property held in the trust will be distributed to Mrs. Mosynary's children or grandchildren, or their trusts, tax-free. (There may be a so-called generation-skipping tax if the trusts are not planned for carefully.) The result is to remove a significant amount of property, plus the appreciation and any excess income during the eleven-year term, from Mrs. Mosynary's taxable estate at no transfer tax cost.

It is also possible for Mrs. Mosynary to obtain an up-front income tax deduction equal to the present value of all amounts that will pass to charity. In this case, the entire deduction is taken in the year the trust is created. (It can, if necessary, be carried forward for use in future years.) This deduction can be tremendously advantageous to offset in one year the income tax on a large capital gain or other substantial nonrecurring income, even though the actual payments to charity will extend over many years. To get this additional benefit, the creator of the trust is taxed on the income generated during the charitable term. If, however, the income is from tax-exempt funds, it remains tax-exempt to the beneficiary. To demonstrate this technique, suppose Mrs. Mosynary has a big capital gain in 1994. At the end of that year she transfers $500,000 of tax-exempt bonds (yielding 7%) to a charitable lead trust to pay Princeton $35,000 yearly for ten years. In 1994, she would have received an income tax deduction of $258,770 — offsetting her income taxes. In the eleventh year, the principal and all appreciation will be returned to her, and the trust will terminate.

A CLAT also can be created in an individual's will to take effect at his or her death. The tax result is essentially the same as creating a charitable lead trust during the individual's lifetime, except that the creator's estate will receive a charitable estate tax deduction instead of the creator receiving the lifetime charitable gift tax deduction.

The most significant difference between a CLAT created at death and a lifetime CLAT is that with the former, there is no immediate benefit to charity and the appreciation on the individual's assets set aside for charity will not be removed from his taxable estate.

The CLUT (charitable lead unitrust) is essentially the same as the CLAT except that the annual charitable amount is a percentage of the changing value of the trust, valued annually, rather than a fixed annuity amount based on its original value.

A recent, very effective use of a CLAT was in Jacqueline Kennedy Onassis's will. In that will, by the way, she referred to herself as "Jacqueline K. Onassis," for no known reason but arguably in deference to the apparent source of much of her wealth — her second husband, Aristotle Onassis.

When Mr. Onassis died in 1975, she had attacked his will and estate plan by challenging the validity of their prenuptial agreement. The challenge was settled with the payment of about $26 million to her, which was substantially in excess of what she was to receive under the terms of that agreement.

The press asserted that by the time of her death, this sum and Jacqueline K. Onassis's other assets, allegedly due to the investment acumen of her companion-lover, Maurice Templesman, had become an estate worth $100 to $200 million.

What then, did Jacqueline Onassis do with her substantial estate?

Her will was designed to take maximum advantage of the estate tax laws by her special use of the charitable lead annuity trust. After leaving, *inter alia*, a Greek alabaster head of a woman to Maurice Templesman, some specific cash legacies including $250,000 to each of her children, Caroline and John Jr., and her Martha's Vineyard property and New York City apartment to her children, she put the bulk of her estate into a CLAT to be called the C&J Foundation.

The terms of the CLAT require payments to charitable entities of 8% per year of the original value of the CLAT for twenty-four years, and then distribution of the remaining property at the end of the twenty-four-year period to Jackie's then living grandchildren (but not to her children). The will includes a precatory statement that the trustees (Caroline, John, Templesman, and Jackie's lawyer, Alexander Forger) give "preferential consideration" to charitable organizations "committed to making a significant difference in the cultural or social betterment of mankind or the relief of human suffering." (Interestingly, each of the four trustees is given the unilateral power to name an individual or a bank or trust company as his or her successor as trustee. Since Mr. Templesman is 65 and Mr. Forger is 72, time will tell if the successors they in due course designate will get along well with Caroline and John.)

Why did Jackie skip her children in the disposition of the bulk of her estate? The Kennedy family apparently had many generation-skipping trusts that benefited Caroline and John on the death of their father, President John F. Kennedy. In addition, the marital trust for Jackie under President Kennedy's will was appointed directly to Caroline and John by Jackie's will, but the death taxes attributable to that trust were to be paid from its assets and not from Jackie's other assets.

By the use of the CLAT, most of her estate would pass death-tax-free at Jackie's death, because of the large charitable estate tax deduction the CLAT creates. But, as previously explained, the property would be subject to the new generation-skipping tax twenty-four years after her death (at its 55% rate) when it passes to her grandchildren. A fine estate plan. Let me explain why. Assume a 10% total yield (4% income and 6% appreciation) on her estate. If Jackie's estate at her death was $100 million (many media estimates were as high as $100 to $200 million built upon her settlement of $26 million from the Onassis estate), then in twenty-four years the grandchildren, who would still be quite young, would receive approximately $126 million and charities would have received about $192 million over the twenty-four-year post-death period. There would be the substantial generation-skipping tax (about $148 million), but payable only twenty-four years after Jackie's death.

An excellent result — deferral of all death taxes for a quarter of a century, substantial sums to the grandchildren when they can use them, and a great deal to charity as well! Her estate plan vividly demonstrates my prior admonition that with sophisticated planning, the estate tax can become for many, in effect, a voluntary tax payable when one wants to pay it and with the taxpayer deciding how much goes to the family, how much to charity, and finally how much to the government.

A major consideration in determining whether to use a charitable remainder annuity trust (CRAT) or a charitable lead annuity trust (CLAT) is the monthly interest (or discount) rate tables of the government in effect at the time of the creation of the charitable trust. As rates increase, the CRAT generates a bigger charitable deduction than the CLAT, and conversely, when rates are low, the CLAT generates the bigger charitable deduction. For example, if the applicable rate is 8% and the individual beneficiary of the charitable remainder annuity trust is to receive only 5% per year for life, the tables would conclude that charity is getting the extra 3% each year, hence the bigger charitable deduction for both income and gift tax purposes. With a CLAT, on the other hand, if the rate is 6%, as it was early in 1994, and charity is to receive 8% per year for twenty-four years (as in the CLAT in Jackie Kennedy Onassis's will), then the charitable deduction will be very large (almost 100% of the gift) as the tables assume much of the principal of the trust over the twenty-four years will go to charity to pay it the 8% annual sum while the trust generates only 6% of income per year. For further example, a few years ago, when the applicable rate was 10%, a CLAT paying an annuity of 8% for twenty years provided a 68% charitable tax deduction while at a 6.6% discount rate the deduction was 87.4%.

CRAT–CLAT Combinations

By using a combination of charitable lead and charitable remainder annuity trusts, you can make sure that your children get income for life from the remainder trusts as well as substantial principal from the lead trusts at the end of the charitable terms. By using this combination, with the charitable payments going to a family foundation, you will also be able to provide for your family's community and charitable obligations for several generations with enormous death tax savings.

Recently, I used such a combination for a widower with a $500 million estate. If he had left his estate outright to his children, the death taxes would be approximately $300 million (60% of $500 million on the estate of a New York resident). If, instead, he creates a combination of a charitable life income trust for each child (a CRAT, or perhaps a CRUT, which may be more advisable) and also a charitable lead trust for each child (a CLAT), the death tax savings, over an estate plan simply leaving everything directly to the children, would be about $140 million. One does not have to be particularly charitable to want to use this to reduce the current 55% federal death taxes (plus state death taxes in most states), especially if much of the savings is to be used to meet the philanthropic and civic obligations that rightfully may be expected of any family of great wealth.

Personal Residences

Outright gifts of real estate to charities are commonplace, but a lesser-known offshoot offers interesting planning opportunities. You can give your favorite charity a remainder interest in your personal residence or farm, while reserving the use of it for your lifetime and the lifetime of your spouse. In that case you generate a current income tax charitable deduction for the value of the remainder interest while continuing to use the property for life.

The property must be used as a residence but need not be the donor's principal residence, so a vacation home will qualify. A personal residence includes all land used in connection with it (seventy-seven acres in one case). It can be a cooperative apartment or condominium, and even a yacht if it contains facilities for cooking, sleeping, and sanitation and the donor actually uses it as a residence.

A donor may also give an undivided interest in real estate to charity. For example, a vacation home may be the paradigm for such a gift. Thus, a college or university might receive a one-half or three-fourths interest in the donor's vacation property with the right to rental income for six to nine months, if any, while the donor retains occupancy for the balance of the year.

Here is an example of these techniques:

Mr. and Mrs. W. Blackacre, both age 70, have a home with a current fair market value of $500,000. They have no mortgage. Their original purchase price or cost basis in the home is $75,000.

Using the IRS formula for valuation and assuming certain accounting criteria, a gift of the home to charity at their death with a retained life estate would generate a current income tax charitable deduction of $163,704.

If Mr. and Mrs. Blackacre file a joint income tax return and their combined federal and state brackets are, say, 40%, they may be able to save as much as $65,482 in taxes in the year of the gift or throughout as many as five succeeding years until the deduction is fully used.

With this considerable tax savings, Mr. and Mrs. Blackacre can participate with their family in acquiring a policy of joint and survivor life insurance on their lives, the proceeds of which will be payable to the beneficiaries upon the death of the second to die of the Blackacres. The policy would be purchased utilizing a method whereby the proceeds would not be subject to estate taxes.

By these means, the Blackacres have maximized the value of the home for the benefit of their family while making a significant gift to charity during their lifetimes.

Here is another example:

Mr. and Mrs. S. Bird own a condominium in Florida with a $300,000 fair market value. They spend only three months per year in Florida; from April through December the condo is vacant.

The Birds take the three-fourths interest and deed it to charity (a qualified partial interest gift). They get a $225,000 tax deduction and $100,000 tax savings. They keep making cash gifts to the charity to pay for the upkeep of the condo. They use the $100,000 tax savings to buy second-to-die insurance for their children.

The partial owners (the Birds and the charity) can decide which months the Birds can use the condo.

At the death of the survivor of the Birds, he or she can leave the retained one-fourth interest to the charity and get an estate tax deduction.

Art and Other Tangible Personal Property

A gift of tangible personal property, such as a painting, coin collection, or rare musical instrument, can be deducted for its full market value only if it is used for the charitable purposes of the charitable recipient. A donor who gives some rare paintings to his college or university may deduct their full market value if it can be reasonably anticipated that they will be added to the collection of that school's museum. If not, the deduction is limited, in effect, to the tax basis (usually the original cost) of the paintings.

It should be pointed out that, as in the case of a residence, one can give a fractional interest in a painting to a museum, e.g., the use of it for six or three months of the year. The museum and the donor become co-owners. There is case law (*Winokur*) in which the IRS has acquiesced, and an IRS private ruling, both holding that if the museum has the unqualified right to possess and enjoy the painting the tax deduction is not lost even if the museum does not in fact exercise its rights so that the painting remains in the donor's home during the entire year. By the way, a 25% ownership interest could also mean that the donor has the painting for three years and then the museum for one year rather than splitting each year. Also, it should be noted that the donor generally has been allowed a deduction for the full value of the percentage partial interest given to charity without discounting.

Stock of a Closely Held Business

If you have appreciated stock in a closely held business that you wish to sell, you can give it to charity while avoiding capital gains when you sell the business. But the timing and technicalities are crucial. For example, once there is a sales contract, it's too late to give it to charity to avoid the tax. The tax planning must be very carefully done to achieve the right result.

In addition, a shareholder of a closely held corporation can make a significant charitable gift and bail out corporate earnings and profits without incurring dividend income. The shareholder donates his or her stock to charity. Later, the corporation redeems the stock from the charity. It is crucial that the charity not be legally bound to surrender the shares for redemption, nor can the corporation have the power to compel the charity to surrender the shares for redemption.

Here is another example:

Hardnose, Inc., has a fair market value of $3 million. Mr. Will B. Tuff and his son are the sole stockholders, with Mr. Tuff owning nine shares and his son one share, for a total of ten shares. Each share is valued at $300,000.

Hardnose has $2 million of cash and Tuff wants to get it out tax-free.

Mr. Tuff gives three shares to charity = $900,000. The current income tax deduction of $900,000 saves $360,000 tax dollars.

Hardnose repurchases the stock from the charity for $900,000 in cash. There is no preexisting repurchase agreement with the charity. Hardnose retires the three shares of stock. Now only seven shares of stock exist.

Mr. Tuff has six shares, and his son still has one share. A percentage of ownership has *shifted* in favor of the son, with *no* gift tax implication.

Keep moving the cash to charity, and eventually this son gets a half interest in the company with no gift tax consequences.

In effect, this can be done until the father no longer controls a majority of the stock, thus dramatically reducing its value in his estate.

Your Own Family Foundation

As previously mentioned, there are approximately 36,000 private and corporate foundations in existence in America today. Of these, 24,000 are so-called family foundations, which gave away $6 billion in

1993, an amount that accounted for 75% of all foundation grants. Much of the estimated $6 to $10 trillion that will get transferred in the next few decades from persons now 60 or over will end up residing in these foundations and new family foundations to be created.

A family or private foundation is a tax-exempt legal entity usually created by one person or members of one family or a special group (such as the rock group The Grateful Dead that has formed the Rex Foundation) to carry out all kinds of charitable pursuits. It is usually established either as a corporation or as a trust. I have found a trust generally to be more flexible and practical, for example, in assuring a line of successorship for the future control of the foundation after the creator's death.

These foundations are started during the creator's lifetime or after the creator's death by the terms of his or her will. As previously explained, the family foundation can be the receptacle of all the charitable payments generated by the previously described tax-saving devices called CRATs, CRUTs, CLATs, and CLUTs. Jackie Kennedy Onassis thus created by her will the C&J Foundation to receive the payments from her twenty-four-year charitable lead annuity trust (CLAT). The creator can also set the guidelines for the foundation's charitable giving or require that only a designated group of donees can receive benefits. The foundation can also be required or requested to liquidate itself by a certain time, e.g., the Aaron Diamond Foundation, which was created by the late millionaire New York realtor. It received $150 million in 1987 and was to give away all of its money in ten years and go out of business by the end of 1996. Led by formidable Irene Diamond, the founder's widow, and its excellent executive director, Vincent McGee, the foundation is on schedule for termination while continuing to contribute significantly to minority education, medical research, and the arts — almost all in New York City — and often for controversial causes, e.g., it is the largest private supporter of AIDS research. Ms. Diamond explained the philosophy of the foundation very succinctly: "I don't really like the foundation world. Most foundations concentrate on the pretty things in life, buildings and safe programs. We don't. I don't like the perks, the luncheons, the affluence of some foundations. We don't have huge quarters and big staffs. We don't give luncheons and dinners. We really spend our money on things that are needed desperately. We don't live in a sweet little world."

During its existence, these private foundations are tax-exempt, and the only technical requirement of note is that they must distribute annually 5% of the value of their assets, i.e., $50,000 per year for a $1 million family foundation.

Why do so many rich citizens create their own foundations? Many do it for the most charitable motives; some for privacy or anonymity in their philanthropy; and a few as a protective shelter from excessive charitable solicitations. Others do it for family reasons: to create unity among siblings and cousins or generations of the same family, and to teach the next generations how to engage in constructive and creative philanthropy.

One of the more enjoyable tasks that I have as a family lawyer is to sit on the boards of several private foundations and participate (as a neutral outside director or trustee) in the debates, often heated and even impassioned, between generations of the same family over issues like abortion, AIDS, legalization or decriminalization of drugs, the peace movement in Israel, etc. These debates involve principled differences that must be resolved before money can be allocated among various causes.

Families approach these matters in various ways. The Frey Foundation of Michigan, for example, has created an adjunct board with a small budget so that third-generation Freys will learn about making grants. The Florence V. Burden Foundation in New York demonstrates the immense value of this generational process. This foundation was created in 1967 by a member of the Vanderbilt family to work in two fields, aging and criminal justice. Today, reflecting the wider interests of its third and fourth generation members, it "support(s) non-pretty issues like child sexual abuse that others won't touch," according to Margaret Burden Childs, co-chairperson of the foundation, which also helps persons with AIDS and battered women. "In the old days, we just sat and deferred to our elders, without having input. Now there is no idea we cannot bring to the table, and we treat each other's ideas with respect."

There are, of course, many private foundations that have brought families together and stimulated a series of generations to participate in philanthropy. Two more are the Norman Foundation in Manhattan, made up of children and grandchildren of Aaron E. Norman, an early partner in the Sears, Roebuck empire, and the Cummings Foundation, founded by Nathan Cummings, a Canadian-born businessman who built a small food-distributing company into the Sara Lee Corporation (formerly Consolidated Foods). To imbue her children with the philanthropic spirit, Ruth Cummings Sorenson, a granddaughter of the founder, is taking her 8- and 9-year old children to Israel, where the three will study Hebrew and teach English to immigrant Ethiopian Jews for a year.

Some of these family foundations have enough money to have their own executive directors or other full-time advisers. Some wisely utilize a relatively new group of consultants, like H. Peter Koroff of the Boston nonprofit entity The Philanthropic Initiative (TPI) to help them focus and direct their giving — to get the most bang for their charitable bucks.

But even with all the good and valuable nontax reasons, there are compelling tax reasons for you to create your own private foundation, which also can often serve as the keystone to an overall tax-efficient estate plan. Look at the matter this way.

A married couple with two adult children have accumulated $5 million in their lifetimes, but they have used up their respective $600,000 estate and gift exemptions. At the death of the survivor, the combined federal and state estate taxes could approximate 60%, or $3 million of the $5 million estate, leaving $1 million for each of the couple's surviving two children. Assume the survivor of the couple leaves $1 million to a new family foundation. The children then would have the use of $1 million to meet all of their lifetime charitable obligations to their schools, churches, etc., but each child loses only $200,000 or a total of $400,000, because $600,000 of that $1 million going to the foundation would have gone to pay death taxes (at the 60% rate) and not to the children if that $1 million had instead been left directly to the children. The children can give to any recognized charity from this new family foundation. The only technical requirement, as previously mentioned, is the requirement to pay out to charities each year 5% of the value of the assets of the private foundation.

With larger estates, the family foundation becomes even more attractive. It can provide funds to meet both the children's and grandchildren's lifetime charitable and community obligations. In addition, such a foundation may be able to provide worthwhile and challenging work for a member or members of the family who would administer or help administer the foundation, and who can receive reasonable compensation for doing so.

There is, however, an important tax benefit for private foundations that is scheduled to expire on December 31, 1994. At present, most wealthy persons receive tax benefits by making gifts to their foundations with publicly traded stocks that have appreciated. At the time of the gift they deduct the fair market value of the donated stock against their income taxes. There are also no capital gains taxes when the foundation sells the stock. If Congress, as expected, does nothing to extend this tax break, donors in 1995 and thereafter can deduct only their cost, i.e., what they paid for the stock, and not its market value.

This change in the tax law will cause many philanthropists to refrain from either creating the traditional family foundations or making additional gifts to existing ones. Many such gifts will instead be diverted to community trusts (such as the New York Community Trust and the Jewish Communal Fund in New York City) or to a lesser known charitable entity—the supporting foundation (also called a "supporting organization").

A supporting foundation is organized and operated exclusively for the benefit of or to carry out the purposes of one or more public charities like a university or a museum. While a supporting foundation is not itself a public charity, it must be sufficiently related and controlled by one to be considered public for tax purposes. The technical rules on the required organizational, operational, and relationship tests to qualify as a supporting foundation are beyond the scope of this book. Suffice it to say that given the aforementioned change in the tax law, new supporting foundations (also some existing private foundations may convert into supporting foundations) may proliferate to the great benefit of public charities, such as universities, hospitals, and museums.

What then can we conclude about all of this charitable giving in the United States? The motives of the givers are too difficult to fathom — only the Shadow knows what really lurks in their hearts. But 'tis certainly taxwise to give.

As an example, take Edith Everyperson, who is now in the 39.6% income tax bracket and in a 55% estate tax bracket. She contributes $100,000 to her favorite charitable institution. This gift saves $39,600 in income taxes, and the $100,000 will be out of her estate. In effect, that is a $100,000 estate tax charitable deduction, saving $55,000 in estate taxes. Edith's total tax saving on her $100,000 gift is $94,600. (If she is a New Yorker with a combined federal and state income tax rate near 50% and estate tax of 60%, it can be seen that her tax saving will be in excess of the $100,000 gift.)

It is true that if Edith does not want to give up income on her gift she can make a life income gift to her charity by way of a charitable remainder trust, a CRAT or a CRUT. As previously indicated, this is a trust that pays the creator (and his or her spouse) income for life and then passes to charity at the death of the last income beneficiary. Charitable remainder trusts not only allow the retention of life income but also provide a way to change investments for a higher yield, i.e., for more income, without a capital gains tax. One can, so to speak, have one's charitable cake and still eat a good part of it.

Finally, the real pleasure, regardless of taxes, is in the giving — so give while you are alive and competent enough to enjoy it!

CREDITORS, SPOUSES, EXPATRIATES, PARAMOURS, AND VITAL MISCELLANY

X

How the Rich Stay Richer: Prenuptial, Postnuptial, and Cohabitation Agreements

PRENUPTIAL AGREEMENTS

On the back lawn of a palatial Palm Beach estate, the minister recited the traditional wedding litany, including: "Do you, Paul, promise to endow Claudine with all your worldly goods?" The groom, who is very rich, turned to the small audience, raised his eyebrows, winked at me, and asked, "*All* my worldly goods?" Then, quickly, he turned back and said, "I do."

The guests naturally assumed this humorous aside was the groom's way of acknowledging that his bride would legally be entitled to a substantial portion of his $250 million. The wink to me was because he knew that his assets were fully protected from his new wife. If he died or they divorced, she would get only what he intended her to have. This was because, weeks earlier, his bride's lawyer and I had negotiated a detailed prenuptial agreement. The marriage took place a few years ago and is doing exceedingly well.

*"That was from my heart.
And now, something from my lawyer."*

But another man who recently sought my advice told a tale of marital woe. Fifteen years ago, he and his wife married, each for the second time, after they signed a premarital contract substantially limiting her economic rights on death or divorce. For the past several years, his wife has been a virago about that contract, angrily telling him it proved his lack of love and trust. Finally, he had his lawyer revoke the contract. Then, not too long afterward, his wife (having moved in with her boyfriend) asked for a divorce and 50% of the property he had acquired during the marriage. The agreement had become a cancer in their marriage, and its excision obviously could not save it. But was the revocation fraudulently induced and therefore not legally valid? The fighting continues — in court.

Like these two couples, many men and women of property now

insist that their spouses sign prenuptial contracts, also called premarital or antenuptial agreements. Prenuptial contracts have, like wills, been around a long time. Babylonian agreements in 1000 B.C. spelled out the bride's dowry as well as the financial consequences of the dissolution of the marriage or the death of either party, e.g., whether the dowry would return to the bride's family if she died without children.

Some say anyone with $500,000 or more should consider having a premarital agreement. Even without $500,000 now, you may have that much or more by the time a divorce occurs, which in America still happens to about half of new marriages. Many see such a step merely as the prudent thing to do. Others, I think, see it as a way to control their spouses through money and its power. For still others, their property is more important and satisfying than their personal relationships; they have worked hard for it and care more about it. But, as the two cases cited above demonstrate, the effects and dangers of premarital agreements vary considerably. Every thoughtful person should analyze whether such a contract is advisable — economically, legally, and psychologically.

The way many rich men and women negotiate prenuptials can easily turn their prospective spouses into confirmed misandrists or misogynists. Occasionally, however, the very rich are smarter than their lawyers about these agreements. When drafting prenuptials for the very rich, lawyers will often advise complex economic formulae. These formulae may provide for a certain amount per year of marriage ($1 or $2 million), capping at a designated amount. Or the amount may depend on the length of the marriage without any cap or whether there is a child of the marriage or both. Alternatively, some agreements even self-destruct after a fixed number of years of marriage or upon the birth of a child.

One wealthy entrepreneur was advised to utilize a formula with a cap of a substantial amount. He also was counseled that even with no agreement his enormous wealth at the time of marriage, if kept separate during the marriage, would remain free from claims at divorce, but would be subject to statutory inheritance rights on his death, usually one-third of the estate, including premarital property. (There are complex ways to put all of one's property in a trust or trusts and avoid even rights upon death.) He patiently listened to the many alternatives and determined he would cut through all the financial constructs. He decided to give his fiancée, who was approximately 25 years younger, a gift of money upon their engagement, as a token of good faith and to give her financial freedom. He would give her $10 million immediately after marriage, $15 million more if there was a divorce, and $25 million if he predeceased her. Remember these were minimums — the wealthier spouse could always do more for the other. He wisely wanted his marriage to start on a basis of mutual love and respect and not on the basis of his control of all the wealth.

The kinds of provisions in prenuptial agreements can boggle the mind. For example, I have seen one that substantially reduces benefits to a spouse who, after the marriage, puts on more than ten pounds above her marital-date weight. The weigh-in this provision seems to require may be nonpugilistic at the start, but plenty of fighting is likely to occur later. It has been reported that the prenuptial agreement between the actor William Hurt and his former wife, Heidi (the daughter of bandleader Skitch Henderson), tied alimony to both parties' ability to stay sober and free of substance abuse. The two had met at the famous Hazelden treatment center in Minnesota. Clauses may divide up special season seats to athletic (the Knicks) and cultural (the Metropolitan Opera) events. One can provide for almost anything that is not against public policy, including the minimum times per week for sexual relations. In a litigated divorce case from Louisiana, a husband sought to avoid alimony on grounds that the wife had violated the prenuptial agreement, which limited sexual intercourse to once a week, by "seeking coitus thrice daily." The court wisely held that "the fault here alleged by the husband is not, in law, any fault." Or, one could add, in life.

Another agreement required that a substantial sum of money be set aside, whether on death or divorce, to finance the husband's intention to preserve his remains by cryonic suspension. (Cryonics is the process of preserving clinically dead persons at subfreezing temperatures in hopes of returning them to life and health when medicine has found a remedy for what "killed" them.)

The truth is that a premarital agreement will work, in psychological terms, only if both parties consider it essentially fair as the financial constitution for their union, and only if it embodies promises and expectations agreed upon from the start. Otherwise, in due course, in one way or another, the agreement will be a destructive force, increasing the likelihood that the marriage will end in divorce.

The harmful effect sometimes can be felt even before a marriage takes place. A prospective bride, particularly if this is her first marriage, will often break with her fiancé when he asks for an agreement. After all, a romantic prenuptial contract seems to be an oxymoron. Many women — and men, too — will simply not enter a marriage, an arrangement traditionally based on trust, with a legal document that envisions its future hypothetical demise.

It is not only the very rich and previously divorced people who are now using these agreements. A woman lawyer once said to me, "A premarital may be all right in some cases, but in a first marriage for both it is tacky." Perhaps this is true, but in my experience this, too, is happening more and more frequently. With first marriages, there is a good argument that only inherited property, preexisting family trusts, and closely held family businesses should be covered by the prenuptial. Thus earnings during the marriage and investments of such earnings would become marital property.

One reason for many premarital contracts is the desire of a once-divorced person to avoid the acrimony and costs, including legal fees, of another divorce. Of the 50% of American marriages now ending in divorce, 85% of the divorced persons remarry, usually within five years, with 60% of *those* marriages ending in divorce.

Unfortunately, though it can help in some cases, there is no guarantee that a prenuptial agreement will spare the couple these difficulties, and, in fact, its validity often becomes a separate, hotly contested legal issue. To mention a few highly publicized confrontations, consider Joan Collins's young husband's lawsuit over their prenuptial agreement; the unsuccessful effort of Tim Peters, former husband of Sallie Bingham of the Louisville newspaper dynasty, to set aside their premarital agreement; Ivana Trump's war with Donald Trump (more on this later); and Jackie Kennedy's successful attack on her agreement with Aristotle Onassis, leading to substantially more money for her

($26 million) than had been provided for in their prenuptial agreement. On the other hand, there is little doubt that Johnny Carson and Ed McMahon, who did not learn from Johnny's marital woes, could have done far better with prenuptial agreements than they did without them. And the less famous also fight all the time over these agreements.

Because of the frequency with which they are attacked, these agreements require great legal precision and sophistication. Steven Spielberg wrote his own prenuptial agreement with Amy Irving on a scrap of paper just between them without consulting a lawyer. He proved the old adage that a person who represents himself has a fool for a client. The agreement did not hold up under attack, and Spielberg reportedly paid $100 million to Irving in one of Hollywood's largest marital settlements. Since that time, he has, among other things, produced the movie *Jurassic Park*, so his fans need not grieve over Amy Irving's good fortune. *Forbes* estimates that Mr. Spielberg will net approximately $250 million personally from his share of the profits of *Jurassic Park*.

Prenuptial agreements seem to be challenged much more frequently than separation agreements or other contracts, partly because they are often enforced many years after they were signed. But the fact that they are challenged often does not mean they are frequently overturned.

The usual grounds for attack are (i) fraud; (ii) failure to disclose assets; (iii) duress, either physical or psychological; and (iv) in some jurisdictions, failure to have separate legal representation. Also, in some states, such as New York, there is an "unconscionability" test that requires an agreement, even if fair when signed, not be unconscionable, often twenty or thirty years later, when it is enforced. This unconscionability test, as you might guess, is a developing area of prenuptial law fraught with uncertainty, given the ambiguity of the concept, which ends up being determined in the discretionary eye of the judicial beholder.

Before Donald Trump became a megarich celebrity, but at a time when he was wealthy by most standards, his lawyer, Roy Cohn, negotiated in 1977 a prenuptial agreement with his fiancée, Ivana, a Czech national who was modeling in Canada. Ivana, a stranger to prenuptial agreements and the complex ways of New York's divorce lawyers, had no attorney. Roy Cohn arranged for her to be represented by a former associate, Lawrence Levner.

In 1979, 1984, and 1987, the Trumps, as they became richer, signed postnuptial agreements giving Ivana a larger share of the marital estate than when the prenuptial agreement was signed. In 1990, when the parties' separation became more important to much of the media than the release of Nelson Mandela, Donald and Ivana litigated the issue of the validity of the pre- and postnuptial agreements. Ivana's attack was primarily based on a failure to be adequately represented; she claimed that Levner was Cohn's alter ego.

After spending legal fees in excess of $1 million, Ivana ultimately agreed to accept the provisions of the agreements, which provided her with $25 million in cash, a Connecticut mansion, a New York apartment, use of the couple's 118-room Mar-a-Lago mansion in Palm Beach for one month a year, and continuing obligations of support of $650,000 per year. The decision was apparently made because the provisions of the agreements executed by Donald looked good to Ivana at that time when compared to the diminishing value of his assets during one of our worst real estate recessionary periods.

An interesting aspect of the Trump case was its confidentiality clause:

> Without obtaining [the husband's] written consent in advance, [the wife] shall not *directly or indirectly* publish, or cause to be published, any diary, memoir, letter, story, photograph, interview, article, essay, account, or description or depiction of any kind whatsoever, whether fictionalized or not, concerning her marriage to [the husband] or any other aspect of [the husband's] personal, business or financial affairs, or assist or provide information to others in connection with the publication or dissemination of any such material or excerpts thereof. . . . Any violation of the terms of this Paragraph (10) shall constitute a material breach of this agreement. In the event such breach occurs, [the husband's] obligations pursuant to Paragraph (9) hereof, to make payments or provisions to or for the benefit of [the wife], shall there-

upon terminate. In addition, in the event of any such breach, [the wife] hereby consents to the granting of a temporary or permanent injunction against her (or against any agent acting in her behalf) by any court of competent jurisdiction prohibiting her (or her agent) from violating the terms of this Paragraph.

Mr. Trump charged that Ivana's book, *For Love Alone*, was a transparent fictionalization of their relationship and violated the clause. The book was about a Czech skier-model who is pursued relentlessly by a very rich American businessman very much like Donald Trump. The husband betrays her, she boots him out of a posh ski chalet where they are vacationing, etc. Mrs. Trump said her book did not violate the clause, and that, in any event, the clause violated her First Amendment rights of free speech. A New York appellate court upheld its enforceability, and perhaps this as well as Trump's declining financial situation led Mrs. Trump to accept the settlement, which essentially carried out the terms of their pre- and postnuptial agreements.

The difficulty with these confidentiality clauses — besides the problem of proving a violation — is that they often have no enforcement mechanism. In *Trump*, it had real *in terrorem* effect, because a violation resulted in the cessation of very substantial support payments. There may be other ways to try to give these confidentiality clauses teeth, such as a fixed amount of damages (so-called liquidated damages) for a violation when there are no other payments under the agreement to terminate, as there were in the Trump case.

Also, it was interesting that Ivana's lawyers had agreed to a unilateral clause — that is, she could not write or speak about him, but he, a celebrity not noted for being reticent, was not restricted in what he could divulge.

Whether or not one is famous, prenuptials put each individual's *Weltanschauung* into play. For example, it is frequently a parent or grandparent who will demand a premarital agreement, hoping to eliminate the possibility of family assets going to an in-law. Familial control is asserted even though the offspring to be married may have no real knowledge of the family assets.

A strong-minded bride or groom may resist as a matter of principle, causing permanent family estrangement, as well as partial or total disinheritance. Is the shrewder approach to sign the agreement to placate the family and, in due course, secretly revoke the contract, thereby keeping one's inheritance and, perhaps, one's principles? (What principle justifies the secret revocation?)

In my experience, the most successful agreements are those arrived at after open and full discussion and negotiation with independent, competent lawyers for both parties, and thereafter never again looked at, with the rich spouse providing for the other well in excess of the financial requirements of the agreement.

What is generally not understood is that with sophisticated legal advice before the marriage, the primary economic advantages of an agreement may be substantially achieved without actually having one, either by the precise segregation and valuation of premarital property, the use of an irrevocable trust, or other legal strategies.

A major problem with prenuptial agreements that many clients (and lawyers) often miss is that they are not self-enforcing or self-executing — that is, they do not themselves constitute a grounds for or grant the parties a divorce or even a physical separation. So, the party wanting to stay in the marriage can simply refuse to consent to a divorce in a fault state like New York or refuse to vacate the marital residence in a no-fault state, thus delaying, often for a long time, the implementation of the agreement. So, in New York and elsewhere, savvy lawyers include substantial financial penalties if the nonmonied spouse does not vacate all marital residences within a short period of time after a notice to vacate from the other spouse. Once the parties are not living like two scorpions in a bottle, the delay in effecting a divorce or enforcing the total agreement is quite bearable.

The practical problem becomes acute in an agreement when both parties waive all their respective rights, since the nonmonied spouse can suffer no detriment by being obstructionist in order to gain some financial benefit from the dissolution of the marriage. In New York, some lawyers think a clause providing that written notice by either party transforms the prenuptial (or postnuptial) agreement into a separation agreement will trigger the statute allowing a divorce one year thereafter—the ground for divorce being living under a *separation* agreement for one year or more. No case, however, has yet adopted this view.

In any event, a premarital agreement should almost always have a powerful deterrent clause against attacks, which assesses the legal fees of both husband and wife against the one of them who unsuccessfully attacks the agreement.

Divorce litigation is also forcing ever newer twists to these contracts. An investment partnership I know of weathered, with pain, a divorce action by the wife of one of its partners. The firm decided that all future marriages by any partner must be preceded by a premarital agreement in which the new spouse waives all economic rights in the partnership. Partners who are already married must sign a postnuptial agreement for the same purpose.

Should a partnership try to assert control in this area? I think that such agreements, imposed in this way by a third party, may damage the businesses as well as the marriages involved.

One of the best solutions to the prenuptial agreement problem is that of a young friend of mine who has substantial inherited wealth and is marrying a young woman—the first marriage for both. After reviewing the various considerations, he decided he needed an agreement relating to his inherited wealth, most of which was in a family business, and thought his bride would consider it fair. Nevertheless, he decided to marry first and then ask her for a postnuptial agreement. If she did not want to sign after the marriage, he told me, he would live with that.

After all, marriage, in all cases, is a risk. Many persons, if they know themselves and their mates well, can afford to take the risk without a prenuptial agreement. If I were a betting man, I would wager that my young friend's marriage will last; at the least, a premarital agreement will not be the beginning of the end, or even cause the end before there is a beginning.

POSTNUPTIAL AGREEMENTS

A postnuptial agreement, as its name indicates, is entered into after marriage. The then Trumps, as previously mentioned, had both. Postnuptial agreements seem to occur less often than premarital contracts, perhaps because often by the time they are needed a divorce is more likely to take place. In fact, negotiations over a postnuptial agreement often can lead to a divorce.

Many postnuptials are an attempt by the more monied spouse to get a better economic deal than he or she would achieve in a contested divorce situation. This is often done because in a postnuptial negotiation the spouses are still relatively civilized with each other, and the less monied spouse may think, sometimes quite wrongly, an agreement will save or preserve the marriage.

When should postnuptials be used? Take an example. A couple has been married for twenty-seven years. He is a successful doctor. She has a small practice as a lay analyst. Almost everything has been put in the husband's name because of his wish to control all the family assets. She wants independence and her own money. She threatens to leave. A two-part compromise is suggested. They consider an agreement that if either of them wishes to dissolve the marriage the economic division of the property will be as set forth in the postnuptial agreement and, in addition, some assets will now be placed in the wife's name and under her control. Thus, she does not need to stay in the marriage for economic reasons, as her rights will be clear, as agreed upon, if she leaves. The marriage continues successfully to this day.

On the other hand, consider this case. A very rich spouse accumulates over $200 million through great business success, all achieved during the thirty-two-year marriage. It and the other assets of the marriage, except for one of three homes that is in joint name, are all in the name of the monied spouse. The nonmonied spouse complains vehemently of this economic inequality. There are other tensions in the marriage. A postnuptial agreement is negotiated, with abundant legal advice on both sides. This agreement, by which either spouse, at any time, can trigger the dissolution of the marriage, provides in that event for an immediate transfer of $40 million and one major residence to the nonmonied spouse. A few months after it is signed, the monied spouse leaves the marriage — permanently. Without the postnuptial agreement, the nonmonied spouse would probably have been able to obtain $80 to $100 million (40% to 50% of the $200 million marital estate).

A postnuptial agreement can sometimes work to hold together a marriage if it has underlying viability and vitality. Do I believe in them? Yes, because I have seen them work. But it is relatively rare. As an outgrowth of the feminist movement and the awareness it generates, postnuptial agreements may become more common in the future. Like prenuptial agreements, the postnuptial agreement itself, in New York and other fault states, does not provide a ground for divorce, and effecting a divorce can cause renegotiation and further financial concessions. In some states, such as California, a provision in a postmarital agreement restricting or waiving spousal support rights is invalid, as it is said to violate the public policy against promoting divorce.

COHABITATION AGREEMENTS

A cohabitation or living-together agreement is the final member of this marital agreement trilogy. According to the Census Bureau, in 1990, 2.9 million unmarried couples were living together, up 80% from 1980 and up 454% from 1970. This dramatic increase in the number of couples living together without marrying has spawned this relative newcomer to the field of marital agreements.

Attention has focused on cohabitation agreements because of the famous case involving the movie star Lee Marvin. In 1970, his seven-year relationship with his live-in companion, Michelle Marvin, broke up and she sued him for support and a division of the property acquired during the time that they lived together. Although she was eventually unsuccessful in proving that a contract regarding their property had been entered into, California's highest court indicated that damages would be obtainable if one could prove such a contract, even a contract that was not created by words or explicit agreement between the parties but rather was implied or inferred simply from the mutual relationship and the acts and conduct between the parties, including pooling financial resources, having children together, and using the same surname. The Marvin case begot a plethora of "palimony" decisions. Allegedly, some Lalaland Lotharios were so nervous after the Marvin case they actually had waivers on their nightstands for sleepover paramours to sign.

These Lotharios must have breathed at least a small sigh of relief when another California court ruled that in order for a palimony claim to succeed, the parties must have lived together. From 1981 through 1988, Duane Wood, a former president of Lockheed, maintained a relationship with Brigit Bergen, a German actress, who was 45 years old when she met Wood, who was then 65. During their relationship, the couple attended social events and traveled together. Bergen acted as Wood's social hostess, and Wood provided Bergen with money for her support. The couple had a sexual relationship but never lived together. She maintained an apartment in Germany, and when in California she kept a room in a Beverly Hills hotel. After the couple's relationship broke up, Bergen sued Wood, claiming, among other things, that there was an agreement between the parties that Wood would support her. A California appellate court ruled that the agreement was not enforceable because the couple had never lived together and living together is a necessary prerequisite to a palimony action.

In New York, property rights have also been found to exist between nonmarital partners under certain circumstances, but these claims are more difficult to prove. In New York, palimony rights cannot be implied or inferred merely from a relationship and the acts and conduct between live-in partners as in California but can exist only if the terms of an agreement are explicitly and actually entered into between the partners, either orally or in writing.

For example, in 1978, rock musician Peter Frampton separated from his live-in partner, Penelope McCall, and was sued by her for a share of the substantial property and earnings that he had accumulated during their five-year relationship. Frampton had met McCall in 1972, when she was married to the manager of Frampton's rock group. McCall claimed that Frampton asked her in 1973 to leave her husband

and her then employment and to devote all of her resources, time, and efforts to the promotion of Frampton, and that she did so. Although the case was ultimately settled out of court, the court stated that if the proof demonstrated that a partnership contract had been agreed to between the parties under which McCall agreed to work to promote Frampton's professional career in return for a share of his earnings, she was entitled to damages. One of Frampton's biggest hits in 1975 was "I'll Give You Money," but we do not know what monetary tune he had to sing over the apparent settlement.

Leonard Trimmer, the male companion of a wealthy woman, one Catherine Bryer Van Bomel, tried to extend the concept of palimony in what a New York court called an action for "companionmony." During the couple's five-year relationship, they attended social events together and dined and traveled in Europe together at the woman's expense but did not live together or have a sexual relationship. The rich Mrs. Van Bomel, with assets stated to be in excess of $40 million, clothed the 67-year-old Trimmer in expensive hand-tailored suits purchased in London and Italy, shoes from Gucci, and accessories from Saks. She also bought him three cars, paid his rent after he moved to a larger apartment, gave him a monthly allowance, and promised that she would take care of him. He gave up his employment as a travel tour operator, at which he made no more than $8,900 per year, to spend the requested time with her. Trimmer's action against her for damages when their friendship ended was dismissed because this promise was found to be too vague to be an agreement, and he was unable to prove that anything more than a friendship existed between the parties. "Friendship like virtue must be its own reward," concluded the court. Trimmer could find solace in the fact that he had already received $300,000 and a very much enhanced lifestyle over the course of the friendship.

There are, of course, no statistics on cases that are settled out of court. To be safe, the rich (and anyone else who wishes to avoid the problem) should enter into nonmarital or cohabitation agreements indicating that such togetherness out of wedlock, whether it be called palimony or companionmony, creates no legal rights in either party.

XI

*How the Rich Keep Their Assets
from Creditors: Creditor-Conscious
Estate Planning*

A major goal of estate planning has always been asset protection, but
usually it has been such protection from the Internal Revenue Service,
from predatory relatives or other heirs, or from intended beneficiaries
who have spendthrift or other deleterious habits.

   In recent years, more and more U.S. citizens have become fearful
of the loss of assets to a different body of claimants. Tort creditors,
especially those gaining malpractice judgments in excess of insurance
limits, garner the most publicity; the costs of such litigation have even
become a separate issue in the national debate on medical care. Other
proliferating claimants include contract creditors (e.g., by judicial extension of corporate liability to officers and directors beyond anticipated and insured risks or by the extension of a guaranty beyond its
contemplated scope); regulatory enforcers (especially for environmental liability under federal law, e.g., CERCLA, the Comprehensive Environmental Response, Compensation, and Liability Act, or similar
state laws); and spousal claimants in the context of a divorce or at

death, where statutory rights may exceed what is desired or even provided for in a prenuptial agreement.

In order to explain the estate planning techniques that may legally protect one from creditors' claims, I have picked for analysis three hypothetical persons — in this case, accountants with quite different factual situations — but the analysis of their situations and alternatives could apply equally to three lawyers, three doctors, three businessmen, or any three readers of this book.

INTRODUCING THREE HYPOTHETICAL MEN

At a recent accountants' conference, Messrs. Clean, Jitters, and Guile were discussing the surge in litigation brought against individual accountants and accounting firms during the last few years. They agreed that their profession was truly an industry under siege and, for the first time, expressed their genuine concern about the safety of their personal assets. Were their homes, pensions, and other assets in jeopardy, or would they somehow be protected against the claims of creditors that might someday arise?

Although these three gentlemen all share the same concerns, their individual circumstances are actually quite different. And, as this chapter discusses, it is these differences that will determine whether various means of asset protection are available to them and what level of protection these alternatives provide. Our analysis begins with a review of each of the accountants' particular circumstances.

Mr. Clean lives and works in New York, where he is a member of a highly lucrative partnership that primarily represents real estate developers. He also comes from a very wealthy family and recently inherited $2 million from his aunt. Mr. Clean has never been sued, and there are no claims on the horizon that he can reasonably foresee. Nevertheless, given the litigious climate in the country and the nature of his clientele, he is concerned that someday, someone will come forward and make a claim against him. It is that eventuality from which he hopes to protect himself. His personal financial statement is as follows:

Assets

New York house (owned individually)	$ 550,000
Furniture and furnishings	50,000
Cash and securities	2,250,000
Life insurance ($500,000 whole life policy with cash surrender value of $50,000)	50,000
Qualified pension plan — 401(k)	300,000
Nonqualified retirement plan	80,000
Total assets	$3,280,000

Liabilities

Mortgage on house	($ 200,000)
Loan against insurance policy	(45,000)
Net worth	$3,035,000

The second accountant, Mr. Jitters, is a longtime resident of Florida and a partner in the Miami office of a Big Six accounting firm. Because of the firm's high-profile work in general, and its representation of a number of bankrupt savings and loan institutions in particular, a rash of lawsuits have been brought against it. Mr. Jitters has not been named individually as a party in any of these suits. Furthermore, while he is somewhat aware of the total amount sought against the firm, he has no way of assessing his personal exposure, given the inherent uncertainties associated with litigation, the firm's substantial assets, and the availability of insurance. His personal balance sheet is as follows:

Assets

Florida house (owned individually)	$450,000
Qualified pension plan — 401(k)	500,000
Cash and securities	500,000
Life insurance (term, $1.5 million; whole life, $500,000 with a cash surrender value of $50,000)	50,000
New York co-op (owned jointly with wife)	125,000
Total assets	$1,625,000

Liabilities

Mortgage on Florida house	($ 175,000)
Net worth	$1,450,000

The last accountant, Mr. Guile, is a sole practitioner in New York, where he also resides. A local bank recently obtained a $1 million judgment against Mr. Guile in connection with the preparation of a fraudulent financial statement for one of his construction company clients. The bank has yet to execute upon the judgment. Mr. Guile's assets and liabilities are as follows:

Assets

New York house (owned as tenants by the entirety with his wife)	$ 650,000
Qualified pension plan — 401(k)	250,000
Rollover IRA	150,000
Conventional IRA	50,000
Total assets	$1,100,000

Liabilities

Judgment	($1,000,000)
Net worth	$ 100,000

In addition to the above, immediately after being named a defendant in the lawsuit, Mr. Guile paid off the then outstanding $150,000 mortgage on his home and put his approximately $100,000 in liquid assets in his wife's name.

Each of these accountants has received the usual cocktail-party advice about protecting his assets, such as transferring property to spouses and children or creating offshore trusts. In fact, as noted above, Mr. Guile has already put some of these suggestions into effect. But is it really possible to avoid a creditor's claim simply by making a gratuitous transfer of property while essentially maintaining control over it? The answer is no, but to a large extent this depends on the transferor's particular circumstances and the law of fraudulent conveyances.

THE LAW OF FRAUDULENT CONVEYANCES

The law of fraudulent conveyances will be relevant whenever an individual (the "transferor" or "debtor") makes a transfer of property for less than adequate value (consideration) with a view toward protecting such property from creditors. In essence, this area of the law provides that if a transfer is made with an intent to defraud creditors, whether present or future, the transferor's creditors or trustee in bankruptcy can have the transfer set aside. If a transfer is set aside, the transferred assets will once again be considered the transferor's property and, as such, will be subject to the creditors' reach. There are two types of fraudulent conveyances, those made with actual intent and those made with constructive intent.

Actual Intent to Defraud Creditors

Elements of Actual Fraud.   Under both state law and the federal Bankruptcy Code, actual fraud exists when a transfer is made with an "actual intent to hinder, delay, or defraud" any present or future creditor. Because of the "intent" requirement, finding actual fraud will involve a subjective inquiry into the transferor's behavior and state of mind to determine what motivated him in making the transfer.

In making this inquiry, courts will often look to see whether any "badges of fraud" were present at the time of the transfer. Some of the most common badges of fraud are (i) a transfer involving family members; (ii) the transferor's continued possession or control over the property after the transfer; (iii) secrecy involved in the transfer; (iv) a conveyance of substantially all of the transferor's assets; (v) inadequate consideration received for the transfer; (vi) the transferor either having been sued or threatened with suit at the time of the transfer; and (vii) a transfer occurring shortly before or after the debt was incurred or the judgment was entered. This list is by no means exclusive, and actual fraud can be found even if none of these elements exists. Conversely, simply because one or more of these badges is present will not necessarily result in a finding of fraud. There are no hard rules; each transfer must be evaluated on a case-by-case basis.

Types of Creditors.   Finding actual fraud will, in large part, depend on the transferor's circumstances with respect to creditors at the time of the transfer. Consider, for example, our accountants. Doesn't Mr. Guile's transfer to his wife after he has been sued strike us as materially different from Mr. Clean's making a gift of property to his wife or children? And would our view change even if we knew that Mr. Clean's gift was at least partly motivated by a desire to protect the gifted property against creditors who might someday arise?

Obviously, these are very different situations, with the differences stemming not so much from the transfers themselves but rather from the status of the claim against the transferor at the time of the transfer. In Mr. Guile's case, a very real claim has been made against him at the time he transfers property to his wife, even though no judgment has been obtained. Thus, in fraudulent conveyance parlance, the local bank seeking restitution from Mr. Guile is considered to be a "present creditor," and any transfer made with a view toward avoiding payment to that creditor will be set aside. It is important to note that present creditors include those whose obligations are not fully matured — i.e., holders of unliquidated, unmatured, and contingent claims — which is precisely Mr. Guile's situation.

Mr. Clean, on the other hand, has no present creditors, nor does he expect anyone in particular to assert a future claim against him. His creditors are therefore referred to as "possible future creditors," and any transfers made with an intention of defeating their rights should *not* be considered fraudulent *so long as Mr. Clean is not rendered insolvent as a result of the transfer.* The law does not prevent an individual from planning for his future well-being, and one need not preserve one's assets for unknown future claimants. Traditionally, in order for a transfer to be set aside as fraudulent, a particular creditor with some legal foundation for his claim must either exist or be reasonably anticipated at the time of the transfer.

Thus, it seems clear that Mr. Guile's transfer to his wife and any subsequent transfers will be voidable by his creditors, while Mr. Clean should be free at present to make whatever transfers he chooses, so long as they do not make him insolvent. But what of Mr. Jitters? He is a general partner in a firm with lawsuits pending against it, but no claims have been made against him personally. Thus, although he is aware of the existence of particular claims that could ultimately be asserted against him, he also understands that unless these claims exceed the firm's considerable assets and insurance coverage, he will have no personal exposure. His situation is therefore quite different from both Mr. Clean's and Mr. Guile's. The question is whether his knowledge of these potential claims puts him in the murky middle ground of fraudulent conveyance law relating to "probable future creditors."

Probable future creditors are essentially claimants-in-waiting, i.e., creditors who may not yet be in existence, but whose claims are likely and expected. Any transfer made with the intention of avoiding such claims will be fraudulent even though the transfer may have been made before the debt was incurred. In determining whether the requisite fraudulent intent is present, courts will generally look at the following factors: (i) whether at the time of the transfer the transferor had a particular creditor in mind whose claim he was hoping to avoid; (ii) whether the debt was incurred (i.e., the claim matured) shortly after the transfer; and (iii) whether the transferor knew at the time of the transfer that he was about to incur the obligation. In order for actual fraud to be found, courts will require clear and convincing evidence that each of these factors, as demonstrated by the transferor's conduct, is present.

In Mr. Jitters' situation, it is difficult to predict whether a transfer made by him at this point could ultimately be set aside by one of the parties currently litigating against his firm. Certainly, the claimant would assert that Mr. Jitters was aware of the potential claim against him and made the transfer with that particular obligation in mind. On the other hand, depending upon how long the lawsuit against the firm takes, it could be years before the claimant proceeds against Mr. Jitters personally. Thus, if he makes an immediate transfer, the debt will not mature until long after the transfer and the second factor will not be present. The third factor—whether Mr. Jitters knew at the time of the transfer that he was about to incur the obligation — is perhaps the most questionable of all. This is a question of fact and will depend upon such factors as his knowledge of the lawsuits against the firm, of the likelihood of the claimants prevailing, of the amount they are likely to recover, of the extent of the firm's assets and insurance, etc. It would appear that in order for the claimant to have the transfer set aside, the claimant would have to show that Mr. Jitters not only expected the claims against the firm to be sustained but expected that the firm would be unable to satisfy them out of its assets and insurance.

Conversion of Nonexempt Property into Exempt Property. As will be discussed below, certain assets are specifically exempted from creditors' claims under either federal or state law. For example, a Floridian's primary residence cannot be reached by creditors regardless of when a debt arises. Similarly, Florida, New York, and federal bankruptcy law exempt annuities, insurance, spendthrift trusts, and various types of IRAs and pension plans. The existence of these exemptions raises another interesting issue.

As we have seen, Mr. Guile's transfer of his liquid assets to his wife will probably not withstand judicial scrutiny and should be set aside. But what if, rather than giving his cash to his wife, Mr. Guile purchased property that is specifically exempted from creditors' claims under either federal or state law? For example, can Mr. Guile take advantage of the Florida homestead exemption by purchasing a home in Florida at this point and thereby avoid his creditors? Again, the answer depends on whether any of the other elements of actual fraud are present.

Consider, for example, the case of Bowie Kuhn, the former Commissioner of Baseball. Mr. Kuhn was a senior partner in a now defunct New York City law firm that was forced into dissolution by its many creditors. In an apparent attempt to escape these creditors, Mr. Kuhn suddenly "disappeared" from the New York metropolitan area, only to reemerge some weeks later in Florida. In the interim, he had sold his New Jersey home, which was about to be attached by creditors, and reinvested the proceeds in a $1 million house just off the Intercoastal Waterway in southern Florida. Mr. Kuhn's creditors promptly sought to have the Florida home purchase set aside. The court ruled that Mr. Kuhn's attempt to convert nonexempt property (i.e., the New Jersey home) into exempt property (i.e., the Florida home) was evidence of an intent to defeat creditors, and thus could be deemed a fraudulent transfer. In making its determination, the court noted the secretive nature of Mr. Kuhn's behavior, one of the classic badges of fraud.

As the Kuhn case demonstrates, the mere conversion of nonexempt property into exempt property does not by itself constitute actual fraud; courts will usually require the existence of some other evidence of fraudulent intent in addition to the conversion. This is not to say, however, that the combination of a conversion and some other element of fraud will necessarily result in a finding of actual fraud. As with all these cases, such findings are highly subjective and will turn not only on the circumstances surrounding the conversion but also on the individual perceptions of the judge or jury hearing the case.

The extent to which subjectivity plays a role in these decisions was well demonstrated by the Tveten and Johnson cases, both of which came out of Minnesota. In these companion cases, two doctors had both invested in the same ill-fated real estate venture, both owed the same $19 million as a result of personal guaranties, and both converted approximately $700,000 into exempt assets. In the Tveten case, the judge ruled that while the bare act of converting nonexempt property to exempt property does not constitute actual fraud, Dr. Tveten's awareness of one judgment and several other suits against him, when considered along with the conversion, created an inferred intent to hinder, delay, and defraud his creditors. In the Johnson case, however, the judge found that Dr. Johnson's activities merely sought to maximize the benefit of statutory exemptions that he had available and did not contain the "deceptive animus that is the atavar of an intent to defraud."

Thus, here you have two identical cases tried in the same court but before different judges with directly contradictory results. How does one reconcile these decisions? It is possible, though unlikely, that one of the doctors either was unaware of the judgment against him or was less clandestine about the conversion of his assets. It is far more likely that the two judges simply saw these cases differently and had differing attitudes as to how to apply the law in this murky area. More than anything else, these cases illustrate the unsettled nature of the law of fraudulent conveyances and the difficulty of predicting the outcome of any case involving actual fraud.

Constructive Intent to Defraud Creditors

As we have seen, finding actual fraud requires an examination of the debtor's behavior with a view toward determining what motivated him at the time of the transfer. The other type of fraud, constructive fraud, is far more mechanical in nature and does not require a finding of fraudulent intent. Essentially, a transfer will be set aside on the basis of constructive fraud if the transferor (i) receives less than "reasonably equivalent value" for the property transferred, *and* (ii) is insolvent at the time the transfer is made or is rendered insolvent as a result of the transfer. There is no precise definition of what constitutes "reasonably equivalent value" under either federal or state law. It is clear, however, that this concept does not require exact economic equivalence. In what has developed as a judicial rule of thumb, courts seem to require that the transferor receive at least 70% of the fair market value of the assets transferred in order to avoid having the transfer set aside. Of course, this 70% test could change at any time.

The test for insolvency is a simple balance sheet test, i.e., whether the fair market value of the transferor's liabilities (including contingent liabilities) is greater than the fair market value of the transferor's assets. Also considered is whether the transferor had an unreasonably small amount of capital at the time the transfer was made and whether the transferor was about to incur debts beyond his or her ability to pay.

ASSET PROTECTION ALTERNATIVES

Thus far, we have been examining whether our three accountants are in a position to transfer some portion of their assets with a view toward protecting them from potential creditors' claims. What we have learned is that their individual circumstances actually put them in very different positions. It seems clear, for example, that Mr. Clean is free to make whatever transfers he chooses, as long as he is not rendered insolvent by the transfer. Mr. Guile, on the other hand, is in precisely the opposite position. Any transfer he makes at this point is almost certain to be set aside on the basis of actual fraud. Our third accountant, Mr. Jitters, poses the most problematical situation. His success is likely to depend on the type of transfer he makes and, in the event the transfer is challenged, the court's perception of his motivations in making it.

Let us now explore the various methods of protecting one's assets from the reach of potential creditors, assuming no fraudulent conveyance is involved. In general, these alternatives seek to take advantage of various provisions of federal or state law that exempt certain property from creditors' claims. As we will learn, while Mr. Guile is probably precluded from taking any additional steps at this time, some of his assets are, in fact, already protected. Mr. Clean, on the other hand, and possibly Mr. Jitters, will have a number of alternatives available to them.

This section begins with a discussion of how to protect the one asset that is of greatest importance to most persons — their personal residence. It then moves to a discussion of various types of investment vehicles — retirement plans, annuities and life insurance, and spendthrift trusts — that are specifically exempted from creditors' claims under both state and federal bankruptcy law. The section concludes with a discussion of offshore trusts, also called APTs (asset protection trusts), an increasingly popular form of asset protection.

Residential Property

Florida Homestead Exemption. As noted above, Bowie Kuhn's sudden interest in Florida had little to do with the weather. He was clearly seeking to take advantage of what is perhaps the most generous exemption available to Florida debtors, the Florida homestead exemption. Under this exemption, absent any actual or constructive fraud, the home of a Florida resident cannot be reached by creditors. The exemption protects not only the debtor's house but also the land on which it is located. In a city it protects half an acre, but in the country up to 160 acres.

In practical terms, this exemption protects the owner's equity in the house as opposed to the house's absolute value. Thus, if the owner has a substantial mortgage on the house and has used the mortgage proceeds to invest in securities or other nonexempt assets, these other assets will be reachable by creditors. Accordingly, in order to obtain the maximum protection afforded by this exemption, the owner should reduce his debt on the house to the lowest amount possible without compromising his needed liquidity.

Florida, because of this homestead exemption, put in its constitution 130 years ago to attract residents, has become the choice of domicile for many sophisticated debtors. Paul Bilzerian was convicted of violating federal securities laws a year after he won control of the Singer Company in a $1.06 billion hostile takeover in 1988. He served twenty months in prison. He went into personal bankruptcy in 1991 but has retained his Florida house — a complex with twenty-one bathrooms, a full-size basketball court, an indoor squash court, etc. Marvin Warner, whose Ohio banking empire went under, in 1985 paid $3.5 million cash for a 400-acre horse farm in Ocala, Florida. He kept 160 acres as permitted by Florida law, and transferred 240 acres to his wife and son. He filed for bankruptcy in 1987 and was able to keep this estate and his thoroughbred horses.

The Florida homestead and other exemptions discussed below are available only to Florida domiciliaries — i.e., those individuals who claim Florida as their *principal* residence. Those individuals who are new to Florida will be required to demonstrate that they intend to establish Florida as their place of domicile. Numerous factors are considered in determining whether such an intention exists, such as whether the individual has given up his prior out-of-state residence, registered to vote and obtained a driver's license in Florida, joined local clubs and religious organizations, etc. Another important factor is whether the individual has filed a sworn statement with the clerk of the circuit court for the county in Florida in which he resides. The affidavit must state that the individual resides in that county and intends to maintain such residence as his permanent or principal home and that he intends to continue as such.

The Florida homestead exemption obviously represents good news for Mr. Jitters, our only Floridian. He can rest assured that even if a judgment is ultimately obtained against him, his home, or at least the $275,000 equity in it, will always be safe. But what if he takes a portion of his liquid assets and pays off the $175,000 mortgage on the house? Will these additional funds also be protected?

This kind of transfer is essentially what Bowie Kuhn did — i.e., attempt to convert nonexempt assets (cash) into exempt assets (house). Thus, once again the question is whether actual fraud is involved in making the payment. If a judge later determines that the payment was made with a view toward defeating the rights of the parties currently suing Mr. Jitters' firm and that Mr. Jitters was aware when he made the payment that he would soon be indebted to these parties, the payment will be set aside and Mr. Jitters' creditors will be able to reach the $175,000. If, on the other hand, Mr. Jitters can demonstrate that it was not at all clear at the time of the payment that he would have any personal exposure with respect to the claims against the firm, the payment should stand.

What about Mr. Guile? Upon learning of the Florida homestead exemption, he will undoubtedly look to buy the most expensive home in Florida he can find. This purchase is certain to be viewed as a fraudulent conveyance and, once challenged, should be set aside.

New York Residences. In contrast to Florida's generous homestead exemption, New York law provides that a debtor may only exempt up to $10,000 of value of "property owned and operated as a principal residence." Despite this limited exemption, it is still possible to protect an individual's interest in a New York residence if title to the residence is held in the proper form. Thus, in certain instances, it may be advantageous for a married New York resident to change the form in which he holds title to his home, or if that is impracticable, to transfer his interest in the house to his spouse or some other individual.

In most cases, married New York residents hold title to their homes in one of three different forms: (i) outright ownership by one spouse;

(ii) as "tenants by the entirety"; or (iii) as "joint tenants with right of survivorship."* Only spouses may hold title as tenants by the entirety, whereas any two individuals may create a joint tenancy with a right of survivorship. The difference between a tenancy by the entirety and a joint tenancy is based on a legal fiction that assumes that a husband and wife are really a single legal and economic unit and thus the "unit" is deemed to hold the property as if a single person owned it.

Both tenancies by the entirety and joint tenancies have a survivorship right, which means that on the death of the first spouse, the surviving spouse immediately becomes the owner of the entire property by operation of law. The key difference between these forms of ownership is that joint tenancy property is subject to voluntary partition, whereas tenancy by the entirety property is not. With a joint tenancy one spouse may unilaterally terminate the survivorship rights of the other and force a sale of the property. This would not be possible with a tenancy by the entirety, where both spouses must join to terminate the survivorship right and sell the property.

As a result of this distinction, a creditor will find it considerably more difficult to satisfy a claim against a debtor's interest in a tenancy by the entirety than a joint tenancy. With a tenancy by the entirety, a creditor may levy against the debtor's (in this case, the husband's) interest in the home and obtain title to it. In that case, the creditor will become a tenant in common with the debtor's wife and will be entitled to share in the rents, profits, and occupancy of the house. However, the wife cannot be forced out of the house, and even the debtor may continue to reside there as his wife's guest. Furthermore, the creditor's interest will be subject to the wife's right of survivorship, which means that if the husband dies first, the wife will automatically become the owner of the entire property and the creditor will be left with nothing.

Thus, as a practical matter, executing on a tenancy by the entirety interest is of little value, since residential property rarely generates any rent and the creditor is unlikely to want to move in with the debtor and his family.† In fact, the only situation in which a creditor can

---

* Although this discussion focuses only on New York law, the principles discussed here will be applicable in most states.

† While a creditor has a technical right to occupancy, New York courts have the discretion not to enforce it.

obtain satisfaction with a tenancy by the entirety is if the wife dies first, in which case the creditor can have the house sold and take one-half of the proceeds.

Compare this with a joint tenancy. In this situation, when the creditor levies upon the debtor's interest, he can force the immediate sale of the home, assuming it cannot actually be divided into two separate premises, and receive one-half of the sale proceeds. Such a sale will extinguish the wife's survivorship right and essentially require the debtor's entire family to vacate the house.

One caveat to bear in mind here is that if the debtor becomes the subject of a federal bankruptcy case (i.e., he has either filed a bankruptcy petition or has been forced into involuntary bankruptcy), *both spouses* may be forced to relinquish their rights in the marital home, regardless of whether the property is held as tenants by the entirety or as joint tenants. Section 541(a) of the Bankruptcy Code provides that the debtor's interest in a tenancy by the entirety passes to the trustee in bankruptcy. Under Section 363(h) of the Bankruptcy Code, a trustee has the right to sell the debtor's interest, *together with the interest of the nondebtor spouse*, if all of the following conditions are met: (i) a partition in kind (i.e., an actual division of the property) would be impracticable; (ii) a sale of the debtor's interest in the home would realize significantly less than if the house were sold free of the debtor's wife's interest; and (iii) the benefit to the debtor's estate derived from the sale would outweigh the detriment to the wife. If a bankruptcy court were to permit such a sale, the wife would receive her one-half share of the net sale proceeds. It is important to note that a New York bankruptcy judge has found this provision unconstitutional, since it allows the wife's interest in the property to be "taken" to satisfy the debtor's private debts. Although no other court has yet followed this decision, if its view prevails tenancies by the entirety will have the same degree of protection under both federal and state law.

Mr. Guile, who owns his house with his wife in a tenancy by the entirety, will obviously be glad to hear that his house should be safe, as long as he is able to stay out of bankruptcy court. He should be especially delighted because his wife is 25 years his junior, which means that there is a strong likelihood that she will survive him and thus terminate any interest his creditors may obtain. Mr. Guile does have some exposure with respect to the $150,000 payment he made on his mortgage shortly after being named a defendant in the lawsuit. In view of the timing of the payment, this might well be a fraudulent conveyance and thus could be set aside.

Mr. Clean holds title to his New York home in his own name. Given his concerns, he probably would be well advised to change the form in which title is held, since his present form of ownership would provide no protection against future creditors. He has several alternatives. First, he could simply transfer title to his wife. Although this is a gratuitous transfer, it should not be a fraudulent conveyance, since Mr. Clean has no present or probable future creditors. The problem with this alternative is that although the house would be protected against Mr. Clean's creditors, it would not be safe from Mrs. Clean's creditors, if any should ever exist. Thus, he is probably better off creating a tenancy by the entirety or transferring the house to a spendthrift trust, which is discussed below in greater detail.

What if Mr. Jitters were a New York resident and owned his house with his wife in a joint tenancy with right of survivorship? Would there be anything he could do to protect his house other than create a tenancy by the entirety? One possibility would be to "sell" his one-half interest in the house to his wife or some other third party for adequate consideration. For example, Mrs. Jitters could purchase his interest for a promissory note with a face value equal to one-half the value of the house. This note would have to be bona fide in all respects, including bearing a market-level interest rate. Furthermore, Mrs. Jitters would have to pay the interest on the note out of her own separate assets, assuming she has any. She could not draw on a joint account that was primarily funded by Mr. Jitters.

If a judgment were ever obtained against Mr. Jitters, his creditors would be able to execute on the note, but their rights would be no greater than his. Mrs. Jitters would therefore only be required to pay them interest on the note. If she were able to sustain these payments long enough for Mr. Jitters to get back on his feet, she could ultimately pay off the principal balance on the note out of her separate assets and Mr. Jitters' creditors would simply become a bad memory. In the meantime, the Jitters would have successfully protected their most treasured asset — their home.

Pension and Other Retirement Plans

As is typical with many Americans today, a substantial portion of all three of our accountants' wealth is held in pension and profit-sharing plans and individual retirement accounts (IRAs). Holding property in these forms is rather fortunate, since a recent decision of the United States Supreme Court held that all pension benefits payable under an ERISA qualified plan are exempt from the reach of creditors. Thus, the substantial 401(k) plans maintained by Messrs. Clean, Jitters, and Guile will all be protected.

It is important to note that IRAs are not qualified plans and thus do not have the same protection under federal law. However, both New York and Florida law now provide specific exemptions for IRAs and Keogh plans. Thus, the various IRA accounts owned by the three accountants will also be protected.

Annuities and Life Insurance

In addition to protecting pension benefits, many states, including Florida and New York, specifically exempt annuities and life insurance from creditors' claims. The New York insurance law, which is essentially the same as its Florida counterpart, defines an annuity as follows:

> any obligation to pay certain sums at stated times, during life or lives, or for a specified term or terms, issued for a valuable consideration, regardless of whether such sums are payable to one or more persons, jointly or otherwise. . . . [N.Y. Ins. Law §3212(a) (2)]

In New York, the exemption is subject to the following limitations: (i) the annuity contract must have been purchased more than six months prior to an individual's filing of a bankruptcy petition; (ii) a court may order the annuitant to pay to a judgment creditor a portion of the benefit if such portion is deemed by the court to be unnecessary to meet the annuitant's ordinary financial needs; and (iii) an annuity contract purchased with actual intent to defraud creditors will not be deemed exempt.

Given this exemption, both Mr. Clean and Mr. Jitters should consider investing a portion of their assets in annuities. In the case of Mr. Clean, the amount invested will depend upon his "ordinary financial needs," since in New York, any benefits payable in excess of that amount will not be protected. But that phrase should allow him to maintain a comfortable standard of living. Only amounts above that would or could be deemed nonprotectable excess.

One interesting question here is whether the annuity must be a commercial annuity issued by a life insurance company or can be a so-called private annuity. With a private annuity, the annuitant would give cash or other property to another person in exchange for that person's obligation to pay the annuitant a fixed amount for life. Thus, assume Mr. Jitters transfers $250,000 in cash and securities to his wife in exchange for her promise to pay him $20,000 per year for life. Would the $20,000 payments to him be exempt? There is nothing in either the New York or Florida statute that would suggest otherwise. Furthermore, the $250,000 transfer to Mrs. Jitters should not be a fraudulent conveyance, since it was for adequate consideration, i.e., the payback of $20,000 per year to Mr. Jitters for his life.

New York and Florida also provide an exemption for benefits payable under life insurance policies, but with certain small differences. New York protects all aspects of an insurance policy, including its death benefits, cash surrender value, premiums waived, and dividends, except where the insured receives the dividends in cash. The Florida exemption is somewhat more limited in that it shelters only the cash surrender value of the policy.

Both Mr. Clean and Mr. Jitters own life insurance. Mr. Clean has a $500,000 whole life policy with a cash surrender value of $50,000. In addition, he has borrowed out $45,000 of the policy's loan value. Mr. Clean should consider repaying the loan, since any amounts repaid will be added to the policy's cash surrender value and thus be protected under New York law. Such repayment is a simple means of converting nonexempt property into exempt property. He might also consider transferring ownership of his policy to an irrevocable insurance trust, which is a spendthrift trust. As discussed in the next section, spendthrift trusts are also exempt from creditors, so that by putting an insurance policy in such a trust, an additional layer of protection will be obtained. Insurance trusts also provide an extremely valuable estate planning feature in that the proceeds payable to an insurance trust will usually avoid estate taxation. See pp. 124–129 on Irrevocable Insurance Trusts.

Mr. Jitters has two insurance policies, a $1.5 million term policy and a $500,000 whole life policy with a cash surrender value of $50,000. Under Florida law, the $50,000 cash value of the whole life policy will be protected, but the term policy, which has no cash value, will not be.

Spendthrift Trusts

The term "spendthrift trust" refers to any trust that expressly prohibits its beneficiaries from transferring their right to receive trust income or principal to any other person. As a general rule, assets held in a spendthrift trust for the benefit of someone other than the trust's creator, or grantor, will be exempt from the reach of the grantor's creditors. The integrity of spendthrift trusts is premised on the right of the trust's creator to determine how the trust property will be used, which includes the right to protect the beneficiaries from their own financial mismanagement.

The vast majority of states (forty-two plus the District of Columbia) recognize the validity of spendthrift trusts. Only five states, New Hampshire, Rhode Island, Ohio, North Carolina, and Georgia, do not recognize spendthrift provisions, and an additional three states, Alaska, Idaho, and Wyoming, have not addressed the issue. In New York, all trusts are spendthrift trusts as to income unless the trust instrument expressly provides otherwise. Thus, no beneficiary can transfer his right to trust income to anyone else unless the trust specifically allows such a transfer.

As noted above, the spendthrift trust exemption will protect the trust assets from the beneficiary's creditors as long as the trust was created by someone other than the beneficiary himself or herself. Thus, assume Mr. Guile's 90-year-old mother, who loves her son dearly and knows he can do no wrong, plans on leaving her entire multimillion-dollar estate to him outright. If she does, his creditors will be able to reach that property the moment he receives it. What makes more sense is for her to create a spendthrift trust that gives the trustee (someone other than Mr. Guile) complete discretion to distribute as much or as little of the trust income and principal to Mr. Guile as the trustee considers advisable. The trust will last for Mr. Guile's lifetime and pass to his children upon his death.

Because distributions from this trust are entirely in the discretion of the trustee, Mr. Guile cannot compel the trustee to make any distributions to him. Also, Mr. Guile's creditors cannot compel distributions, since their rights can be no greater than his. The result is that the trust assets are completely protected. Of course, to the extent that trust income or principal is actually distributed to Mr. Guile, his creditors will be able to reach these distributions.

One solution to this problem is to have Mr. Guile's mother include his wife as a discretionary beneficiary of the trust. The trustee could then make distributions of trust income and principal to Mr. Guile's wife for as long as his creditors' problems continued. If Mr. Guile's problems with creditors should ever disappear, there is nothing to prevent the trustee from exercising his discretion to distribute the entire trust principal to Mr. Guile and thereby terminate the trust.

This arrangement is fine for Mr. Guile, but what about Mr. Clean and Mr. Jitters, who don't have wealthy old mothers or fathers? Can they transfer assets to a spendthrift trust for their own benefits and thereby shield these assets from creditors? The answer is no, and this will be true regardless of their intent or solvency at the time the trust is created. The New York statute, which resembles a great many others, is quite explicit and makes no distinctions: "A disposition in trust for the use of the creator is void against the existing *or subsequent* creditors of the creator" (emphasis added).

When a grantor creates a trust for his or her own benefit, the general rule is that the grantor's creditors can reach the maximum amount that can be distributed to the grantor under the trust provisions, even if no distributions are actually contemplated. Thus, if Mr. Guile, rather than his mother, had created the trust described above, his creditors could reach the entire trust, since his trustees have the discretion to distribute all of the trust income or principal to him at any time.

This is not to say that spendthrift trusts are of no benefit to individuals such as Messrs. Jitters and Clean, since they can be quite useful as long as the grantor does not retain an interest in the entire trust property. For example, assume Mr. Clean creates a trust that provides that all income must be distributed to him annually but that principal may only be distributed in the trustees' discretion to his wife and children. With this type of trust, Mr. Clean's creditors would only be able to reach the trust income, since the trustee does not have the discretion to distribute trust principal to Mr. Clean. Taking this one step further, if Mr. Clean had no interest in either the trust income or the principal, the trust would be entirely exempt.

Gift and Estate Tax Consequences.   One problem with trusts in which the creator does not retain an interest is that they could generate a gift tax. Thus, if Mr. Clean transferred $1 million of his inherited money to a trust described above for the exclusive benefit of his wife and children, he would be making a taxable gift of the entire trust corpus and would owe $153,000 in federal gift tax, assuming he had made no prior gifts.* One means of avoiding this tax is for Mr. Clean to retain a so-called limited power of appointment over the trust principal. (With such a power, rather than the trust property passing directly and automatically to his children at his wife's death, Mr. Clean would have the ability to direct in his will or some other lifetime instrument the beneficiaries who would receive such property and in what shares.) When this element of control is retained, the gift is considered to be "incomplete" for gift tax purposes so that no tax results. Significantly, however, retaining this power of appointment does *not* make the trust property subject to creditors' rights.

One consequence of avoiding a gift tax is that the trust will be subject to estate tax in Mr. Clean's estate at his death. While this may be preferable to paying a present gift tax, from an estate planning perspective it often does not make sense. Paying gift tax is generally more tax-efficient than paying estate tax for two reasons. First, unlike estate tax, gift tax is tax-exclusive, which means that no tax is paid on the funds used to pay the tax itself. Thus, assuming the same 50%

* This is after giving effect to his $600,000 exemption from federal gift and estate tax.

estate and gift tax bracket is applicable, it will cost a total of $1.5 million to make a lifetime gift of $1 million ($500,000 in gift tax and $1 million in gift), whereas a testamentary bequest at death of $1 million in a will would cost $2 million ($1 million in estate tax and $1 million in bequest).

The second reason for paying gift tax is that the tax is based on the present value of the property transferred, which means that any income or appreciation earned by the property after the transfer will not be subject to tax. For example, assume the $1 million Mr. Clean transferred to the trust grows to $2.5 million by the time he dies in thirty years. If that amount is included in his taxable estate, it could be subject to as much as $1.5 million in federal and New York estate tax, depending on the value of his other assets at his death. His children will thus be left with $1 million. If, on the other hand, he had not retained a limited power of appointment to make the gift incomplete, but instead deliberately subjected the trust to gift tax at the time of its creation, the children would receive the entire $2.5 million at a tax cost of only $153,000.

Unified Credit and Lifetime QTIP Trusts.   Mr. Clean could avoid both a federal gift and an estate tax by establishing a trust and funding it with $600,000, the maximum amount an individual can give away free of federal estate and gift tax under current law. By limiting the trust to this amount and not retaining a power of appointment, he would be able to pass on any income and appreciation earned by the trust during his lifetime to his children tax-free. Thus, if the trust were to grow to $1.5 million over his lifetime, he would be able to transfer this entire amount to his children tax-free, and at the same time, shelter the trust assets from his creditors. Furthermore, to the extent the Cleans ever needed any funds from the trust with which to pay their living expenses, the trustee would be free to make distributions to Mrs. Clean. Since Mr. Clean is not a beneficiary of the trust, these distributions could not be reached by creditors.

Both the asset protection and estate planning benefits of this trust could be doubled by Mr. Clean's giving his wife $600,000 (assuming she has no independent funds of her own) and having her create a similar discretionary trust for the benefit of the children and Mr. Clean. Since Mrs. Clean would be the creator of the trust, Mr. Clean's creditors would not be able to reach it, even though Mr. Clean can receive trust property in the discretion of the trustee. In addition, the Cleans would be able to pay the children's expenses, such as camp and college tuition, from the trust if it ever became necessary. If the trust experienced the same growth over Mrs. Clean's lifetime, an additional $1.5 million would be passed on to the children tax-free.

If Mr. Clean is still uncomfortable with sheltering only $1,200,000 of his liquid assets, he could go one step further and create a so-called lifetime QTIP trust for his wife with the balance of his funds. Under the terms of this trust, all income generated from the principal of the trust must be paid to Mrs. Clean for her lifetime, and principal could be made available to her at the discretion of the trustee. At her death, the trust principal would pass to the children. This trust qualifies for the federal gift tax marital deduction, which means that no gift tax will be due upon its creation. It will, however, be subject to estate tax in Mrs. Clean's estate. Thus, while it accomplishes little from an estate planning standpoint, it does provide a means of shielding additional assets from creditors without incurring a gift tax.

Like the other asset protection devices described in this section, a spendthrift trust will act as a shield against creditors only to the extent that no fraudulent conveyance is involved in the initial funding of the trust. Thus, while Mr. Clean is free to create any of the trusts described here, the other two accountants will be subject to the same degree of scrutiny previously discussed.

Offshore Asset Protection Trusts

Certainly one of the hottest current topics on the cocktail party circuit, and also among estate planners, is the offshore asset protection trust, or APT. In recent years, APTs have become increasingly popular as a means of shielding one's assets from potential creditors. APTs are basically trusts established in foreign jurisdictions with laws specifically designed to make it very difficult to collect U.S. judgments or those of other countries outside the jurisdiction of the trust. Asset protection, or, more accurately, the attraction of foreign funds, has become a highly competitive industry in these jurisdictions, so local legislatures are continually amending existing statutes or enacting new ones to provide even better protection against creditors' claims. Some of the jurisdictions currently in favor are the Bahamas, Belize, Bermuda, the Cayman Islands, the Channel Islands (Jersey and Guernsey), the Cook Islands, Gibraltar, the Isle of Man, Liechtenstein, Nevis, and the Turks and Caicos Islands.

Often the primary purpose of offshore asset protection statutes is to place both physical and legal obstacles in the path of creditors seeking to enforce judgments. For example, many jurisdictions either do not recognize U.S. judgments or will do so only after the case is heard or retried under local law. Thus, after obtaining a judgment in the United States, the creditor is forced to travel to the foreign jurisdiction and start the case anew. This additional expenditure of time and money, in itself, may be enough of an impediment to cause the creditor to look elsewhere for satisfaction or at least to compromise the claim.

The legal obstacles normally appear in the form of an exceptionally short statute of limitations (the time period in which one can enforce a claim), which, from a practical standpoint, renders the judgment uncollectible. For example, in the Cook Islands, which are located in the South Pacific east of Australia, if a creditor fails to bring an action within one year of the trust's creation or within two years from the time the creditor's right arose, the trust assets will not be reachable. Thus, if the trust is funded shortly after a claim arises, by the time the U.S. creditor sues on the claim and obtains a judgment, which could take years, the local statute of limitations will have run and the trust assets will be safe.

The terms of APTs are quite straightforward. In many respects, APTs are similar to the spendthrift trusts described above. Typically, they are totally discretionary trusts, with the trustee having the sole ability to distribute income and principal among a class of beneficiaries. The most significant difference between an APT and a domestic U.S. spendthrift trust is that the creator of the trust may also be a discretionary beneficiary of the trust without making the trust reachable by creditors. Thus, should the creator's creditor problems ever disappear, the trustee would have the discretion to terminate the trust by distributing the entire trust principal back to the creator.

APTs are usually irrevocable and last for a designated period of time, which can be extended if new creditors arise. If the creator dies during the trust term, the trust assets will pass either in accordance with the terms of his or her will or the terms of the trust.

APTs also contain certain unique provisions. One is an "anti-duress" clause that allows the foreign trustee to ignore an order from a U.S. court directing either the creator or a U.S. trustee (if there is one) to turn over the trust assets to the grantor's creditors. Another is a "transfer of situs" provision that gives the trustees the authority to change the jurisdiction of the trust in the event any legal action threatens the trust or its assets. Thus, if a creditor is close to enforcing a judgment in the Bahamas, the trustee could pay over the trust property to a Gibraltar bank, and the creditor would be required to start all over again in Gibraltar.

The trustee is usually a foreign bank or trust company. In selecting a trustee, it is best to avoid a bank that is either a subsidiary of a U.S. corporation or has a U.S. subsidiary, since either might be the basis for obtaining U.S. jurisdiction over the trust. In addition to the trustee, the trust will have a "protector," who will normally be a close friend or adviser of the grantor. The protector may be given a number of powers over the trust, such as the right to remove the trustee and name a successor and to add or delete beneficiaries. Either the grantor or the protector can be given the authority to name investment advisers, assuming the grantor does not wish to leave investment decisions to the trustee.

The grantor will determine whether the trust assets will be held in the trust jurisdiction or elsewhere, which may include the United States. There are both advantages and disadvantages to leaving the trust assets in the United States. The advantage is the comfort of knowing the assets are held in a reputable, presumably sound U.S. institution. The disadvantage is that it makes the assets one step closer to the grasp of the grantor's creditors. In order to guard against this, some practitioners suggest creating a limited partnership and transferring the underlying assets to the partnership. The APT will then own the partnership interest rather than the assets directly. That way, even if the assets are located in the United States, creditors will not be able to proceed against the assets directly, since they will be owned by a partnership, which in turn is owned by the APT. The result is that the creditors will still be forced to commence an action in the foreign jurisdiction to reach the actual assets.

The tax consequences of creating an APT will depend on its terms. Most APTs are grantor trusts for income tax purposes, which means that the creator (grantor) will continue to be taxed on all income earned by the trust. This income tax presents an added estate planning benefit in that the trust will grow on a tax-free basis, since the creator will pay the income tax out of his own assets that would otherwise be attributable to and payable out of the trust. Thus, if the trust principal is ultimately payable to the creator's children, the creator will have succeeded in essentially making additional tax-free gifts to the children equal to the amount of income tax paid.

Like a domestic spendthrift trust, an APT can be structured as either a complete or an incomplete gift for federal gift tax purposes. Again, this will depend in some cases on whether the creator of the trust has retained a power of appointment over the trust principal to make the gift incomplete. But one key difference between a domestic (U.S.) trust and an APT is that a gift to an APT may be complete even though the creator is a discretionary beneficiary of the trust. As noted above, under U.S. law, creditors can reach the maximum amount that can be distributed to the creator under the trust provisions. Thus, if the trustee has the discretion to distribute any part or all of the trust income or principal to the creator, the creator's creditors will be able to reach all of the assets held in the trust, since theoretically the trustee could give them all back to the creator. This ability of creditors to reach the assets of U.S. trusts in which the creator has a discretionary interest makes transfers to such trusts incomplete gifts.

This is not the case with APTs. No jurisdiction in which APTs are commonly created allows creditors to reach the assets of a trust that includes the creator as a discretionary beneficiary. Thus, under U.S. gift tax law, transfers to such trusts are completed gifts, provided the creator does not retain a power of appointment. This is a very major advantage over U.S. spendthrift trusts since, with an APT, the creator can get the estate planning benefit of making a completed gift and thus excluding the trust assets from his estate, while at the same time preserving the ability to get the trust assets back in the event his creditor problems someday disappear.

When Mr. Guile first hears of APTs, he is likely to make an immediate call to his travel agent and book the next flight to the Bahamas. He will undoubtedly assume that he has nothing to lose by creating an APT and that there is a strong possibility his creditors will never even learn about it. He will further assume that even if they do, forcing them to proceed offshore will make them settle for a fraction of the amount of the outstanding judgment against him.

Mr. Guile's assumptions are probably overly optimistic. First, it is doubtful that any reputable offshore bank will consent to acting as his trustee if it knows of the outstanding judgment against him. All of the jurisdictions commonly used for APTs have a threshold requirement that no fraudulent conveyance be involved in creating the trust, and banks commonly require a statement as to the creator's assets and liabilities, including contingent liabilities. Furthermore, it is quite likely that attorneys for Mr. Guile's creditors will not only discover the existence of the trust almost immediately through postjudgment discovery, but also will be able to commence an action within the appropriate jurisdiction before the statute of limitations runs out. Finally, in view of Mr. Guile's position, transferring funds offshore at this point is likely to be viewed as one more "badge of fraud" and seems certain to result in a finding of actual fraud.

Mr. Guile represents one extreme. But what if Mr. Clean were to create an APT? Would the simple fact of his transferring assets offshore necessarily be viewed as fraudulent in the event a claim is someday asserted against him? Certainly it should not be, since APTs serve important functions beyond mere asset protection. Primary among these is worldwide investment diversification, which has become so advisable in these days of global markets. While it may not be necessary to have an offshore trust to invest overseas, many of the banks that act as trustees of APTs have investment advisers with far greater knowledge and expertise about foreign investments than U.S. money managers. Another reason for an APT is the anonymity and confidentiality they provide with respect to personal financial matters. Such privacy is a matter of increasing concern for wealthy individuals.

Finally, APTs provide an estate planning function that domestic trusts lack. As noted above, it is possible for the creator of an APT to be a discretionary beneficiary of the APT and still have the trust excluded from his or her taxable estate, i.e., by making a completed gift. This result is ideal for those who want to pass on the income and appreciation earned by the trust to their children tax-free, but are concerned that someday, irrespective of potential creditors' claims, they may need to get the trust funds back. With an APT, the trustee would have the authority to make such a distribution back to the creator.

For all of the above reasons, Mr. Clean should have ample legal justification for creating an APT. Such justification would exist even if asset protection were his primary objective, since there is nothing wrong with an individual who has no present or likely creditors taking steps to secure his financial future.

Mr. Jitters, on the other hand, is more problematical. Because his concerns are more immediate, he runs the risk of creditors later claiming that merely creating the APT was evidence of fraudulent intent. In order to avoid such a claim, he should be certain to fund an APT with only a small portion of assets, leaving plenty behind with which to satisfy creditors' claims. In addition, there should be some independent purpose for creating the trust, such as the clear tax advantage of locking in the benefit of his $600,000 gift and estate tax exemption (or $1.2 million with the use of his spouse's exemption). If he proceeds in this manner, he should be able to create an APT without any additional concerns.

This chapter has explored various means of protecting one's assets from existing and potential creditors. As our analysis of Messrs. Clean, Jitters, and Guile has revealed, the degree of protection available will depend on the particular circumstances of the individual seeking it. For example, Mr. Clean is still free to choose from the entire array of asset protection devices described here, while Mr. Guile is probably not in a position to take any further action. Nevertheless, even Mr.

Guile has certain exemptions available to him, such as those for his 401(k) and IRA accounts.

For Mr. Jitters, proceeding with caution is advisable. Before he makes any transfers, a careful analysis of the likelihood that a claim will be asserted against him and upheld will be required. Furthermore, if he does choose to proceed, he should be sure to retain a sufficient portion of his assets so as to avoid a claim of constructive fraud.

As the Jitters case demonstrates, there are few clear answers in this murky area of the law. The success of the techniques described in this chapter will, in large part, turn on very subjective factors and the judge's or jury's perceptions of them. For this reason, for the great many individuals whose situations are not as clearcut as either Mr. Clean's or Mr. Guile's — and probably there are many shaky Mr. Jitters out there — seeking expert legal advice before taking any action is imperative.

XII

How the Rich Provide for Mistresses, Paramours, and Other "Secret" Beneficiaries

Given the mandate of the Seventh Commandment, it would seem that paramours have been around as long as there have been marriages.

Mistresses have been much more in the news of late because of the unveiling of Prince Charles's relationship with Camilla Parker Bowles. Their relationship, which contributed to the split between Prince Charles and Princess Diana, began on a note of irony. When the then Camilla Shand met the prince in 1972, she told him sassily, "My great-grandmother was the mistress of your great-great-grandfather. I feel we have something in common." In fact, Camilla's great-grandmother, Alice Keppel, was the last love of Queen Victoria's eldest son, Bertie. The 56-year-old Prince of Wales had had affairs with actresses Sarah Bernhardt and Lillie Langtry when he met Alice, the 29-year-old wife of George Keppel, an army officer. (Another irony is that Camilla's husband, Andrew Parker Bowles, is also a military officer.) Even after Bertie became King Edward VII, he vacationed on the Continent with his "confidante" in a relationship that was so openly acknowledged that Queen Alexandra invited her to the king's bedside when he was dying in 1910. Of all the royal confidantes, Alice Keppel may have described the role most deftly. "A royal mistress," she is reported to have said, "should curtsy first, then leap into bed."

Earlier British kings or kings-to-be had far more notorious liaisons. Charles II (reigned 1660–85), for example, had no legal heirs by his wife, Catherine of Braganza, but fathered some fourteen illegitimate children by seven of his countless mistresses. One of his liaisons, the actress Nell Gwyn, bore Charles two sons, the first of whom she threatened to throw from a high window because he had been given no royal title. Charles allegedly resolved the crisis by calling out, "Nell, don't kill the Duke of St. Albans!"

Of course, American presidents have not been a great deal purer. From the infamous relationship between Thomas Jefferson and Sally Hemings to Franklin Delano Roosevelt's longstanding love affair with Lucy Mercer Rutherfurd to John F. Kennedy's relationships with Marilyn Monroe and others, the private lives of our presidents have never been models for happy marriages. Grover Cleveland fathered an illegitimate child. Warren Gamaliel Harding, everyone's choice for the president who most looked like a president should, had a long extramarital relationship with Carrie Phillips as well as a torrid affair with Nan Britton, which included lovemaking in a White House cloakroom while a Secret Service man stood guard. Alice Glass, Lyndon Johnson's mistress for almost thirty years, with a bow to Lysistrata, denied him sex because of her opposition to the Vietnam War. Even Dwight David Eisenhower seems to have had a mistress, his wartime chauffeuse and secretary, Kay Summersby.

Men or women with disclosed paramours generally would not have the problem of providing for them secretly. They can do so openly. I have earlier discussed my advice on the legal and tax advantages of adopting a mistress (see pp. 86–92).

But what of the person who wants to provide for a lover but also hopes to spare his or her mate and children the pain and embarrassment of learning about the other relationship? Also, assume that the person has a naturally suspicious or very curious surviving spouse. Creating financial benefits for a paramour under these circumstances and in a legal and private manner is not a simple thing to do.

It was once thought that giving one's paramour an insurance policy on one's life might solve the problem. However, insurance generally does not work well in these cases. The owner of a policy on someone's life has to have a legally insurable interest, and loving is not enough to create that interest. However, such an interest could be created indirectly.

Also, any life insurance policy on an insured's life will have to be disclosed at death in the insured's estate tax return, even if the insured did not own it at death and even if it is not includable in the insured's taxable estate, so there goes the secrecy. Finally, the money to pay the premiums is a gift each year and may present both gift tax and disclosure problems. In some cases, however, if the insured has a compliant executor and a spouse who is likely to take a passive role in the insured's estate administration and who is generally not suspicious, insurance may well be the best route for the insured to take in order to provide for a lover.

What, then, is the legally most discreet and effective way to benefit a lover during life and at death?

A person can make small lifetime gifts (i.e., $10,000 or less per year), directly or indirectly, without detection, since there is no need to report such gifts. Tax reporting requirements apply to gifts in excess of $10,000 a year to any one beneficiary, which seemingly rules out larger direct lifetime gifts to a secret paramour. With larger gifts, the donor is required to file a gift tax return identifying the beneficiary and to pay a gift tax. Further, at the donor's death the gift tax returns are filed with the estate tax return. However, a person may not wish to make lifetime gifts in any event but rather to provide for the mistress only at death in case the relationship ends before the person's death.

Lifetime gifts or bequests at death of any size can probably be made indirectly. But in order to make this arrangement work, the donor must resort to a "beard"—a ruse that has been used to camouflage illicit liaisons since Shakespearean times. In this case, the "beard" is not a convenient escort or "faux-lover" but a trusted—and hopefully, trustworthy—friend who will agree to be the nominal beneficiary of the gift but will in fact act secretly to transfer the gift or bequest to the person's lover. Although the person's family will probably become aware of the gift or bequest, the gift or bequest should not arouse much suspicion, since the trusted friend or adviser is arguably "a natural object of the person's bounty."

Thus, an individual could give property outright during life or leave a legacy in his will to a trusted friend who has secretly agreed to convey it outright to the decedent's lover or hold it in a trust for the lover's benefit. Remembering Samuel Goldwyn's admonition about the value of an oral contract, it is generally preferable for such a secret agreement to be a written secret agreement.

Another approach is for a person to create a "secret trust" during lifetime to provide for a lover at death. For example, this could work as follows:

A man puts $250,000 into a revocable trust of which he is sole trustee during his lifetime. The income and principal of the trust could be distributed to the trust creator in the discretion of the trustee. Upon the creator's death, the remaining principal is to be distributed in equal shares to two trusted friends or, if only one of them is living at that time, to the survivor of them. The friends are also to act as successor trustees.

Simultaneously, with the creation of this trust, the trust creator enters into a "nominee agreement" with his friends in which each of them agrees to distribute all property received from the trust to the creator's mistress. If the mistress predeceases the creator or there is a falling-out between them, the creator would revoke the trust. If his mistress predeceases him and he fails to revoke the trust, the nominee agreement provides that the friends would let the trust property pass pursuant to the terms of the creator's will.

Since the creator is the sole trustee during his lifetime and the trust is revocable in his sole discretion, he has complete control over the assets during his lifetime and can alter or revoke at any time what will ultimately pass to his mistress. Also, because of such retained powers in the trust creator, there are no gift tax or income tax consequences to the creator during his lifetime, or any need to disclose the trust to the tax or other authorities. Further, although his family may become aware of his lifetime transfer to a trust at his death because the trust proceeds will be includable in the creator's estate and the trust agreement will be filed with the creator's estate tax return, this transfer should not arouse any suspicion, since his two friends were arguably among the "natural objects of his bounty." Finally, since there were two friends who agreed to effectuate his intentions, he minimized the risk that the disposition for his mistress would be defeated if one friend predeceased him.

An elaborate variation on this theme was devised by one very rich fellow with a plethora of mistresses to whom he wanted to make lifetime gifts. This fellow created a large trust and named his friends, descendants, and employees as trust beneficiaries. He paid a gift tax and named trusted friends and advisers as trustees. The trustees were authorized to add and remove trust beneficiaries during this man's life. Thus, as new affiliations with confidantes were made, the trustees could add them as beneficiaries and distribute trust assets to them. When relationships ended, the paramours could be removed entirely as beneficiaries. Although, at the man's death, the trust agreement would have to be filed with his estate tax return, presumably these separate designations and removals of trust beneficiaries would not have to be. This very flexible trust worked quite nicely in that case.

However, in order to structure a transaction in any of these ways, one must be able to rely on a friend or some other trusted individual, adviser, or nonamorous confidante to carry out one's intentions in a discreet and secret manner.

These are only a few of the approaches to the problem of discreetly bestowing financial benefits on a lover. The same problems — legally and morally — apply to providing secretly for a child born out of wedlock. It is difficult to explore this topic in more detail, because each factual situation seems unique and requires very careful, thoughtful, and sensitive legal planning if the goal of secrecy is to be achieved. Considering the difficulties involved in planning and executing the legal maneuvers necessary to provide for a secret lover, it is no wonder the Restoration playwright William Wycherley mused: "Next to the pleasure of meeting your new mistress, is the pleasure of getting rid of your old one."

XIII

The Last (Best?) Refuge
of the Rich: Expatriation

As previously explained, almost every U.S. citizen of wealth faces federal estate taxes of 55% at death (or the death of his or her spouse)
with an 80% to 85% toll because of the generation-skipping tax for
transfers to grandchildren or more remote descendants.

Furthermore, the United States is virtually the only industrial country in the world (Norway may be the other) that seriously imposes
significant income and death taxes on the worldwide income and assets
of every citizen even if the citizen is domiciled elsewhere. Almost all
other countries impose income and death taxes only on persons actually residents of or domiciled within that country or on income earned
there or on property actually located there.

Given our hefty taxes, the demise of Communism, the relative
safety and comfort of other jurisdictions, the speed of travel, and the
sophistication of telecommunications, more U.S. citizens seem to be
considering renouncing their citizenship, i.e., expatriation, obtaining a
new citizenship, and taking up a domicile in a foreign country.

I used to think that expatriates were like ghosts: everyone talks about them but no one has seen one. Yet, in fact, there are Americans, usually sophisticated and usually quite rich, who will do almost anything to avoid taxes, and perhaps the last, best refuge of such tax avoidance addicts may be expatriation. It has been called the ultimate estate plan.

And there may be many more expatriates than meet our eyes. William Holden, the actor, years ago generated much publicity when he changed his legal domicile to Kenya. Ted E. Arison, the billionaire owner of Carnival Cruise Lines, has expatriated in favor of Israel, where he was born. Some years ago, a State Department publication indicated that about 350 persons renounced their U.S. citizenship annually. In 1993, 306 Americans took the step.

An extraordinarily rich Chinese American not long ago gave up his U.S. citizenship for citizenship from the People's Republic of China (yes, China, not Taiwan) to save many millions *yearly* in income tax, not to mention the enormous gift and estate tax savings. Two other Chinese Americans, residing and prospering in Hong Kong, renounced their U.S. citizenship, took up citizenship in Ireland while continuing to live in Hong Kong. A prosperous New York lawyer decided to retire, took up residence in the Bahamas, renounced his U.S. citizenship and purchased a passport (and citizenship) from the small Caribbean island, St. Kitts.

Another expatriate who did recently get attention in the press is billionaire Kenneth Dart, a member of the family that owns Dart Container, which makes more than 50% of the thirty billion polystyrene cups sold every year in the United States. He and his family are also Salomon Inc.'s second-largest shareholder. Mr. Dart, who is president of Dart Container, gave up his U.S. citizenship and became a citizen of Belize (formerly British Honduras), a small Caribbean country known mostly for two things — its scuba diving and its status as a tax haven. Belize does not tax any income earned outside of it and has no death or estate taxes. Apparently Mr. Dart's wife and children have remained in Sarasota, Florida, from where he and his father run and control Dart Container.

Other current countries of choice for U.S. expatriates appear to be

Ireland, Israel, Portugal, Switzerland, Monaco, Costa Rica, and various Caribbean countries. Some of these countries, like Ireland and Israel, are easier to become citizens of if the person expatriating has ancestral, religious, or other ties (often economic) to the new country. One can apparently secure a Swiss "forfait" whereby one buys a Swiss residency (not citizenship) by making a payment to the Swiss authorities. The amount of the payment, as well as the Swiss income and estate tax consequences, are negotiable with the Swiss cantonal authorities.

What then is expatriation all about and how is it done? What are the basic tax and legal issues that arise if a U.S. citizen gives up his or her citizenship and moves to a foreign jurisdiction?

RENUNCIATION OF CITIZENSHIP

Renouncing citizenship is a very significant act that involves more than just tax considerations. I have strong reservations against it, although my reservations are personal rather than legal.

There is, of course, a practical, nontax aspect to renunciation, namely, the need to have already obtained, or to obtain simultaneously with the renunciation, citizenship in another country. The consequences of being stateless are unacceptable to any thinking person. Some persons believe that one should seek citizenship only in a "first world" country such as Canada or Ireland. Others are not so choosy about where they take citizenship, especially when they then become domiciled in a country other than the one granting citizenship. It appears, for example, that Mr. Dart will not be domiciled in Belize but in the Cayman Islands or some other jurisdiction more suitable to his lifestyle. There are countries where citizenship and the corresponding passport are for sale for from $15,000 to $40,000.

In acquiring an actual domicile in another country, which, as I have mentioned, often is not the new country of citizenship, political and economic stability obviously must be fully taken into account. Also, the laws of the new country must be carefully examined, since they may affect whom your fiduciaries can be and how easily and to whom you can dispose of property. For example, there may be forced heirship rights, as in France, or other restrictions on death-time dispositions of property, as in Japan.

The actual renunciation is easily accomplished. One files an Oath of Renunciation at a U.S. embassy or consulate in a foreign country. There seems to be no recognized method for renouncing citizenship while one is physically present in the United States. Renunciation results in the automatic revocation of one's U.S. passport, which must be physically turned over to the U.S. consular official at the time of renunciation.

So, in summary, before the tax avoidance addict actually goes through the renunciation process, he or she should have secured a viable citizenship (and passport or other travel documents) in another country.

GIVING UP A U.S. RESIDENCE

Of major significance is that for a U.S. citizen to avoid income and estate taxes on worldwide assets and income it is not enough to renounce citizenship. He or she must also establish a domicile outside the United States and must limit the number of days spent in the United States in any given year.

U.S. residence has different meanings depending on which U.S. tax is involved.

For gift and estate tax purposes, residence means "domicile." The relevant IRS regulation states

> A person acquires a domicile in a place by living there, for even a brief period of time, with no definite present intention of later removing therefrom. Residence without the requisite intention to remain indefinitely will not suffice to constitute domicile, nor will intention to change domicile effect such a change unless accompanied by actual removal.

Thus, to change domicile to a foreign country an expatriate must prove he or she has acquired a foreign residence and has abandoned his or her U.S. residence with no intention of returning to it. These are some of the most important steps to be taken:

1. Purchase a residence in the foreign country and spend "considerable" time there.

2. Sell any United States residence (or change ownership, perhaps by gift). This is not absolutely essential but is highly desirable if consistent with the pattern of life envisioned after changing domicile. If possible, it should be done before the date on which change of domicile is to take effect.

3. Inform the local board of elections, stating that you no longer reside in the United States, and have your name removed from the voter registration rolls. If possible, register to vote in the foreign country.

4. Make sure all tax returns reflect your new status as a foreign resident and citizen.

5. In your next will, and in all other documents that recite residence, use the new foreign address.

6. Cancel any driver's license issued by a state in the United States and obtain a foreign driver's license. (It also may be desirable to obtain an international license.) Do not keep cars registered in any state in the United States.

7. Convert religious and club memberships and other U.S. affiliations, to the extent possible, to nonresident status.

8. Comply with any procedures required for permanent resident status in the foreign country, if different from the new country of citizenship.

Residency is tested differently for income tax purposes than it is for estate and gift tax purposes. Domicile is not the test. Even if you are "domiciled" in another country, you may be deemed to be a U.S. resident for income tax purposes in a year in which you spend too many days in the United States. Thus, if a person spends a total of 183 days or more of a calendar year in the United States, he or she will be deemed a resident for that year. If a person spends 30 or fewer days in the United States in a calendar year, he or she will not be a resident for that year. Any part of a day in the United States, even one minute, can count as a full day.

The rules are somewhat complicated for time spent in the United States of more than 30 days but less than 183 days in one year. To simplify these rules in a nutshell, after a period of time an expatriate can arrange his affairs so if he spends 121 days (in total about four months, but the 121 days need not be consecutive days) or fewer each year he will not become subject to U.S. income taxes on his or her worldwide income.

U.S. ESTATE AND GIFT TAX CONSEQUENCES OF EXPATRIATION

If U.S. citizenship is renounced and a non-U.S. domicile is successfully acquired, then the expatriate generally will be treated the same as any nonresident alien, and thus be subject to U.S. estate tax only on property located in the United States (often referred to as U.S. situs assets). Property located in the United States includes real estate and tangible personal property (e.g., art, furniture, and furnishings) *physically located* within the United States, shares of stock of U.S. corporations, and debt securities of most U.S. issuers, including U.S. corporate bonds, municipal bonds, and Treasury securities.

The generally accepted way nonresident aliens (expatriates included) avoid U.S. estate tax on their property located in the U.S. is simply to transfer such property to a foreign corporation, which will not itself be deemed to be located in the United States. However, U.S. real estate, e.g., a house or cooperative apartment, transferred to a foreign corporation will itself trigger a U.S. capital gains tax. What a wealthy nonresident alien who wishes to keep a residence here or who cannot sell it without a huge taxable gain may do is borrow out by a nonrecourse mortgage most of the value of the residence so that the net equity of the U.S. residence, which is subject to U.S. estate tax, will be quite small.

The federal gift tax applies only to gifts by nonresident aliens (expatriates) of real property and tangible personal property located in the United States. It does not apply to the transfer of intangible personal property (stock or funds) by nonresident aliens, even if such property has a U.S. situs.

U.S. INCOME TAX CONSEQUENCES OF EXPATRIATION

An expatriate not conducting a U.S. business or working here is generally taxed only on some U.S. "source income," which is income from U.S. situs assets, as explained above, including such income as rents, dividends, interest, and salary. Under current law, gains realized by an expatriate upon the sale of assets (other than U.S. real estate) are generally exempt from U.S. income tax.

However, there are special "anti-avoidance" tax provisions. These are special rules that attempt to tax the expatriate who has surrendered citizenship and taken up domicile elsewhere if one of the principal purposes of the expatriation was tax avoidance. If so, the expatriate, then called, somewhat pejoratively, a "tax expatriate," can remain subject to special United States tax rules for a ten-year period from and after the date of the renunciation of citizenship.

The initial burden is on the Internal Revenue Service to demonstrate that one of the principal purposes for the loss of citizenship is tax avoidance. To meet that burden, the Internal Revenue Service must only establish that it is reasonable to believe that the expatriate's loss of U.S. citizenship would result in a substantial reduction in taxes. Once that has been established, the burden of proving that avoidance of taxes was not one of the principal purposes for the loss of citizenship shifts to the taxpayer. For example, it would appear from the information in the public press that Mr. Dart, newly a citizen of Belize, has a real problem with this anti-tax-avoidance rule.

Under these special tax rules, the tax expatriate is subject to U.S. income tax on all gains from the sale of (i) property located in the United States; (ii) stock of U.S. corporations; and (iii) debt securities of U.S. issuers (including the U.S. and municipal governments). As noted above, nonresident aliens normally are not subject to tax on such capital gains. These taxes are in addition to regular U.S. income taxes on U.S. dividends, interest, rents, and other U.S. income. In addition, for such ten-year period, the tax expatriate is taxed at the higher of (i) the usual tax applicable to nonresident aliens (i.e., currently a flat 30% withholding tax) and (ii) the tax applicable to U.S. citizens and residents (now about 40%). Thus, for the ten-year period, for income tax purposes, the tax expatriate would consider realigning his portfolio to hold debt securities of foreign issuers or tax-exempt U.S. securities. If such a realignment is made, even if an individual is determined to be subject to the special tax rules because of a tax-motivated expatriation, he or she should not have any U.S. income tax liability. However, the tax expatriate may be faced with huge U.S. capital gains in changing his or her assets to foreign, non-taxable assets. There may be ways to avoid such capital gains on U.S. assets (other than real estate), e.g., by the use of an intermediate foreign corporation, that are beyond the scope of this book to explain in detail.

In the estate and gift tax areas, anti-avoidance rules also apply. Simply using a foreign corporation to hold U.S. assets (other than U.S. real estate) does not work for the tax expatriate as it does for the typical nonresident alien. Nevertheless, because of changes in the estate tax law implemented after the enactment of this special anti-avoidance rule, the rule has little practical effect. The only impact of the anti-avoidance rule seems to be that for the ten-year period after the loss of citizenship, stock of certain closely held foreign corporations owned by the tax expatriate at his or her death is included in the U.S. estate but only to the extent the foreign corporations own assets located in the United States.

In the gift tax area, if the anti-avoidance rules apply, for the ten-year period after the expatriation, the tax expatriate will be subject to gift tax on gifts of stocks of U.S. corporations. However, there seems to be a relatively easy way around this problem. If the tax expatriate places his or her U.S. assets in a foreign corporation, he or she can then give away the stock of the foreign corporation without incurring gift tax. A tax expatriate, like any nonresident alien, can give away non-U.S.-located assets at any time without a gift tax.

If all of this seems very complicated, it is. Expatriation may lead one to a tax avoider's Nirvana, but it's not bad for lawyers either. In all events, extreme caution and highly complex legal and financial planning are needed if expatriation is not to be a trap for the unwary instead of a refuge for the sophisticated.

XIV

How to Compensate Fiduciaries and Lawyers

FEES FOR EXECUTORS AND TRUSTEES

The compensation of your executor and trustee is fixed by statute in most jurisdictions. In some cases, precise dollar amounts are stipulated, based on the size of the fund administered. In many states a standard of "reasonable compensation" is set forth in the governing law. These fees or commissions can be substantial.

For example, a statutory fee for an executor in New York is 5% of the first $100,000 in assets disposed of by the will, 4% of the next $200,000, 3% of the next $700,000, 2.5% of the next $4 million, and 2% of the balance.

The New York statute allows up to three full commissions to be paid to individual executors and trustees by an estate or trust for persons dying or lifetime trusts established on or before August 31, 1993. For persons dying or lifetime trusts established after August 31, 1993, no more than two full commissions can be paid unless the decedent specifically provided otherwise in a signed writing. Milton Petrie, a New Yorker, died in 1994 at age 92, leaving an estate estimated at $900 million. His eight executors (an unusually large and, I think, excessive number) will share two full commissions, roughly 4% of the estate, or approximately $4.5 million each.

California's executors' commissions are 4% of the first $15,000, 3% of the next $85,000, 2% of the next $900,000, and 1% of the excess over $1 million.

Until recently, Florida's commissions for a personal representative (the Florida equivalent of an executor) were based on "reasonable compensation." Under a law that took effect for decedents dying after October 1, 1993, commissions are 3% of the first $1 million, 2.5% of the next $4 million, 2% of the next $5 million, and 1.5% of the excess over $10 million.

Trustees' commissions are generally paid on an annual basis and can also vary from state to state. In New York, the annual commission for an individual is 1.05% of the first $400,000 of principal, 0.45% of the next $600,000, and 0.3% of the value of the principal over $1 million, plus a 1% commission on all principal assets paid out of the trust. In New York, this annual fee is charged one-third to income and two-thirds to principal, unless otherwise directed.

Florida has no statutory scheme for the payment of trustees' fees. Accordingly, rates vary widely throughout the state. One large bank in Palm Beach County charges the following annual fees, based on market value of principal, for acting as trustee: $1,500 base fee *plus* 1% of the first $1 million, 0.75% of the next $1 million, 0.50% of the next $8 million, and 0.375% of the excess over $10 million. This annual fee is charged one-half to income and one-half to principal, unless otherwise directed.

Also in Florida many corporate trustees charge a fee of 1% of the value of principal paid out by distribution or termination.

An important point, which many people seem to be either unaware of or too inhibited to raise, is that fiduciary fees are negotiable. Leading corporate fiduciaries can be very flexible and reasonable. Even the banks least likely to negotiate their fees will do so if the circumstances are right, i.e., in most cases — if the estate is large enough. Two of the best corporate fiduciaries, which generally refuse to negotiate their fiduciary fees, agreed (at least in two cases with which I was involved) to make reasonable, special fee arrangements for estates of $100 million or more.

It is interesting to compare executors' and trustees' fees of leading New York corporate fiduciaries, as the differences that exist, or can be negotiated, are often quite substantial. But, of course, one must also be aware of the different strengths and weaknesses of the various institutions.

Depending on your relationship with the particular bank, you may wish to negotiate fiduciary fees directly or to interpose your lawyer or other adviser as the negotiator.

Ideally, fees should be discussed with your fiduciaries while you are alive and then set forth by letter agreement or by the provisions of the will or trust. It is equally important to agree upon fees for your individual executors and trustees.

While it is advisable to set fees before death, it is not impossible to do so even after death, depending on the terms of the will or trust, particularly its provisions on successor fiduciaries and on the power to remove a corporate fiduciary. However, inexperienced widows and non-business-oriented children are least inclined to negotiate such matters after death. It is a great disservice to leave open such fee matters, as was demonstrated vividly in the fight over trustees' fees in the estate of Henry Ford II.

I am always surprised when hard-nosed businessmen, accustomed to negotiating all sorts of fees with their investment bankers, lawyers, and accountants, seem neither to know how nor to want to negotiate fees with their executors and trustees. I attribute this, at least in some cases, to a general psychological reluctance to confront issues relating to death. Especially in large estates, it is inadvisable to leave fee questions up in the air, as this many times leads to disputes and acrimony later.

FEES FOR LAWYERS

Lawyers who represent estates often charge by the hour; or, like an executor, by a fixed fee based on a percentage of the estate; or by some variation of these alternatives. The trend seems to be to handle most estates, like most other legal matters, on a strict time basis, but the practice varies a great deal from state to state and even from one law firm to another.

The danger of compensating lawyers by a percentage fee like an executor was dramatically demonstrated in the estate of Andy Warhol. The sole executor of the estate, Frederick W. Hughes, agreed to pay Edward W. Hayes, the lawyer, whom he selected to represent the estate, 2% of the value of the estate. Mr. Hayes, a former Bronx County prosecutor, collected $4.85 million, and then in April 1992 he sued the estate (and later Mr. Hughes personally), alleging that the Warhol estate was grossly undervalued. Surrogate Eve Preminger of New York County ruled that the art appraisals were off by a factor of four, and that the estate was worth $509 million, not $220 million as had been estimated. Mr. Hayes stands to gain approximately $5 million more in fees, but the legal fight continues, at what seems a greater legal cost than a settlement, with the estate arguing that Mr. Hayes did so little he should return part of his earlier fee.

In fact, under a new Florida statute that is effective for estates in existence after October 1, 1993, lawyers are entitled to receive, without court order, 2% of the value of the estate's probate assets and the income earned on the estate during administration *plus* 1% of the value of the nonprobate assets *plus* the lawyers' time charges (and the time charges of the individuals working under the lawyers' supervision) at a reasonable hourly rate. These fees are presumed to be reasonable compensation for estate administration. They too, of course, are negotiable. Another question that often arises is the appropriate compensation of a lawyer who is to serve in a dual capacity — usually as an executor and as legal counsel to the estate.

Most states permit a lawyer to have dual service, i.e., to act as a fiduciary (executor or trustee) and as lawyer for the fiduciary. It is often appropriate when the lawyer has a long-standing relationship with the client and also, in many cases, with the client's family. A lawyer serving in both capacities should clearly inform the client of the alternatives and the costs of such dual service. This notification is particularly important because of the loss of the check that a separate fiduciary provides on the amount of fees sought by the lawyer and vice versa. A client is properly informed if the lawyer explains the role and duties of the fiduciary, the ability of a nonlawyer to serve as fiduciary with legal and other professional assistance (e.g., investment advice), and the comparative costs of appointing the lawyer or another person or institution as fiduciary.

In 1993, California adopted legislation restricting the methods by which a client may appoint the client's lawyer as a fiduciary. If an individual who has a fiduciary relationship to the transferor who drafts, transcribes, or causes to be drafted or transcribed any instrument of transfer (i.e., will, trust, deed, etc.), including relatives, cohabitants, and partners and employees of such individuals, such individual is defined as a "disqualified person." Such an individual who is named as a sole fiduciary may be removed unless the court finds that it is fair, just, and equitable that he or she continue to serve as such. "Disqualified" status may be avoided if the otherwise disqualified person is related by blood or marriage to or is a cohabitant with the transferor or if an *independent* attorney certifies (on a statutorily prescribed form) that the transfer was not the product of fraud, menace, duress, or undue influence. The legislation also places limits on dual compensation for an attorney who is also acting as a fiduciary.

A related matter is the propriety of a lawyer's drawing a will or trust that directs a fiduciary to retain the lawyer as his or her counsel. It is usually unnecessary to designate any particular lawyer to serve as counsel to the fiduciary or to direct the fiduciary to retain a particular lawyer. Before drawing a document in which a fiduciary is directed to retain the lawyer-draftsperson as counsel, such lawyer should advise the client that it is neither necessary nor customary to include this direction in a will or trust. A client who wishes to include such a direction should be advised as to whether or not it is binding on the fiduciary under the governing law. In most states such a direction is usually not binding on a fiduciary, who is generally free to select and retain legal counsel of his or her own choice without regard to such a direction.

Lawsuits have been brought against lawyers for overreaching in this area of dual compensation. To prevent such conflict, two surrogates (probate judges) in Queens and Suffolk counties of New York have established their own court rules requiring that if an attorney is named in a will as a fiduciary, the testator execute an affidavit stating (i) that he was advised that the attorney/fiduciary may be entitled to legal fees *as well as* a statutory commission for serving as executor or trustee or both; (ii) that the testator was advised of the possibility of multiple commissions if the attorney is named as a cofiduciary; and (iii) the testator's reasons for nominating the attorney to serve as fiduciary. Although this rule goes further than many courts and others would require, proof that the client made his or her choice with an awareness of its financial consequences does seem appropriate. Such proof can be established far more civilly by a specific fee letter between the lawyer and the client or specific fee provisions in the will or trust. Under the new Florida statute, a lawyer for an estate who also acts as personal representative (executor) for the estate is entitled to be compensated in both capacities.

What is the appropriate arrangement for a lawyer acting in the dual capacity of fiduciary/lawyer? Generalizations, as usual, don't work well. As previously indicated, in some cases the client genuinely wants the lawyer for the two separate roles and expects to compensate the lawyer for both. Fees for either or both roles are negotiable in any event, and that does not change because the lawyer is acting in two capacities. Bear in mind that the lawyer has two responsibilities and therefore can be held liable for damages for quite different conduct in each separate role. If the lawyer operates at risk in both roles, why should he or she be compensated for only one?

It seems unfair that a lawyer's actual time spent in carrying out both roles should not be compensated for in some manner, but there are no hard and fast rules in this area. Some lawyers will charge one-half an executor's commission as well as their agreed-upon legal fee. Others will take no executor's commission as such on the condition that their time for all services — legal and executorial — be compensated for on the same basis, usually their normal hourly billing charge, or by a single executor's commission, whichever is greater.

Many lawyers who are willing to waive executor's commissions will not waive trustee's commissions, partly because the trustee's functions are ongoing and often involve exercising more sensitive discretionary powers, and the annual fees are much less than the one-time, large executor's commission. Also, there may be little practical difference between paying a lawyer the trustee's commission or his or her customary time charges.

All too frequently, persons are intimidated or otherwise unwilling to discuss the matter of fees with their lawyers during their lifetimes. Widows and widowers often are less well equipped to do so, especially in the first months after the death. But whatever the arrangement, fiduciary and legal fees should be openly and thoroughly discussed, understood, and agreed upon before your death.

XV

Living Wills, Health Care Proxies, and the Right to Die

If there is one legal document that you should have, whether rich or poor, old or young, it is a health care proxy or some other recognized legal document that explains your intentions concerning your future medical care.

Why should everyone no matter what his or her wealth have a living will or other health care directive? Remember Sunny Von Bulow. She has remained in a deep, irreversible coma with no reasonable chance of recovering any meaningful mental function since December 1980. The cost of her care at Columbia-Presbyterian Hospital in New York City, with a private room and private nurses, is estimated to be over $500,000 per year. Her loving children, Alexander and Ala von Auersperg, continue to keep the machines on, so she stays alive technically. (Ironically and tragically, their father also suffered an irreversible coma as a result of an automobile accident.) One assumes if Sunny Von Bulow had left a living will expressly stating her wishes to terminate such measures in her circumstances, then her children would feel free to have the machines turned off and utilize that money for one of their favorite charitable causes.

A health care directive may authorize your named representative (usually a spouse, a child, or a close friend) to make health care decisions for you if you cannot do so yourself for any reason, for example, because of injury or mental incapacity. It can also instruct your treating physician to cease all heroic measures to keep you alive if there is no quality left to your life and no hope of your recovery.

These advance directives for health care have different names in different states — "living wills," "health care proxies," "durable powers of attorney for health care," "declarations relating to the use of life-sustaining procedures" — and set different limits on the authority you can delegate and the circumstances under which you can refuse treatment. Generally, these documents are of two varieties: a statement of the kind of treatment you do or do not want in the event you are diagnosed with a terminal illness or an illness from which there is no medical probability of your recovery, and your designation of a person authorized to make medical treatment decisions for you if for any reason you are unable to make them yourself.

The events triggering the use of these documents differ, and although some states have adopted a narrow definition of terms such as "terminal condition," "permanent unconsciousness," "dementia," and "persistent vegetative state," one thing is clear: by executing an advance medical directive you are doing all you can to ensure that if you are ever ill and cannot make your own medical decisions, your wishes will be carried out to the extent allowed by law.

The benefits of a living will or other health care directive are economically as well as psychologically important. A recent study in *Archives of Internal Medicine* of Medicare patients indicated that for 342 patients who had not left oral or written instructions about what kind of treatment they wanted, the average in-patient charges during the final hospital stay of their lives was $95,305, whereas for 132 patients who did leave instructions, the average charges were $30,478. In short, older people with living wills or other documents setting forth the extent of medical care that they want spend about one-third as much on their final hospital stays as those without such provisions. Nevertheless, other studies show that fewer than 15% of Americans have living wills or their equivalents, and the estimated cost of life support systems for people whose families claim they did not want their lives prolonged is $10 billion annually.

You must keep in mind a few important things when you execute an advance directive setting forth your health care wishes:

First, although all fifty states now have some type of law governing advance directives, the rules vary widely from state to state. (See the Appendix for maps illustrating the various state laws.) Therefore, make sure that the documents you sign are valid in the state where you live and that they are executed properly, in the presence of the required number of witnesses and, if necessary, notarized. Also, if you spend significant time in other states, where you have a summer home or a business office, for example, you should execute health care documents for those states as well. Appropriate forms (which you can prepare yourself without formal legal assistance) and instructions for completing and signing them can be obtained through your doctor or lawyer, a local senior citizens' organization, or Choice in Dying, a national organization that promotes the dissemination of information concerning advance directive rights. (See the Appendix for examples of forms used in New York, California, New Jersey, and Florida.)

Second, you should know the philosophy of your chosen health care agent and of your doctor and the health care facilities with which he or she is affiliated. For example, if your brother, as your designated health care agent, believes in prolonging life at all costs, it will probably be difficult, if not impossible, for him to make the decision as your agent to remove you from life support systems. Also, have a frank discussion with your doctor about his or her philosophy and approach concerning the continuation of care for a terminally ill patient, since some physicians are more willing than others to avoid hospital red tape in order to carry out a patient's wishes. Consider too whether a particular hospital's religious affiliation may make it more difficult for your intentions to be carried out. For example, if a hospital has a policy of refusing to terminate life support systems, a patient must be transferred to another facility before treatment can be withdrawn.

Third, remember that an advance directive becomes effective *only* when you can no longer make medical decisions yourself. Therefore, you must make sure your health care agent, your family, your friends, and your doctor know what decisions you want them to make. Do you want to be kept alive on a respirator even though there is no real hope you will ever regain consciousness? At what point, if any, do you want the administration of food and water withdrawn if you are terminally ill? Do you want to stop all medicines except those necessary to alleviate pain and make you as comfortable as possible?

The existence of advance medical directives, coupled with a clear understanding of your wishes, can save your loved ones a great deal of time and expense, not to mention the emotionally draining (and separately expensive) experience of fighting with hospital administrators or going to court to have your medical intentions carried out. As difficult as it may be to initiate these conversations, talking about your feelings in advance is crucial — and be certain that your conversations conform to your wishes as expressed in your written health care documents. Hospitals (and, unfortunately, courts) often place a great deal of weight on how explicitly and how consistently patients, when healthy, expressed their wishes about death and the continuation of treatment in a terminal situation. Of course, open discussions with your family and friends also may help to lessen their anxiety and trauma if it ever becomes necessary for them to make the difficult decision on your behalf to terminate life support measures.

Finally, give copies of your signed health care documents to your designated agents and to your doctors. In addition, if you are admitted to a hospital, have copies of these documents added to your hospital records. Carrying out your wishes may be impossible (or at least made much more complicated) if the persons involved in your care are unable to locate and produce the written authority needed.

The increasing number of living wills, health care proxies, and other advance medical directives that are signed every day reflects society's recognition that we each have the right, while competent, to make binding decisions about our future health treatment.

But what about the ill person who wants to take an even more aggressive approach to ending his or her life but who, because of circumstances, is unable to do it alone? Often, actions taken by family, friends, or medical personnel in such situations cross the line between legally withholding or withdrawing life support on the one hand and assisting suicide on the other.

Consider this example:

Barry was diagnosed as being HIV-positive three years ago, and until recently he was relatively free of symptoms. In the past few months, however, he has developed Kaposi's sarcoma skin lesions, and he has just recovered from a bout of *Pneumocystis carinii* pneumonia. Barry, who has watched many of his friends die slow, debilitating, and painful deaths from AIDS, is determined not to suffer that way. He tells his longtime companion that he intends to commit suicide before his illness progresses any further. To this end, Barry has already obtained a combination of drugs that, if taken together, should be sufficient to cause him to fall asleep and not wake up.

In his final hours, Barry plans to check into a luxurious New York City hotel, take in a Broadway play, have dinner at an elegant restaurant, and catch the last Bobby Short show at the Carlyle. Later, at the hotel, he will ingest the fatal medication. Because he is afraid to die alone, Barry asks his companion to accompany him for the evening, be in the hotel room when Barry takes the drugs, and stay with him until he dies. His friend can then leave the hotel unnoticed.

Although this sounds like a workable and, some would say, even civilized and humane plan, it is not without potential complications, both for Barry and for his companion. First, there is always the possibility that the medication will not result in Barry's death and that he will awaken in an impersonal hotel room or, perhaps worse, in a hospital. If death does occur, who will hotel personnel call when Barry's body is discovered? Since the cause of death is questionable, will an autopsy be required? Should Barry leave a note explaining his actions? Is Barry aware that if his death is recorded as a suicide and he recently purchased life insurance, his insurance company may not pay the insurance benefits? (In some states, including New York, an insurance company can withhold benefits if death is a result of suicide within two years from the date the policy was issued.)

In addition, Barry's friend must seriously consider not only his emotional ability to cope with the situation both during and after Barry's suicide, but also his actual response if things don't go as planned. For example, if Barry's death does not occur from the overdose of medication, will his friend expose himself to possible legal prosecution by taking some overt action to assist the suicide? Will he call for medical aid or will he simply walk away?

Even if he does nothing further, has Barry's friend committed a crime under state law? For example, some state laws (such as California) say that a person who deliberately aids, advises, or encourages another to commit suicide is guilty of a felony, whereas other states (such as New York) define the crime of promoting a suicide attempt as intentionally causing or aiding another person to commit suicide. Depending on the state in which a person's death occurs, as well as what actions the assisting friend or family member takes, these subtle and often indistinguishable variations in state laws can mean the difference between susceptibility to legal prosecution and conduct that does not cross over the line into illegality.

Barry's friend should also consider his real motives for helping Barry to die. Will he benefit financially, either through insurance or by will, from Barry's death? If so, could his assistance deprive him of his inheritance? If he stays with Barry (whether or not he actually assists in the suicide), will his friends and family view him as a murderer or as a compassionate ally?

Here is another example:

For five years, Elizabeth has been suffering from amyotrophic lateral sclerosis (Lou Gehrig's disease), a fatal degenerative disease. The disease is now progressing quickly, but although she is weak, Elizabeth still has some mobility. From time to time over the years, Elizabeth has complained to her doctor about insomnia and has received prescriptions for small doses of sleeping pills. Because of the increasing frequency of these complaints and Elizabeth's not-so-subtle questions regarding the toxicity of the drugs being prescribed, her doctor believes that Elizabeth is hoarding the pills so that she can accumulate enough to commit suicide.

By prescribing drugs that are appropriate to Elizabeth's condition but that can kill her if taken in large quantities, is Elizabeth's doctor actually assisting in her suicide? Once the doctor reasonably believes that Elizabeth actually intends to hoard the drugs and kill herself, is he ethically required to discuss the matter with her? Does the doctor then have an obligation personally to administer all prescribed drugs that are potentially life-threatening, thereby removing even more of Elizabeth's autonomy, or is he justified in "looking the other way" and allowing his patient to determine her own fate? Although one grand jury in New York State has refused to indict a physician for similar conduct, the law in the United States is by no means settled, and doctors who believe they are acting appropriately and compassionately may nonetheless run the risk of legal action and professional reprimand.

Still another example:

Maggie, a 55-year-old woman suffering from end-stage cancer, has a life expectancy of three to six months. She executed a living will explicitly authorizing the cessation of all chemotherapy and other treatment except medication to ease her pain, and for many years she discussed with her family her desire to die as quickly and painlessly as possible when her cancer progressed to this point. Maggie is being cared for at home, and although she appears mentally alert about a third of the time, she is physically unable to go anywhere without assistance. Maggie has asked her adult daughter to obtain a lethal dose of barbiturates, grind the pills up, mix the powder with applesauce, and leave the dish and a spoon by her bedside.

This is unlike the two previous examples, because there is no doubt that if Maggie's daughter complies with her mother's wishes, she will actively be assisting in a suicide, which is a felony in most states. Since the risk of prosecution, fines, and perhaps even imprisonment is clear, Maggie's daughter should think about her actions very carefully. Even if Maggie appears to remain firm in her wishes, does she in fact still have the mental capacity to make a decision of this magnitude? Is there another way to help Maggie live her remaining months peacefully — perhaps in a hospice or by altering her medication? Can her daughter alone evaluate her mother's convictions, or should she confide in another family member, a member of the clergy, a psychiatrist or her mother's doctor?

A final example:

Sam, who is 83, has resided in a nursing home for three years. During this time, his Alzheimer's disease has worsened to the point where he has no sense of time or place, cannot speak or respond to conversations, and does not recognize his family, friends, or medical caregivers. Sam is not able to manage for himself any of the "activities of daily living" (feeding, dressing, bathing, etc.). However, he will swallow food if spoon-fed by an aide, and he exhibits some minor responses to physical stimuli. Sam spends his days diapered, strapped in a wheelchair, alone in the hospital-like hallway.

Once a respected financial consultant with a thriving business and an active, exciting life, Sam repeatedly told his son that he never wanted to end up as a "vegetable" and that he would rather die than "rot away" in a nursing home. Seven years ago, when Sam first exhibited some early symptoms of Alzheimer's disease, he designated his son as his health care agent and made him promise to do whatever was necessary so that Sam could die with dignity. So long as Sam continued to have mental capacity, he reiterated those wishes. Now, when there is obviously nothing more that can be done for his father medically, Sam's son, in his capacity as health care agent, wants to direct the nursing home to stop providing his father with food and water.

These facts present perhaps the most difficult situation of all these cases. Even though Sam's son legally has the authority to make all health care decisions for his father (including the decision to withdraw or refuse life support), the nursing home will almost certainly initiate a court proceeding in response to a direction to stop feeding Sam. Understandably, the nursing home will be afraid to take the drastic step of withholding all food and water from a patient who is still able to swallow, and it will refuse to do so without the protection of a court order directing it to comply with the health care agent's instructions. And despite the fact that courts in many states define "medical treatment" to include not only the administration of medication but also the provision of nutrition (food) and hydration (water), the fact that Sam will eat if he is fed makes it unlikely that any court would order the nursing home to allow Sam to starve to death.

What, then, is the alternative? Sam's son could take his father out of the nursing home and allow him to die at home — although without proper medical care and supervision, the process would almost certainly be painful and frightening. Additionally, if Sam's son attempts to remove his father, the nursing home might go back to court and seek the appointment of an adult guardian for Sam who would have authority to override the son's decision.

The four situations described above raise many serious questions to which there are no real answers. Yet, these and other types of assisted suicides do, in fact, occur — more often than our legal system recognizes, despite the fact that the majority of states in this country have statutes expressly criminalizing such behavior (see Appendix for a map illustrating the various state laws), and more often than many patients, doctors, families, and friends are willing to admit publicly.

Few issues confronting us today are as politically, morally, and emotionally charged as the question of assisted suicide. However, as the publicity generated by *Final Exit* (a book that discusses in great detail practical aspects of suicide by a terminally ill individual) and Dr. Jack Kevorkian's recent actions in Michigan demonstrate, a significant segment of this country's population believes that assisted suicide — particularly physician-assisted suicide — should be legalized in certain circumstances. The more difficult question is what standards for physician aid in dying should be established, and who should establish them.

Perhaps the day may come in the not-too-distant future when our law will allow a terminally ill patient to end his or her life with dignity if certain narrowly tailored criteria are present. For example, such a proposed new law might include the following requirements:

1. The patient's condition must be terminal, and that diagnosis must be confirmed by at least two physicians, one of whom has had no prior relationship with the patient. All physicians must concur that the patient's death is imminent, which would be defined as meaning death is reasonably expected to occur naturally within a certain period, for example, three months.

2. The patient must be fully competent and understand his or her medical condition, prognosis, and treatment options.

3. The patient must request assistance in dying on more than two separate occasions. These requests must be in writing and must be witnessed by independent persons.

4. If possible, the patient's family and friends should be informed in advance of his or her decision to request assistance in dying.

5. The patient may change his or her mind at any time, either orally or in writing. If the patient's mental capacity diminishes and he or she is no longer capable of making medical decisions for himself, the request for assistance in dying will be deemed revoked.

6. The patient must have sole authority to determine the timing of his or her death. The patient must reaffirm the request to die immediately before any assistance is given.

7. Death will be assisted by a licensed physician as painlessly, quickly, and humanely as possible.

Obviously, these guidelines do not cover every situation, and many patients, such as those suffering from Alzheimer's disease, could not benefit from a law along these guidelines. But such guidelines may help to focus the attention of lawmakers, health care professionals, and the general public on the need for available options that truly reflect the attitudes and beliefs of our population.

The right to choose death with dignity, including a physician-assisted death, may well be the next great constitutional right, arising out of the right to privacy, to be fashioned by the U.S. Supreme Court as we approach the twenty-first century. It is, in my opinion, an idea whose time has come, and that needs the protection of our laws.

Section Five

MY LAST
WORDS

XVI

Some General Advice
for Wise Estate Planning

Let me conclude by trying to distill some general guidelines, advice, and recommendations about estates, wills, and trusts based on more than a quarter of a century of experience on the family firing lines.

INTRAFAMILY LITIGATION

A French lawyer left the following will: "I give 100,000 francs to the local madhouse. I obtained this money out of those who pass their lives in litigation; in bequeathing it for the use of lunatics I only make restitution."

The enmity, publicity, and costs of a family fight in court over money do not ordinarily justify the fight. In all events, talk, and then talk some more, to try to avoid it.

Do not pretend it's a matter of principle when usually it's only a matter of money. One of the worst mistakes is to sue and then negotiate on the theory that bringing the lawsuit will help settle the matter. The opposite is often true: as positions become fixed, publicity starts, discussions end, a court-designated guardian *ad litem* may be immediately appointed, and the genie is forever out of the bottle.

You can always draw up court papers, to show the other family member what is legally at stake, without filing them.

SELECTION OF FIDUCIARIES

Spend a lot of time picking an executor, trustee, or guardian. Consider the use of a reputable bank or trust company as an executor or trustee or both. Be clear on who the successors are to be, or — if you have not done so in the governing instrument — how successors are to be selected. Be explicit about fees — who is to get what, if anything, for serving. Review your choices periodically, and feel free to change your selections from time to time. Be certain your fiduciaries understand your familial and financial situations. Do not hide from them what they need to know to be effective, including any so-called skeletons in the closet.

Try to find fiduciaries whom your beneficiaries will respect and whose advice they will follow. The greatest gift that you may give your family may be your prudent selection of fiduciaries, to protect both the money and your beneficiaries.

CAVEATS TO EXECUTORS AND TRUSTEES

Remember that it may turn into a real pain in the neck to be an executor or trustee. Serving as a fiduciary is often neither an honor nor a game for beginners; it requires technical skills, experience, and an ability to get along with family members. It may take much more of your time than you ever contemplated and can result in substantial cost for liability for errors. Furthermore, be certain that you are adequately compensated for your time as well as for your exposure to liability. The latter can be a very serious matter. For example, a trustee may be held personally liable for cleanup of a hazardous waste site owned by the trust even though the trustee was not involved in the contaminations. And depending on the law governing the trust, the trustee may be held liable for one bad investment even though his or her overall investment performance is excellent.

Don't rush to be someone's fiduciary unless you fully understand what the position requires. Not only should the testator or testatrix know his or her executors and trustees; it may be equally important for fiduciaries to understand the testator's situation.

Often, people agree to be a fiduciary when they are unaware of existing or lurking family financial or personal problems that will cause all hell to break loose after death. If you are the right person to serve, you are entitled to know all the relevant facts. Obtaining such knowledge may require discreet or indiscreet questioning from you before your acceptance, but even if the questioning is awkward, it is better than not knowing.

HOW MUCH TO TELL YOUR CHILDREN

This is an age-old quandary. You do not want to stifle their initiative by telling them that they will inherit a lot of money. On the other hand, you don't want to hide the truth from them either — particularly if your own lifestyle is obviously affluent. You don't want to create anxiety over matters that they otherwise would not be concerned about one way or the other. You do want them to know what you expect of them.

Certainly, there is an age before which children will not even comprehend much about their future inheritance. Each situation requires separate analysis (if not psychoanalysis). I think the best approach is to teach your children good values about money early, and with luck the rest may fall into place, including a desire on their part to be productive. That, of course, is always easy to say, but not so easy to do.

SOPHISTICATED ESTATE PLANNING TAX ADVICE

Too many people who would never make a move in their businesses without the most up-to-date tax advice will leave wills and estate plans that achieve no real tax savings. They often leave all of their estates to their spouses (only thereby deferring, but not avoiding, the 55% federal death taxes) and then to their children.

They do not consider whether GRITs, GRATs, CRATs, CLATs, and family partnerships, explained in earlier chapters, fit their situations, as well as other death-tax-saving devices like irrevocable insurance trusts, lifetime gifts, and the creative use of private charitable foundations. If you would prefer to leave your money to your family and/or charity rather than to the government, get the very best tax advice as early as practicable.

The crucial fact to realize is that estate and gift taxes can be made essentially voluntary by the sophisticated person. For example, with the judicious use of a private foundation and a wealth replacement trust (irrevocable insurance trust), you can determine how much of your estate you want to go to the government in taxes, and how much you want to go to your family and to your charitable causes through your own foundation.

YOUR LAST WORDS

Few men or women of accomplishment think of death without also contemplating what will be said about them after they are gone.

Last words at death can be revealing, sensitive, sad, bitter, or quite confusing. Beethoven's were poignant: "I shall hear in heaven." William Saroyan said what every lawyer might say: "Everybody has got to die, but I've always believed an exception would be made in my case." In the context of a terminal illness, such as cancer, last words can sometimes be very hurtful to the surviving family. One rich man, almost at the moment of his death, turned to his children and former wife gathered around his bed and uttered, "That's it. F*ck you," dying shortly thereafter. Was he cursing the specter of death or was he conveying his own narcissistic message to his family, a message arguably consistent with many of his lifetime attitudes toward them? No one will ever know for sure what he meant. In any event, we should be thoughtful about leaving last words for our loved ones and posterity.

Some persons actually try to leave a last message not with words, but with their remains or "cremains"—the six or seven pounds of bone fragments and ash that remain after cremation. The usual place for them is in an urn on a mantel, but one testator asked that his remains be put in the sand trap on the tenth hole of his country club's golf course, remarking that since he never could get out of it during his lifetime he might as well end up there. Another woman wanted her ashes dumped on her compulsively neat mother-in-law's favorite rug, but divorce made her request academic. Canuck's Sportsman's Memorials in Des Moines, Iowa, run by Jay "Canuck" Knudsen, Sr., has stashed cremains in a bowling ball and a set of golf clubs. A special job was for a sportsman who had his cremains divided among and placed in five duck decoys, which were then bequeathed to five buddies so the deceased could, in effect, still go gunning with them posthumously. The list of favorite objects in which one's last remains could be placed—to convey one message or another—seems endless. At his death, the prolific mystery writer Robert Block, author of the novel *Psycho*, left notes, saying he wanted to give his many readers a surprise ending. In those notes, he directed cremation and that his ashes be placed in a book-shaped urn at the University of Wyoming, to whose American Heritage Center he left his personal memorabilia.

YOUR OBITUARY

Usually the last public words *about* us will be in our obituaries, which unfortunately and all too often can be deficient in many respects. These obituaries may be quite inaccurate, or focused on one publicized peccadillo in a largely useful and blameless life (e.g., an SEC consent decree or the like), or with most of the emphasis on the unimportant or the trivial. Recently the art critic Hilton Kramer wrote a whole piece

"*In view of my firm belief in reincarnation, I do hereby direct
that my entire estate be held in trust, pending my return
to this earth.*"

lambasting and refuting quite tellingly what he termed a "stupid" and an "uncomprehending hackwork" obituary in the *New York Times* of the esteemed art critic Clement Greenberg.

What, if anything, can be done about this problem of the bad obituary that is due to ignorance, indifference, or sloppy writing and not to one's own either faulty or uneventful life?

Recently several of my clients of stature have decided to try to eliminate or minimize this problem by their own hands, or, to be more precise, their own pens.

What they have done is to write their own obituaries, and then to keep them up-to-date, much as they keep current their refined wills and estate plans.

The advantages of this self-help device seem self-evident. First, the important basic facts of your life will be comprehensive and accurate (assuming, of course, the veracity of the writer and, in any event, the verifiability of such facts). Second, the emphasis on what really mattered to you will be clear. For example, in one case, the not-yet-decedent in his advance obituary explained which of his many philanthropic activities meant the most to him. In another, a business tycoon explained which mercantile success was most significant to his extraordinary career and why it was. Finally, any guiding principle, motto, or ethical precept can be set forth with clarity and personal meaning.

The remaining part of the problem is how to ensure that the self-written obituary with your own last words will be published, and published accurately. That, of course, cannot be guaranteed. But with both a lawyer and a public relations person acting together, expeditiously and effectively, the right journal (or journals) will immediately have the self-written obituary available at the death of its composer. Even though those journals may not use it *in haec verba*, as we lawyers say, the theory is that they will use the gist of it and will have complete and accurate facts of your life provided for them, and also your own views on what mattered in your life. There seems to be little doubt that this cannot but help — and probably significantly — the assigned obituary writer. Even if it doesn't, I have noticed that with those few of my esteemed clients who have attempted to write their own obituaries, the process has a side benefit — it focuses their minds on their lives and accomplishments, and even on what they want to do with the rest of their lives. Not a bad result in any event.

Churchill was probably right when he said, "Any man who says he is not afraid of death is a liar." So perhaps the fear of the Great Unknown may be slightly lessened for those who have reason to think that their own last words will make meaningful the last words written about them. Thus, if you want to have a say about the last say about you, prepare your own obituary while you can. If you don't get around to it, at minimum prepare some quotable final words for yourself so you don't end up like Pancho Villa, who said as he died: "Don't let it end like this. Tell them I said something."

AN ETHICAL WILL

Persons should consider alternative means of expression. Once upon a time, a will was studded with personal concerns, philosophy, and admonitions to heirs. It was as much a personal statement as a disposition of property. Benjamin Franklin, among his many accomplishments, was one of the drafters of the Declaration of Independence (as well as the author of the famous essay "Advising a Young Man as to the Selection of a Mistress," in which he strongly recommended "old women to young ones"). Franklin left his daughter Sarah "the King of France's picture, set with 408 diamonds — requesting that she not form any of those diamonds into ornaments — and thereby introduce or countenance the expensive, vain, and useless fashion of wearing jewels in this country." Most wills today seem to deal only with legal and tax details.

There is a lovely custom in Judaism of writing what is called an ethical will. The first (unwritten) ethical wills are in the Bible. Jacob gathers his children around his bedside and tells them the ways in which they should live after he is gone. And David, before he dies, prepares Solomon by warning him whom to watch out for when he becomes king, and by asking him to complete the task that he has begun. The Apocrypha, the Talmud, and medieval and modern Hebrew literature contain many examples of ethical wills that parents left to their children.

An ethical will is, in effect, a love letter from the beyond. Usually addressed to one's nuclear family, this testament is generally revealed only after death. It is often moving, poignant, and wise. It is not morbid or grim, and can be quite humorous in parts. It is a means of passing one's wisdom about living to those one loves. An ethical will can, of course, be part of a regular will, but more often it is a separate, private document.

Some examples may help clarify this concept. A grandmother asked her children to care for her bachelor brother and explained his needs to them. A father asked that his children call their mother every day, visit her once a week, and make her laugh. Sholem Aleichem, the great Jewish humorist, asked in his ethical will, among other things, that his family gather together on the anniversary of his death and read from his stories, especially the funny ones.

As mentioned, the crux of an ethical will need not be in a separate document but sometimes is placed within a traditional will otherwise consisting of only the usual legal language. A beautiful, intelligent woman who had survived the Holocaust inserted the following in her will:

So that my children and grandchildren may better understand some of the provisions appearing in this will, they should remember that my oldest child, their maternal grandparents, their mother's brothers and practically all other members of her family, and other members of my own family died tragically in Europe during the last great war, and they died because they were Jews and for no other reason. I feel that the tragedy of their deaths would be compounded and in vain if any of my estate might be devoted, eventually, to any religious purpose other than the perpetuation of the Jewish faith and traditions, or to the assistance of people other than the Jewish people to whom so much of my thought is directed. I implore my children and grandchildren never to abandon the Jewish faith and, what is equally important, not to raise their children in any faith other than the Jewish faith and religion.

Jack Kelly, the Philadelphian who rose from bricklayer to multi-millionaire contractor, was best known as Grace Kelly's father. But this colorful Irishman was also known for his own accomplishments. He included some of his philosophy of life in his unusual and very personal will. These excerpts will give the flavor:

> For years I have been reading last wills and testaments, and I have never been able to clearly understand any of them at one reading. Therefore I will attempt to write my own will in the hope that it will be understandable and legal. Kids will be called "kids" and not "issue," and it will not be cluttered up with "parties of the first part," "per stirpes," "perpetuities," "quasi-judicial," "to wit," and a lot of other terms that I am sure are only used to confuse those for whose benefit it is written.
>
> This is my last will and testament and I believe I am of sound mind. (Some lawyers will question this when they read my will; however, I have my opinion of some of them, so that makes it even.)
>
> ....
>
> Godfrey Ford has been with me over forty-five years, and has been a faithful and loyal servant. Therefore, I want him to be kept in employment as long as he behaves himself well, making due allowances for minor errors of the flesh, if being slightly on the Casanova side is an error. I want my survivors to feel an obligation regarding his comfort and employment. In addition, I give him $1,000 outright. I have already turned over to him the bonds I bought for him at Christmas each year. . . .

After providing for his daughters and son John, Kelly approaches the matter of his sons-in-law, among them Prince Rainier of Monaco:

> In the case of my daughters' husbands, they do not share and if any of my daughters dies, her share goes to her children, or if there are no children, then that share goes back into my own children's fund. I don't want to give the impression that I am against sons-in-law — if

they are the right type they will provide for themselves and their families and what I am able to give my daughters will help pay the dress shop bills, which, if they continue as they have started out, under the able tutelage of their mother, will be quite considerable. . . .

....

I can think of nothing more ghastly than the heirs sitting around listening to some representative reading a will. They always remind me of buzzards and vultures awaiting the last breath of the stricken. Therefore, I will try to spare that ordeal and let you read the will before I go to my reward — whatever it will be. I do hope that it will never be necessary to go into court over spoils, for to me the all-time low in family affairs is a court fight, in which I have seen families engage. If you cannot agree, I will direct that the executor or trustees, as the case may be, shall decide all questions of administration or distribution, as the executor and trustees will be of my choosing or yours. . . .

I will try to give each of you all I can during my life so that you will have money in your own right — in that way you will not be wholly dependent on my bequest. I want you all to understand that U.S. Government Bonds are the best investment even if the return is small, and then come Commonwealths and Municipals that have never failed to meet their interest charges. As the years gather you will meet some pretty good salesmen who will try to sell you everything from stock in a copper or gold mine to some patent that they will tell you will bring you millions, but remember that for every dollar made that way, millions have been lost. I have been taken by the same gentry but that was perhaps because I had to learn from experience — when my father died, my hopes were high, but the exchequer low, and the stock market was on the other side of the railroad tracks, as far as I was concerned.

To Kell, I want to say that if there is anything to this Mendelian theory, you will probably like to bet on a horse or indulge in other forms of gambling — so if you do, never bet what you cannot afford to lose and if you are a loser, don't plunge to try to recoup. That is wherein the danger lies. "There will be another deal, my son, and after that, another one." Just be moderate in all things and don't deal in excesses. (The girls can also take that advice.) I am not going to try to regulate your lives, as nothing is quite as boring as too many "don'ts." I am merely setting down the benefit of my experience, which most people will admit was rather broad, since it runs from Port Said to Hawaii, Miami Beach to South America.

I have written this will in a lighter vein because I have always felt that wills were so dreary that they might have been written by the author of *Inner Sanctum* and I can see no reason for it, particularly in my case. My family is raised and I am leaving enough so they can face life with a better than average start, financially.

As for me, just shed a respectful tear if you think I merit it, but I am sure that you are all intelligent enough not to weep all over the place: I have watched a few emotional acts at graves, such as trying to jump into it, fainting, etc., but the thoroughbred grieves in the heart. . . .

Not that my passing should occasion any "scenes," for the simple reason that life owes me nothing. I have ranged far and wide, have really run the gamut of life. I have known great sorrow and great joy. I had more than my share of success. Up to this writing my wife and children have not given me any heartaches, but on the contrary, have given me much happiness and a pardonable pride, and I want them to know I appreciate that. I worked hard in my early life, but I was well paid for that effort.

In this document I can only give you things, but if I had the choice to give you worldly goods or character, I would give you character. The reason I say that is with character you will get worldly goods because character is loyalty, honesty, ability, sportsmanship, and, I hope, a sense of humor.

If I don't stop soon, this will be as long as *Gone With the Wind*, so just remember, when I shove off for greener pastures or whatever it is on the other side of the curtain, that I do it unafraid and, if you must know, a little curious.

Jack Kelly signed the will with a flourish — in green ink.

Too often, parents die leaving behind children who will never know what really mattered to their parents or what they wanted for them. I represent a lovely, accomplished woman whose mother died when she was five. Her father and stepmother, with a mixture of motives, never discussed the child's natural mother and, in effect, tried to erase her from the child's memory.

This woman never even had pictures of her mother until she found some after her father died — photos he had kept but had also hidden from her. Think of the solace a letter from her mother, who knew she was dying and who had time to write before death, could have been. Since one never knows the date of his or her death, it can be particularly valuable to leave your children some testament of your feelings and values. Dying wordlessly can cause irremediable psychological damage.

But doing an ethical will is no easy task. You must look inside yourself and determine essential truths you have learned during your lifetime. You must confront your failures and consider what really counts. Creating an ethical will is worth doing for its own sake but will also be worth doing for your children's sake. When you write an ethical will, you demonstrate that you have not completely departed this life if you leave behind others who understand what you stood for and will carry on what you believed in.

Finally, if you want your will to be done on this earth after you have left it, devote as much time, care and thought to your estate plan as you do to your most important business matters. Otherwise, after you are gone, only your heirs and their lawyers and the Internal Revenue Service will determine what happens to your estate — which may not be at all what you wanted to happen. In that event, as Ambrose Bierce put it, "Death is not the end; there remains the litigation."

Glossary

Annual Exclusion   The $10,000 that each person under current law can give every year to anyone in the world without federal gift tax. A married couple can together give $20,000 yearly to anyone even if it all comes from the property of one of them.

Beneficiary   One who either inherits under a will or receives property from a trust, an insurance policy, etc.

CLAT   Charitable lead annuity trust (see p. 158 for definition of and discussion about it).

CLUT   Charitable lead unitrust (see p. 160 for definition of and discussion about it).

Codicil   An amendment to a will.

CRAT   Charitable remainder annuity trust (see p. 155 for definition of and discussion about it).

CRUT   Charitable remainder unitrust (see p. 156 for definition of and discussion about it).

Estate Tax   This is a tax on the transfer of property at death. It is imposed on the estate itself, and not on the beneficiaries. The federal death tax is an estate tax. An estate tax can be contrasted with an inheritance tax that is a tax on a beneficiary's right to receive the property.

Executor   A person or institution named by the will-maker to carry out the terms of the will after the death of the will-maker. Co-executors are two or more executors who are designated to work together.

Family Limited Partnership   This kind of partnership, created under state law, is one of the hottest current devices to reduce gift and estate tax on transfers to the younger generation of a family while retaining control in the older generation of that family.

Fiduciary   A person or institution who serves as a trustee, executor, or guardian.

Generation-Skipping Tax ("GST")   A new federal transfer tax, at the rate of 55% (which is equal to the federal estate tax maximum rate), imposed on property transferred from one person to another, the latter of whom is more than one generation younger than the transferor, e.g., a grandparent to a grandchild. There is an exemption to this GST tax explained immediately below.

Generation-Skipping Tax Exemption   The $1 million that each person can transfer to a beneficiary or beneficiaries two or more generations younger than the transferor. Thus two grandparents can transfer a total of up to $2 million to their grandchildren or more remote descendants free of the GST.

Glossary   A good-faith effort to give plain English definitions for complex terms and concepts with this warning: Let the reader beware of over-simplification.

Grantor   A person who establishes or creates a trust, also called a settlor or a donor.

Grantor Retained Income Trust (GRIT)   Also called a Qualified Personal Residence Trust (or Q-PERT). This is an estate and gift tax saving trust by which a grantor transfers to it a residence (e.g., a home or cooperative apartment). The grantor retains the right to live in the residence for a period of years at which time it passes to the grantor's children or remains in trust for them.

GRAT   Grantor retained annuity trust (see p. 117 for definition of and discussion about it).

Irrevocable Insurance Trust   Also often called a Wealth Replacement Trust. This trust holds insurance for the grantor's family, and yet because it is this special form of trust, the insurance proceeds are not subject to death tax in either the grantor's estate or his or her spouse's estate.

Lifetime Exemption   Also called the unified credit. Under current law, each person can transfer up to $600,000 (a married couple can transfer $1.2 million) free of federal gift and estate tax. These transfers can be made either during life by gift or at death by means of a will or other legal arrangement such as a trust. In some states, these transfers may be subject to those states' estate and gift taxes.

Living Will   It is not really a will but a set of directions, usually made in accordance with a statutory procedure or judicial decisions of a particular state, setting forth an individual's health care decisions to be made during the individual's lifetime.

Premarital Agreement   An agreement, also called a prenuptial agreement, entered into before marriage that limits the rights of one or both spouses in the property of the other upon divorce or death or both.

Private Foundation   Also called a Family Foundation. As used herein, a tax-exempt legal entity (usually a corporation or a trust) created by one or more members of a family or a special group or a corporation to carry out charitable purposes. (In contrast, a public charity, like a hospital, university, or museum, is supported by the general public.)

Testator   The will-maker (male).

Testatrix   The will-maker (female).

Trust   A legal agreement by which one person (the trustee) holds property for the benefit of another (the beneficiary). This flexible legal mechanism has an unlimited number of forms, including insurance trusts (p. 124 and glossary under Irrevocable Insurance Trust), personal residence trusts (p. 112 and glossary under GRITs), dynasty trusts (p. 44), and charitable trusts (p. 156).

Trustee   A person or institution named in a trust with legal responsibility for the disposition of the trust's assets. Co-trustees are two or more trustees who are designated to work together.

Will   Usually referred to as a last will and testament. A will is a legal document containing your wishes as to the disposition of your assets after your death.

ILLUSTRATIVE
MAPS AND
SAMPLE HEALTH
CARE DOCUMENTS

STATE STATUTES GOVERNING LIVING WILLS
AND APPOINTMENT OF HEALTH CARE AGENTS

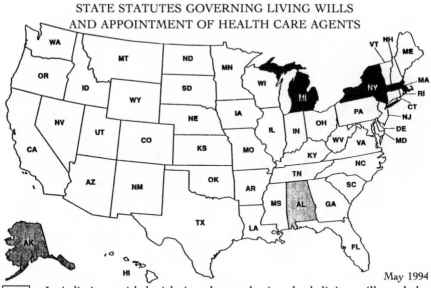

May 1994

Jurisdictions with legislation that authorizes both living wills and the appointment of a health care agent (**the District of Columbia and 45 states: Arizona, Arkansas, California, Colorado, Connecticut, Delaware, Florida, Georgia, Hawaii, Idaho, Illinois, Indiana, Iowa, Kansas, Kentucky, Louisiana, Maine, Maryland, Minnesota, Mississippi, Missouri, Montana, Nebraska, Nevada, New Hampshire, New Jersey, New Mexico, North Carolina, North Dakota, Ohio, Oklahoma, Oregon, Pennsylvania, Rhode Island, South Carolina, South Dakota, Tennessee, Texas, Utah, Vermont, Virginia, Washington, West Virginia, Wisconsin, and Wyoming**).

States with legislation that authorizes only living wills (**2 states: Alabama and Alaska**).

States with legislation that authorizes only the appointment of a health care agent (**3 states: Massachusetts, Michigan, and New York**).

Note: The specifics of living will and health care agent legislation vary greatly from state to state. In addition, many states also have court-made law that affects residents' rights. For information about specific state laws, please contact Choice in Dying.

ARTIFICIAL NUTRITION AND HYDRATION
IN STATUTES AUTHORIZING HEALTH CARE AGENTS

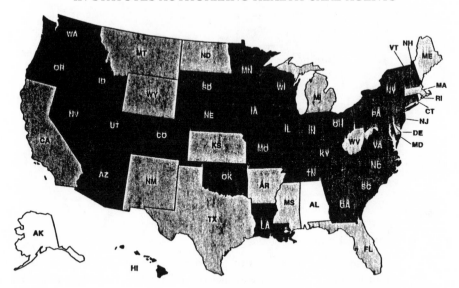

June 1994

■ States with statutes that permit health care agents to order the withholding or withdrawal of artificial nutrition and hydration **(32 states: Arizona, Colorado, Connecticut, Georgia, Hawaii, Idaho, Illinois, Indiana, Iowa, Kentucky, Louisiana, Maryland, Minnesota, Missouri, Nebraska, Nevada, New Hampshire, New Jersey, New York, North Carolina, Ohio, Oklahoma, Oregon, Pennsylvania, South Carolina, South Dakota, Tennessee, Utah, Virginia, Vermont, Washington, and Wisconsin).**

▨ Jurisdictions whose medical power of attorney statutes do not explicitly address the issue of artificial nutrition and hydration **(the District of Columbia and 16 states: Arkansas, California, Delaware, Florida, Maine, Massachusetts, Michigan, Mississippi, Montana, New Mexico, North Dakota, Rhode Island, Texas, West Virginia, and Wyoming).**

☐ States without statutes authorizing health care agents **(2 states: Alabama and Alaska).**

ARTIFICIAL NUTRITION AND HYDRATION
IN LIVING WILL STATUTES

June 1994

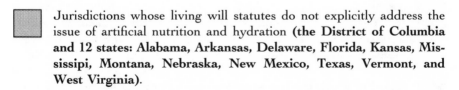

States with living will statutes that **permit** individuals to refuse artificial nutrition and hydration through their living wills **(34 states: Alaska, Arizona,[1] California, Colorado, Connecticut, Georgia, Hawaii, Idaho, Illinois,[2] Indiana, Iowa, Kentucky, Louisiana, Maine, Maryland, Minnesota, Nevada, New Jersey, New Hampshire, North Carolina, North Dakota, Ohio, Oklahoma, Oregon, Pennsylvania, Rhode Island, South Carolina, South Dakota, Tennessee, Utah, Virginia, Washington, Wisconsin, and Wyoming).**

States with living will statutes that **require** the provision of nutrition and hydration except in very limited circumstances **(1 state: Missouri[3]).**

Jurisdictions whose living will statutes do not explicitly address the issue of artificial nutrition and hydration **(the District of Columbia and 12 states: Alabama, Arkansas, Delaware, Florida, Kansas, Mississipi, Montana, Nebraska, New Mexico, Texas, Vermont, and West Virginia).**

States without living will statutes **(3 states: Massachusetts, Michigan, and New York).**

[1] The authority to withhold or withdraw artificial nutrition and hydration is only explicitly mentioned in the sample document, not in the text of the statute.

[2] Artificial nutrition and hydration cannot be withheld or withdrawn if the resulting death is due to starvation or dehydration.

[3] The medical power of attorney statutes in Indiana and Missouri permit appointed agents to refuse artificial nutrition and hydration on behalf of the principal.

ASSISTED SUICIDE LAWS IN THE UNITED STATES

July 1994

States with statutes that explicitly criminalize assisted suicide: **(34 states: Alaska, Arizona, Arkansas, California, Colorado, Connecticut, Delaware, Florida, Georgia, Hawaii, Illinois, Indiana, Kansas, Kentucky, Maine, Michigan, Minnesota, Mississippi, Missouri, Montana, Nebraska, New Hampshire, New Jersey, New Mexico, New York, North Dakota, Oklahoma, Oregon, Pennsylvania, South Dakota, Tennessee, Texas, Washington,[1] and Wisconsin).**

Jurisdictions that criminalize assisted suicide through the common law **(the District of Columbia and 10 states: Alabama, Idaho, Maryland, Massachusetts, Nevada, Ohio, Rhode Island, South Carolina, Vermont, and West Virginia).**

States in which the law is unclear concerning the legality of assisted suicide **(6 states: Iowa,[2] Louisiana,[3] North Carolina,[4] Utah,[4] Virginia,[2] and Wyoming[4]).**

[1] A federal district court has ruled the Washington statute criminalizing assisted suicide unconstitutional.

[2] Case law exists which may be applicable to assisted suicide.

[3] State constitution stipulates that "no law shall subject any person to euthanasia."

[4] State has abolished the common law of crimes and therefore does not explicitly prohibit assisted suicide.

NEW YORK LIVING WILL

INSTRUCTIONS

This Living Will has been prepared to conform to the law in the State of New York, as set forth in the case In re Westchester County Medical Center, 72 N.Y. 2d 517 (1988). In that case the Court established the need for "clear and convincing" evidence of a patient's wishes and stated that the "ideal situation is one in which the patient's wishes were expressed in some form of writing, perhaps a 'living will.'"

PRINT YOUR
NAME

I, _____, being of sound mind, make this statement as a directive to be followed if I become permanently unable to participate in decisions regarding my medical care. These instructions reflect my firm and settled commitment to decline medical treatment under the circumstances indicated below:

I direct my attending physician to withhold or withdraw treatment that merely prolongs my dying, if I should be in an **incurable or irreversible mental or physical condition with no reasonable expectation of recovery.**

These instructions apply if I am (a) **in a terminal condition;** (b) **permanently unconscious;** or (c) **if I am minimally conscious but have irreversible brain damage and will never regain the ability to make decisions and express my wishes.**

I direct that my treatment be limited to measures to keep me comfortable and to relieve pain, including any pain that might occur by withholding or withdrawing treatment.

CROSS OUT
ANY
STATEMENTS
WITH WHICH
YOU DO
NOT AGREE

While I understand that I am not legally required to be specific about future treatments **if I am in the condition(s) described above I feel especially strongly about the following forms of treatment:**

I do not want cardiac resuscitation.
I do not want mechanical respiration.
I do not want artificial nutrition and hydration.
I do not want antibiotics.

However, I **do want** maximum pain relief, even if it may hasten my death.

ADD PERSONAL INSTRUCTIONS (IF ANY)

Other directions:

These directions express my legal right to refuse treatment, under the law of New York. I intend my instructions to be carried out, unless I have rescinded them in a new writing or by clearly indicating that I have changed my mind.

SIGN AND DATE THE DOCUMENT AND PRINT YOUR ADDRESS

Signed _____ Date _____

Address _____

WITNESSING PROCEDURE

I declare that the person who signed this document is personally known to me and appears to be of sound mind and acting of his or her own free will. He or she signed (or asked another to sign for him or her) this document in my presence.

YOUR WITNESSES MUST SIGN AND PRINT THEIR ADDRESSES

Witness 1 _____

Address _____

Witness 2 _____

Address _____

Courtesy of Choice in Dying, Inc.   11/93
200 Varick Street, New York, NY 10014   1-800-989-WILL

© 1993
CHOICE IN DYING, INC.

NEW YORK
HEALTH CARE PROXY

I, _____ , hereby appoint my _____ ,
_____ , who resides at _____ ,
as my health care agent. In the event that _____ is
unable, unwilling, or unavailable to act as my health care agent, I hereby
appoint my _____ , _____ , who resides at
_____ , as my alter-
nate health care agent.

In the event that I become unable to make my own health care decisions,
this health care proxy shall take effect, and I hereby authorize my health care
agent to make any and all health care decisions for me.

My directions and intentions with respect to health care decisions concerning artificial nutrition and hydration are known to _____
and _____ . It is my intention that my agent shall
have authority to make all decisions concerning these matters as fully as I
could if I were able to make such decisions.

I direct my agent to make health care decisions in accordance with my
wishes and instructions as stated above or as otherwise known to such agent.
I also direct my agent to abide by any limitations on such agent's authority
as stated above or as otherwise known to such agent.

I retain the power to revoke this proxy at any time and for any reason. I
understand that, unless I revoke it, this proxy will remain in effect indefinitely.
Date: _____ Signature: _____

Address: _____

_____

I declare that the person who signed this document is personally known
to me and appears to be of sound mind and acting willingly and free from
duress. She/He signed this document in my presence. I am not the person
appointed as agent by this document.

Witness: _____

Address: _____

Witness: _____

Address: _____

FORM OF LIVING WILL FOR USE IN NEW YORK STATE, CONTAINING SPECIFIC STATEMENT OF WISHES CONCERNING TERMINATION OF CARE

LIVING WILL

To my family, friends, doctors, and all those concerned with my care:

Being now of sound mind, I, _____, here state my feelings regarding medical treatment, in the event that I am unable to participate in such decisions.

If, due to injury or illness, I become extremely disabled and it appears that there is no reasonable expectation (i) of my recovery, or (ii) that I will regain a meaningful quality of life, I direct that no medical treatment be initiated. If at that time medical treatment has already been commenced, I direct that such treatment be discontinued.

I therefore ask that, under such circumstances, I be released from this life and not sustained by medication, artificial means, or extreme or heroic measures, including, without limitation:

    (a) respiration by machine if my brain can no longer sustain my own breathing;

    (b) electrical or mechanical resuscitation of my heart if it has stopped beating;

    (c) nasogastric tube, gastronomy tube, hyperalimentation, or other methods of artificial feeding if I am no longer able to swallow;

    (d) saline infusions to prevent dehydration;

    (e) surgery;

    (f) dialysis if my kidneys are no longer functioning;

    (g) blood transfusions;

    (h) administration of antibiotics;

or any other measures, available now or developed in the future, which merely prolong or suspend the dying process without providing any possible cure.

The directives contained in this document shall not be limited to a primary medical condition but shall also apply to any secondary condition, even if that secondary condition is susceptible to treatment.

I do, however, ask that medication be mercifully administered to alleviate suffering even though this may shorten my life.

If it does not impose an undue burden on my friends or my family, I would like to live out my last days at home or in a hospice or similar facility rather than in a hospital.

This statement is made after careful consideration, many years of discussion with those close to me, and in accordance with my strong convictions and beliefs. I have discussed my views regarding life sustaining measures with my _____, _____ and my _____,

_____ . My purpose in listing these names is solely to evidence the consideration I have given to the foregoing statement.

I have made this declaration while in full command of my faculties in order to furnish clear and convincing proof of the strength and durability of my determination to forego life-sustaining treatment in the circumstances described above. The wishes and directions here expressed are to be carried out to the extent permitted by law. Insofar as they are not legally enforceable, I hope that those to whom this instrument is addressed will regard themselves as morally bound by these provisions and will be guided by this statement.

These directions express my legal right to refuse medical treatment. Therefore, I expect my family, doctors, and all those concerned with my care to be free from any liability or guilt for having followed my directions.

Signature: _____

Date: _____

I declare that the person who signed this document in my presence is personally known to me and appears to be of sound mind and acting willingly and free from duress.

Witnessed by: _____

Address: _____

_____

Witnessed by: _____

Address: _____

_____

CALIFORNIA
DECLARATION

If I should have an incurable and irreversible condition that has been diagnosed by two physicians and that will result in my death within a relatively short time without the administration of life-sustaining treatment or has produced an irreversible coma or persistent vegetative state, and I am no longer able to make decisions regarding my medical treatment, I direct my attending physician, pursuant to the Natural Death Act of California, to withhold or withdraw treatment, including artificially administered nutrition and hydration, that only prolongs the process of dying or the irreversible coma or persistent vegetative state and is not necessary for my comfort or to alleviate pain.

If I have been diagnosed as pregnant, and that diagnosis is known to my physician, this declaration shall have no force or effect during my pregnancy.

Signed this _____ day of _____ , _____ .

Signature _____

Address _____

The declarant voluntarily signed this writing in my presence. I am not a health care provider, an employee of a health care provider, the operator of a community care facility, an employee of an operator of a community care facility, the operator of a residential care facility for the elderly, or an employee of an operator of a residential care facility for the elderly.

Witness _____

Address _____

The declarant voluntarily signed this writing in my presence. I am not entitled to any portion of the estate of the declarant upon his or her death under any will or codicil thereto of the declarant now existing or by operation of law. I am not a health care provider, an employee of a health care provider, the operator of a community care facility, an employee of an operator of a community care facility, the operator of a residential care facility for the elderly, or an employee of an operator of a residential care facility for the elderly.

Witness _____

Address _____

CALIFORNIA
DURABLE POWER OF ATTORNEY FOR HEALTH CARE

1. DESIGNATION OF HEALTH CARE AGENT. I, _____, do hereby designate and appoint [insert agent's name, address and telephone] as my attorney-in-fact (agent) to make health care decisions for me as authorized in this document. For the purposes of this document, "health care decision" means consent, refusal of consent, or withdrawal of consent to any care, treatment, service, or procedure to maintain, diagnose, or treat an individual's physical or mental condition.

2. *CREATION OF DURABLE POWER OF ATTORNEY FOR HEALTH CARE.* By this document I intend to create a durable power of attorney for health care under Sections 2430 to 2444, inclusive, of the California Civil Code. This power of attorney is authorized by the Keene Health Care Agent Act and shall be construed in accordance with the provisions of Sections 2500 to 2508, inclusive, of the California Civil Code. This power of attorney shall not be affected by my subsequent incapacity.

3. *GENERAL STATEMENT OF AUTHORITY GRANTED.* Subject to any limitations in this document, I hereby grant to my agent full power and authority to make health care decisions for me to the same extent that I could make such decisions for myself if I had the capacity to do so, including the right to consent, refuse consent, or withdraw consent to any care, treatment, service, or procedure to maintain, diagnose or treat a physical or mental condition, and to receive and to consent to the release of medical information, subject to the statement of desires, special provisions and limitations set out below. In exercising this authority, my agent shall make health care decisions that are consistent with my desires as stated in this document or otherwise known to my agent, including, but not limited to, my desires concerning obtaining or refusing or withdrawing life-prolonging care, treatment, services and procedures.

4. *STATEMENT OF DESIRES, SPECIAL PROVISIONS, AND LIMITATIONS.* In exercising the authority under this durable power of attorney for health care, my agent shall act consistently with my desires

as stated below and is subject to the special provisions and limitations stated below:

Statement of desires concerning life-prolonging care, treatment, services and procedures:

[Insert any specific instructions here.]

5. *INSPECTION AND DISCLOSURE OF INFORMATION RELATING TO MY PHYSICAL OR MENTAL HEALTH.* Subject to any limitations in this document, my agent has the power and authority to do all of the following:

a. Request, review, and receive any information, verbal or written, regarding my physical or mental health, including, but not limited to, medical and hospital records.

b. Execute on my behalf any releases or other documents that may be required in order to obtain this information.

c. Consent to the disclosure of this information.

6. *SIGNING DOCUMENTS, WAIVERS AND RELEASES.* Where necessary to implement the health care decisions that my agent is authorized by this document to make, my agent has the power and authority to execute on my behalf all of the following:

a. Documents titled or purporting to be a "Refusal to Permit Treatment" and "Leaving Hospital Against Medical Advice."

b. Any necessary waiver or release from liability required by a hospital or physician.

7. *AUTOPSY; ANATOMICAL GIFTS; DISPOSITION OF REMAINS.* Subject to any limitations in this document, my agent has the power and authority to do all of the following:

a. Authorize an autopsy under Section 7113 of the Health and Safety Code.

b. Make a disposition of a part or parts of my body under the

Uniform Anatomical Gift Act (Chapter 3.5 (commencing with Section 7150) of Part 1 of Division 7 of the Health and Safety Code).

c. Direct the disposition of my remains under Section 7100 of the Health and Safety Code.

8. *DESIGNATION OF ALTERNATE AGENT.* If the person designated as my agent in paragraph 1 is not available or becomes ineligible to act as my agent to make a health care decision for me or loses the mental capacity to make health care decisions for me, or if I revoke that person's appointment or authority to act as my agent to make health care decisions for me, then I designate and appoint the following person to serve as my agent to make health care decisions for me as authorized in this document:

a. First Alternate Agent: [Insert alternate agent's name, address and telephone.]

9. *NOMINATION OF CONSERVATOR OF PERSON.* If a conservator of the person is to be appointed for me, I nominate the following individual to serve as conservator of the person: [Insert name, address and telephone of proposed conservator.]

10. *PRIOR DESIGNATIONS REVOKED.* I revoke any prior durable power of attorney for health care. I retain the power to revoke this proxy at any time and for any reason. I understand that, unless I revoke it, this proxy will remain in effect indefinitely.

I sign my name to this durable power of attorney for health care on _____, 199_, at _____,

_____.

_____

_____, Principal

I declare under penalty of perjury under the laws of California that the person who signed this document is personally known to me to be the principal, that the principal signed this durable power of attorney in my presence, that the principal appears to be sound of mind and under no duress, fraud, or undue influence, that I am not the person appointed as attorney-in-fact by this document, and that I am not a health care provider, an employee of a health care provider, the operator of a community care facility or residential care facility for the elderly, nor an employee of an operator of a community care facility or residential care facility for the elderly.

I further declare under penalty of perjury under the laws of California that I am not related to the principal by blood, marriage, or adoption and, to the best of my knowledge, I am not entitled to any part of the estate of the principal upon the death of the principal under a Will now existing or by operation of law.

Print name: _____

Date: _____

Address: _____

_____

Print Name: _____

Date: _____

Address: _____

_____

Certificate of Acknowledgment of Notary Public

STATE OF ⟩

        : ss.:

COUNTY ⟩

On this _____ day of _____, 199_, before me personally appeared _____, known to me to be the principal whose name is subscribed to this instrument, and acknowledged that [s]he executed it. I declare under penalty of perjury that the person whose name is subscribed to this instrument appears to be of sound mind and under no duress, fraud or undue influence.

Notary Public

STATE OF ⟩

        : ss.:

COUNTY ⟩

On this _____ day of _____, 199_, before me personally appeared _____ and _____, known to me to be the persons whose names are subscribed as witnesses to this instrument, and they acknowledged to me that they executed it.

Notary Public

WARNING TO PERSON EXECUTING THIS DOCUMENT

This is an important legal document. Before exexuting this document, you should know these important facts:

This document gives the person you designate as your agent (the attorney-in-fact) the power to make health care decisions for you. Your agent must act consistently with your desires as stated in this document or otherwise made known.

Except as you otherwise specify in this document, this document gives your agent power to consent to your doctor not giving treatment or stopping treatment necessary to keep you alive.

Notwithstanding this document, you have the right to make medical and other health care decisions for yourself so long as you can give informed consent with respect to the particular decision. In addition, no treatment may be given to you over your objection, and health care necessary to keep you alive may not be stopped or withheld if you object at the time.

This document gives your agent authority to consent, to refuse to consent, or to withdraw consent to any care, treatment, service, or procedure to maintain, diagnose, or treat a physical or mental condition. This power is subject to any statement of your desires and any limitations that you include in this document. You may state in this document any types of treatment that you do not desire. In addition, a court can take away the power of your agent to make health care decisions for you if your agent (1) authorizes anything that is illegal, (2) acts contrary to your known desires or (3) where your desires are not known, does anything that is clearly contrary to your best interests.

This power will exist for an indefinite period of time unless you limit its duration in this document.

You have the right to revoke the authority of your agent by notifying your agent or your treating doctor, hospital, or other health care provider orally or in writing of the revocation.

Your agent has the right to examine your medical records and to consent to their disclosure unless you limit this right in this document.

Unless you otherwise specify in this document, this document gives your agent the power after you die to (1) authorize any autopsy, (2) donate your body or parts thereof for transplant or therapeutic or educational or scientific purposes, and (3) direct the disposition of your remains.

This document revokes any prior durable power of attorney for health care.

This power of attorney will not be valid for making health care decisions unless it is either (1) signed by two qualified adult witnesses who are personally known to you and who are present when you sign or (2) acknowledged before a notary public in California.

Your agent may need this document immediately in case of an emergency that requires a decision concerning your health care. Either keep this document where it is immediately available to your agent and alternate agents or give eachof them an executed copy of this document. You may also want to give your doctor an executed copy of this document.

If there is anything in this document that you do not understand, you should ask a lawyer to explain it to you.

NEW JERSEY
ADVANCE DIRECTIVE FOR HEALTH CARE

This advance directive for health care includes both a proxy directive and an instruction directive in accordance with the provisions of the New Jersey Advance Directives for Health Care Act (1991).

(1) *DESIGNATION OF HEALTH CARE REPRESENTATIVE.* I, _____[name]_____ , residing at _____ , do hereby designate and appoint (name, address and telephone number of representative) _____ , as my health care representative to make health care decisions for me as authorized in this document. For the purposes of this document, "health care decision" means a decision to accept, to withdraw or to refuse any treatment, service or procedure used to diagnose, treat or care for an individual's physical or mental condition, including life-sustaining treatment, as well as a decision to accept or to refuse the services of a particular physician, nurse, other health care professional or health care institution, including a decision to accept or to refuse a transfer of care.

(2) *GENERAL STATEMENT OF AUTHORITY GRANTED.* Subject to any limitations in this document, I hereby grant to my health care representative full power and authority to make health care decisions for me, in the event I subsequently lack decision making capacity, to the same extent that I could make such decisions for myself if I had the capacity to do so. In exercising this authority, my health care representative shall make health care decisions that are consistent with my desires as stated in this document or otherwise made known to my health care representative, including, but not limited to, my desires concerning obtaining or refusing or withdrawing life-prolonging care, treatment, services, and procedures. The powers granted to my health care representative in this Advance Directive for Health Care shall be immediately effective and shall not be affected by my subsequent disability or incapacity.

(3) *STATEMENT OF DESIRES, SPECIAL PROVISIONS AND LIMITATIONS.* In exercising the authority under this advance directive for

health care, my health care representative shall act consistently with my desires as stated below:

[INSERT SPECIFIC INSTRUCTIONS HERE]

(4) *INSPECTION AND DISCLOSURE OF INFORMATION RELATING TO MY PHYSICAL OR MENTAL HEALTH.* Subject to any limitations in this document, my health care representative has the power and authority to do all of the following:

a. Request, review, and receive any information, verbal or written, regarding my physical or mental health, including, but not limited to, medical and hospital records.

b. Execute on my behalf any releases or other documents that may be required in order to obtain this information.

c. Consent to the disclosure of this information.

(5) *SIGNING DOCUMENTS, WAIVERS, AND RELEASES.* Where necessary to implement the health care decisions that my health care representative is authorized by this document to make, my health care representative has the power and authority to execute on my behalf any necessary waiver or release from liability required by a hospital or physician.

My health care representative shall have the authority to direct and consent to the writing of a "No Code" or "Do Not Resuscitate" order by any health care provider.

(6) *PHOTOCOPIES.* My health care representative is authorized to make photocopies of this document as frequently and in such quantity as my agent shall deem appropriate. All photocopies shall have the same force and effect as any original. I specifically direct my agent to have a photocopy of this document placed in my medical records if such a copy does not already constitute a part of my medical records.

(7) *SEVERABILTY.* If any part of any provision of this document shall be deemed invalid or unenforceable under applicable law, such part shall be ineffective to the extent of such invalidity only, without in any way affecting the remaining parts of such provisions or the remaining provisions of this document.

(8) *GOVERNING LAW.* This document shall be governed by the laws of the State of New Jersey in all respects, including its validity, construction, interpretation, and termination. I intend for this Advance Directive for Health Care to be honored in any jurisdiction where it may be presented and for any such jurisdiction to refer to New Jersey law to interpret and determine the validity of this document and any of the powers granted under this document.

(9) *DURATION.* This power of attorney will exist until it is revoked.

(10) *DESIGNATION OF ALTERNATE HEALTH CARE REPRE-SENTATIVE.* If the person designated as my health care representative in paragraph 1 is not available or becomes ineligible to act as my health care representative to make a health care decision for me or loses the mental capacity to make health care decisions for me, or if I revoke that person's appointment or authority to act as my health care representative to make health care decisions for me, then I designate and appoint the following person to serve as my health care representative to make health care decisions for me as authorized in this document:

First Alternate Health Care Representative:

_____(name)_____ , _____(address)_____ , _____(telephone)_____ .

(11) *PRIOR DESIGNATIONS REVOKED.* I revoke any prior advance directive for health care.

I sign my name to this Advance Directive for Health Care on _____(date)_____ , 199_ , at _____ ,

_____ .

_____

[Name]

Address: _____

_____

I declare under penalty of perjury that the person who signed or acknowledged this document is personally known to me to be _____ , that (s)he signed this advance directive for health care in my presence, that the declarant appears to be sound of mind and under no duress, fraud, or undue influence, that I am not the person appointed as health care representative by this document.

I further declare under penalty of perjury that I am not related to the declarant by blood, marriage, or adoption and, to the best of my knowledge, I am not entitled to any part of the estate of the declarant upon the death of the declarant under a Will now existing or by operation of law.

Print name: _____

Date: _____

Address: _____

_____

Print Name: _____

Date: _____

Address: _____

_____

[Notary Acknowledgment]

FLORIDA
DECLARATION

Declaration made this _____ day of _____, 199_.

I, _____, willfully and voluntarily make known my desire that my dying not be artificially prolonged under the circumstances set forth below, and do hereby declare:

If at any time I have a terminal condition and if my attending or treating physician has determined that there is no medical probability of my recovery from such condition, I direct that life-prolonging procedures be withheld or withdrawn when the application of such procedures would serve only to prolong artificially the process of dying, and that I be permitted to die naturally with only the administration of medication or the performance of any medical procedure deemed necessary to provide me with comfort care or to alleviate pain.

I do [   ] do not [   ] desire that nutrition and hydration (food and water) be provided by gastric tube or intravenously.

In the event that I have been determined to be unable to provide express and informed consent regarding the withholding, withdrawal, or continuation of life-prolonging procedures, I hereby designate my _____, _____, to make such decisions for me and to carry out the provisions of this declaration.

It is my intention that this declaration be honored by my family and physician as the final expression of my legal right to refuse medical or surgical treatment and to accept the consequences for such refusal.

I understand the full import of this declaration, and I am emotionally and mentally competent to make this declaration.

_____

This declarant is known to me and I believe him/her to be of sound mind.

_____
Witness

_____
Witness

FLORIDA
DESIGNATION OF HEALTH CARE SURROGATE

Declaration made this ____ day of _____ , 199__.

In the event that I, _____ , become unable to provide informed consent for medical treatment and surgical and diagnostic procedures, I wish to designate my _____ , _____ , as my surrogate to make health care decisions for me; to authorize my admission to a medical, nursing, residential or similar facility; to enter into agreements for my care; to arrange for and provide, withhold or withdraw consent to medical, therapeutic and surgical procedures for me, including the administration of drugs; to apply for public benefits to defray the cost of health care; and to exercise all of the authority conferred on health care surrogates by law.

I affirm that this designation is not being made as a condition of treatment or admission to a health care facility.

_____

_____
Witness

_____
Witness

Index